LEADERSHIP

for Action in

RURAL COMMUNITIES

LEADERSHIP

for Action in

RURAL COMMUNITIES

Burton W. Kreitlow

Professor of Education and
Professor of Agricultural and Extension Education
University of Wisconsin
Madison, Wisconsin

E. W. Aiton

Director
4H Club and YMW Programs
U. S. Department of Agriculture
Federal Extension Service
Washington 25, D. C.

Andrew P. Torrence

Head
Department of Agricultural Education
Tuskegee Institute
Tuskegee, Alabama

THE INTERSTATE
Printers and Publishers, Inc.
Danville, Illinois

PRELUDE

You are a leader searching for more effective ways to serve. You seek to improve yourself, yet you are what you are by the action and interaction of many factors.

There is no such thing as a self-made man. Each of us is the product of his inheritance from parents plus the effects of the environment or culture. Sitting with you, as you read these pages, are generations of people who taught you to read, to organize and remember, to reason a course of action, to try that course, to move ahead if all goes well and to back up and take a new look and a new course if that appears best. Guiding the pen of the authors are countless individuals who have influenced our thought, experiences, and attitudes toward life.

Personal leadership is a product of three great forces or influences. First is our inheritance, which to some degree determines our physical and mental capacity for leadership. Second are our relationships with other people which develop our personality and stimulate those qualities and attitudes which register as plus or minus as other persons react to us. Finally, our environment, the nature of the community in which we live and grow is the laboratory where our leadership skill becomes trained or fixed. For many, who grow up in a free democratic society, their inheritance, relationships with other people, and community environment are rich media for leadership growth. For others, less fortunate, these factors may limit somewhat the opportunity for leadership growth.

The purpose of this book is to develop an understanding of how these three factors interact with and about an individual leader to help him grow and mature in our rural society. Likewise, it will show how an understanding of these factors will help you as you try to improve your own leadership. More attention will be given to the relationships we have with others and to the community than to inheritance. A study of inheritance as it relates to leadership is very complex and in a large measure is not within the framework of this book. Leadership ability is considered to be an important part of the total personality pattern of an individual.

For the most part, leadership is acquired after birth by our relationships with other people, by our contact with the culture around us, by efforts of others to educate us for leadership, and finally by personal efforts to improve our own leadership ability. This book begins with two assumptions—(1) an individual's leadership ability can be improved, and (2) you want to improve yours.

TABLE OF CONTENTS

TABLE OF CONTENTS—(Continued)

LIST OF ILLUSTRATIONS

THE SETTING FOR
LEADERSHIP AND ACTION

CHAPTER I

You Are the Leader

Have you ever been in a group where you were expected to make the next move? Where others were looking to you for a suggestion? Where you felt the responsibility to make a decision and knew that with that particular group at that particular time your decision would be accepted?

In such a situation have you ever felt that you needed to know just a little more about this leadership responsibility that you have accepted in your group? About the role of leadership which somehow has been assigned to you by neighbors or friends?

Have you ever had the responsibility of helping organize a yearly program of work for a local club or organization? Has it ever been your job to take a group of youngsters on a tour? Did the responsibility ever fall on your shoulders to help get out the vote on a school improvement project? Have you felt that others were waiting for you to make up your mind before they were willing to make up theirs?

Have you ever wondered if you would be able to do the job that someone suggested you could do? Have you ever sunk low in your chair and looked vaguely into space as you heard someone suggest that you should be responsible for organizing a committee to do a community job? Have you ever missed a meeting of your organization and discovered that in your absence you were named as chairman of an important committee or nominated for the position of president for the coming year?

Have you ever had a feeling of inadequacy as your turn came to be a leader in your club?

You may have wondered about the leadership responsibilities that came your way, but in spite of a moment or more of hesitation you went ahead and tried your best to do the job expected of you. You may not have consciously decided to be of service to your community, your group or organization as you accepted these responsibilities, but you know as you look back that you have been. Although being of service in a community and being a leader in a community are not the same, it is through service and a growing dedication to service that leadership can be developed. Wanting to be of service does not guarantee that a person will develop into a leader, but it does provide a base upon which a person's leadership can develop. Leadership cannot always be recognized as being associated with a job or a position in the community or in a group. We easily recognize as leaders, the many persons in rural America who are appointed or elected to certain leadership jobs in the local community or in its organizations. As you think of your experiences in your community, you will recognize that an even greater number of leaders are not named, elected, or appointed. These are the people whose words are also weighed when decisions are made. These are the people who may even by their silence determine action. These are the people who often help in the careful selection of those leaders who are to be named, elected, or appointed. Both the formally named leaders and the greater number of unnamed leaders ask themselves the question, "What could I do to be of greater service to my group or to my community? How can this leadership job I have be done efficiently and well?"

It should help you to know that people who are assigned professional leadership jobs often feel the same as you. These are people who have had professional training for leadership. Yet they get many of the same feelings of inadequacy as do formal or informal community leaders. For example, the teacher of agriculture who recently graduated from a Land Grant College has accepted a position at your high school. After several weeks of school he attends his first Future Farmers of America meeting as a chapter advisor and he has a peculiar feeling in the pit of his stomach. He wonders just how much more he needs to know to do his job well. Yet, he has a strong dedication to be of service to youth. Strong enough, indeed, to cause him to complete four years of professional training for this job. His dedication to leadership of youth is no less, and not necessarily any stronger, than that of the farmer in the same community who is a recognized leader in the 4-H Club program. Both will find themselves in situations where they feel inadequate; but both will have a dedication to service strong enough to override this feeling. If they want to help youth and the community they will move ahead, they'll do their job and learn from their experiences.

The county 4-H Club agent or the associate agricultural agent when new on the job is asked to talk to Mrs. Jones from Happy Corners. She wants help on the organization of a new 4-H Club. This is a professional leadership job, yet the new agent has never acted in this particular capacity before. He wants to be successful in this venture, yet has no specific pattern to follow; but he, too, is dedicated to serve; he wants to do what he can for the boys and girls in Happy Corners. He probably feels less sure of himself than does Mrs. Jones who expects him to call.

The rural librarian is asked for the first time to organize a study group on THE HISTORY OF OUR COMMUNITY. She asks herself, what do other people do? How do they go about it? What procedures do they use? What principles do they follow?

Whether you are a citizen leader in the community or a professional leader, many of the important things to learn about leadership are the same. You have much more that is in common in your leadership than you have that is different.

It is the purpose of this book to help rural community leaders. This, of course, means helping all who have a leadership responsibility in the rural community. It is for the named leader of a local club or organization. It is for the informal counselor who will never be *named* as "leader" but who in a very real sense is responsible for changing the action, attitudes, or knowledge of others in his community. It is for the person who has been college-trained for leadership. He must keep in mind the same principles, use many of the same skills, and depend upon his leadership experiences in much the same way as the formal or informal community leader. Have you ever watched professional leaders, formal leaders, and informal leaders work together in the community? If you have, you will recognize that all three could benefit by a better understanding of the principles of leadership and by viewing and analyzing each others' experiences.

Let's look at several leaders. Mrs. Anderson has been a pillar of her rural church and her community for many years. She has had her turn as chairman of women's organizations. She has been a deaconess, she had aided in the organization of a Girl Scout Program which started in her church but later spread to the total community. She once was a volunteer leader of a 4-H Club. In talking with Mrs. Anderson it is easy to recognize that she has had a major leadership role in her community. With her years of leadership experience one might think she knows all about leadership. Such is not the case. She is the first to admit that the one thing she would like to improve during the next several years is her ability to lead more effectively.

Mr. Upton asks, "How can I do a better job with these young people in our 4-H Club? How can we get done what needs to be done in our community? How can we lead them so that their decisions in the next few years are right?" Mr. Upton asks these questions even though he became a volunteer 4-H leader for the first time in 1940. He is still looking for answers to leadership problems. This isn't because he hasn't learned much from his experience; it is because he has learned that leadership is an ever-changing responsibility, that this year's youth are by no means identical to the youth he worked with in 1940. Yet as Mr. Upton looks back to 1940 and the years immediately following he sees many of the same characteristics. He even asks himself the question, "What did I really do for these young people then? What can I really do for the young people today?"

A study of leadership is certainly for Mrs. Anderson and Mr. Upton. It's also for the professional leader of long experience. Take, for example, Miss Dobbke who is back at a university in graduate school after 20 years as a home agent. What did she tell her advisor she wanted first as she began graduate study? She wanted courses on leadership, on methods of working with volunteer leaders, and a chance to discuss leadership problems with other professional leaders.

Have you ever listened to the "shop talk" of long-time formal leaders in a community or professional leaders as they sit down over a cup of coffee? What are they talking about? They're seeking tips from each other. They're seeking to clarify basic purposes, they want new ideas, they're looking for underlying principles. These are dedicated leaders who by their action tell new leaders (formal, informal, or professional) that leadership is no simple, easily learned skill. They tell us instead that leadership is a way of being of service. It is a field of action in which one can grow from youth through all adulthood. They tell us that even after years and years of leadership they can still learn from others. New leaders can take heart from this. This shouldn't discourage new leaders. Instead, if you have a new leadership assignment, it should emphasize for you the importance of the responsibility which you have accepted.

A little warning flag should be thrown up at this point in our discussion. Although the emphasis in this book will continue to be the individual leader and his or her dedications and ability to be of service in line with these dedications, the authors recognize and wish for you to recognize that the leader (whether he be formal, informal, or professional) *is not an isolated factor* influencing communities, groups, organizations, or other individuals. In a real sense the leader is a part of a group. The nature of the group helps determine the kind of action a leader can take. The nature of the community in which you live does the same and the nature of the situation in which your organization operates has a great influence on the actions a leader can and should take. This tells us that in addition to your role as an individual leader you must function as a member of a group and accept the sanctions of the group. It tells us that in one situation you may be a very effective leader in getting a community job accomplished. In another situation your leadership will not be recognized. For example, we can be sure that some community leaders reading this book will be particularly effective in getting people to work together after a community crisis has passed and a decision has been reached that will change the community. There are other community leaders who will not be effective in bringing peace and a new spirit of working together to a community after it has gone through a crisis. These leaders may act in such a way that the crisis will reoccur. Some community leaders are very effective in awakening a group to its responsibilities but are ineffective in leading to a solution to the problem once the group is awakened. On the other hand a different person may be particularly effective in dealing with this group only when it is ready to take action. This all adds up to telling us why we feel inadequate in some leadership situations. We don't really know what principles to follow. We too often know just a few skills that work only in a few situations. Talking about leadership with other leaders, observing what other leaders do, reading about the experiences of others and about the basis of leadership in a rural community will aid you in being a better leader. Leaders are dedicated people. They should be brave enough to follow the suggestions they gain from other leaders. Brave enough to follow the principles suggested in this book. Brave enough to try the methods and techniques which grow out of the principles, and creative enough to do their own thinking after incorporating these ideas into their own personalities.

We're going to "talk shop" in this book. In talking shop we're going to focus on the improvement of the rural community. Even though we focus on the rural community we know that leadership reaches well beyond the community, beyond the organizations, beyond the groups of people directly influenced by other people.

In Chapter II we're going to talk about the improvement of the rural community. We're going to see how the community in many ways acts just as individuals act. We're going to look at the way a community changes and the role of leadership in this change. We're going to see what the community does to us and what education can do for the community. Then in Chapter III we're going to identify some of the agencies and organizations through which professional, formal, and informal leaders work. It is important to know what groups other than our own are trying to do. In Chapters IV and V we're going to get down to some basic material that is close to home to all leaders; the dedications that get you involved in leadership in the first place and the principles that aid in determining the leadership action to take. This Chapter V on principles is a tough chapter to read but we've talked about these principles with leaders like you and have found that the principles are understood almost immediately. We're convinced that you will understand them too. From then on we're going to discuss your relationships with your group, the skills you need, how to help other local leaders, what to do about controversy and how to use it productively, and then we're going to look at ways community leaders have of cooperating as they work for community improvement.

After that we're going to look in on other leaders. We're going to see what happened to our friends at Carley's Corners, a small farming neighborhood in Eastern Ontario, when they started a farmer's cooperative. Then we're going to look at Beckley, West Virginia and observe how the leaders there changed the economic life of an entire region. Next we will observe leaders in a homemakers' club on the eastern seaboard, a Ruritan Club in Arkansas, a 4-H Club in Maryland, an adult farmer class in a school in Alabama, a county library in Missouri, a farm organization in Virginia, and some rural churches in Tennessee. We've "talked shop" with leaders in these communities.

They've looked back on what they've done. They've identified where they've been successful. They've recognized where they have failed. Through the medium of the printed page this leadership "shop talk" is now reaching you. Let's look at it together.

CHAPTER II

Leadership for Rural Community Development

THE NATURE OF COMMUNITY DEVELOPMENT

Man is a goal-seeking animal. He is endowed with those special talents that help him to overcome obstacles and problems. He has the ability to set goals and to plan in advance the route he hopes to follow as he moves toward them. He sees those things which stand in the way of his goals whether they be his own inadequacies, other individuals, physical blocks, government, or other social institutions.

This same man lives first with himself, second in a social setting which is called the community. Man as an individual with his own goals, or man as a single cell of the community organism, exhibits some of the same characteristics. In so far as a rural community can identify goals, it can use some of the same methods in overcoming them as those used by an individual. Leaders seek to raise the level of individuals by working with them directly, or by seeking to raise the level of the community. By developing the community, the leader believes the opportunities to develop the individual will be improved.

Community development can be described as the efforts of the community to identify its problems and to attempt to establish and reach its goals. Hoiberg[1] defines community planning in a similar way by saying it is "the systematic application of forethought to the problems of community development."

Just as an individual weighs the various evidence that appears as a personal problem arises, so a community weighs the evidence that identifies a community problem. The individual has the distinct advantage in problem-solving since he has only the problem and himself to contend with. The community, on the other hand, has many individuals to whom the evidence may mean many different things; and consensus as to what is a community problem may, in some situations, not even be possible.

[1]Otto G. Hoiberg, *Exploring the Small Community*. Lincoln, University of Nebraska Press, 1955, p. 12.

An individual may weigh the various arguments for or against his purchasing a new car next year. The decision may be difficult to make, but he can make it alone and then if he needs financial assistance he may go directly to a bank or other loan agency to obtain it. The village of a rural community, on the other hand, may weigh the various arguments for or against widening and improving its systems of streets. An officially elected body may have considerable difficulty considering all aspects of the problem before it decides to go ahead with the street improvement project. Even after a decision has been reached it may still be necessary to hold a referendum so that all village citizens can vote yes or no on the necessary bond issue to finance the street project.

As a leader you very likely have engaged in community development projects because through them you believe you can further aid the individual. You are right. You have probably found that planning for community action is far more complex and difficult than is individual planning and action. Often the various individuals and groups in a community cannot, or will not, make the effort to identify their problems. Yet the ability to act in a corporate way is one of the significant criteria which identifies a community. The roads between *ability to act as a community* and *willingness to act as a community* are filled with roadblocks, wrong turns, steep hills, and dead ends.

To help bring a community to action, it is necessary for individuals and groups to provide leadership. Just as the authors accept individual growth as a fact, so community growth and development are accepted. This growth, we believe, takes place in two ways: (1) through leadership toward established goals, and (2) through cultural momentum. Our greatest concern in presenting principle and example will be that of leadership in both the establishment of and reaching of community goals. In addition, cultural momentum will be considered as a phenomenon of community change.

GROWTH TOWARD ESTABLISHED GOALS

The community citizen and leader has a number of choices to make as to the most appropriate time to be effective in his or her leadership. For example, he may wait for a community problem to reach a crisis before suggesting any action and even then make only minor attempts to identify the cause of crisis.

He may anticipate crisis in the future and from the evidence he sees, make plans for action. He may actually help to bring about crisis because of his belief that things won't get done until disaster threatens. Or he may attempt to lead toward the establishment of goals which, when pursued and accomplished, will circumvent crisis.

Just as different leaders make different personal decisions as to the best time to identify goals and solve problems, so communities appear to act in different ways in their reaction to self development and problem solving. Figure 1 represents a theory of community change and identifies four periods through which communities move if no goals are established or action taken to solve problems. It is noted in this example that the period of Community Balance extends for one-half of the time pictured in the figure. It is during this long period that leadership to establish goals and reach them is the least likely to occur. The period of Community Ferment, on the other hand, provides only one-

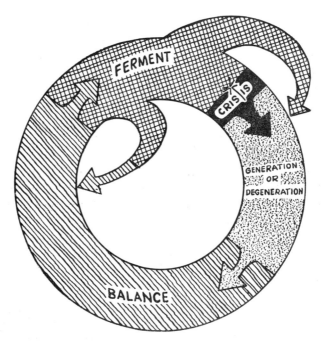

Figure 1. Periods and Conditions of Community Change (Read in clockwise direction)

half as much time to accomplish that which leaders may propose. But it is in this second period that leaders are most likely to make a greater effort to help the community identify its present problems and develop plans to solve them. During this period, other leaders are prone to raise the warning flag of impending crisis, while still others, who believe that only during a period of crisis is change made, will use their efforts to accelerate the movement toward the crisis period. It can be observed that the period of Crisis is shorter still. This is a time when both leaders and community citizens can see that goals must be set and problems solved. It should be noted that the period of crisis is short and if the community problems which cause the crisis cannot be solved, community degeneration may occur. Because of the minimum time available to solve crises, community leaders who are not accustomed to taking action may waste so much time working out the practical details of joint action that they will fail to act at all.

The period of Community Generation or Degeneration is then upon them. The time it takes to adjust to the results of crisis is unknown, but it is certain that a community will again reach a period of Community Balance. This will be with either more or less human and physical potential to be a good community than it had before the cycle began. As this is considered, it is easy to identify some communities that have leaders who are always striving to maintain balance. This is done by advance thought and planning. In other communities, leadership is so active in promoting new ideas that the community is almost always in a period of ferment. Still other communities appear to get no leadership until a crisis arrives. Then, too, there is the community which seems to lack leadership and we observe its loss of stature as a community as it degenerates because of inactivity.

It should be noted in Figure 1 that it is possible for leaders to change the direction of community change, and even to cause certain periods of change to be by-passed. Note especially how the period of Ferment can be turned back into the period of Balance, and how a crisis can be eliminated.

The scope of community planning and action is very closely allied with the planning and action carried on by individuals for their own development. Individual goals of community citizens affect the total community. Likewise, goals and plans of action determined by the community affect the individual citizen.

The Citizen Affects the Community. Even without planning to make his personal action responsible for community change, the individual citizen makes his influence felt. The person who, by individual decision, decides to stay home and watch a popular television program rather than hear a report of a survey committee of twelve, who have considered ways of developing a small industry in the village, is as surely affecting the community as is the formally organized group of twelve citizens who provided leadership for the survey and arranged for its presentation at a public gathering. If these twelve are the only ones in attendance, the potential of their group project will be more highly influenced by the individual decisions of the several hundred who determined to stay home. The action of this large group can in no way be labeled a group action; rather it is the result of concurrent individual actions.

The concurrent actions of several hundred citizens may be just as positive as it was negative in the previous example. In fact, concurrent individual action is often the visible sign to the leader that group action is possible. If at the public gathering referred to, several hundred citizens had arrived in addition to the committee of twelve who already were involved in the survey, the wise leader would have recognized the large attendance as a sign that many individuals were interested in action on the problem. After careful consideration of the various individual views, a proposal for group action might have been made. If the results were positive, we could see how closely allied are group action and individual action. In addition, one should not overlook the fact that in the former situation where all but the committee stayed home, the common action of those staying at home may have been just as significant in determining total group action, even though it would have been a different action. The citizen has an effect on the community and its groups regardless of his individual decisions. That these effects are positive or negative has been clearly demonstrated.

The Community Affects the Citizen. A large number of people in every small town or farming area take little active part in community decision making. They are affected by the actions of others who, in a very real sense, set community goals for them. Essert[2] points this out when he identifies a number of distinct characteristics of adult education for community development. In one of these he describes the effect of organized community groups on other citizens of the community. In describing the community development form of adult education he states that: "it reaches beyond the limitations of the membership of any particular group or class and offers educational experiences to the citizen in his daily affairs; whether he is or is not enrolled in a formal class, discussion group, membership group, or school."

Just as concurrent individual decisions and actions make for community-wide decision and change, so group action for the community by formal and informal leadership makes for changes among the individual citizens. This effect may be direct or indirect. A town board decision to dissolve a one-room school district and attach it to a 1-12 grade system, will directly affect every family with children in the dissolved district. An organized group of businessmen in the village may be considering keeping the stores open on Wednesday nights as well as on Friday nights. They make no actual changes, yet they do affect the individual citizens by their group action. The effect is indirect and many individuals may not be aware that any group planning or decision was made.

Growth Due to Cultural Momentum. Community development, in one sense, is a matter of "keeping up with the Joneses." Community X must have a new gymnasium for its high school because Community Y just built one. "We can't let the community down the road have a better piece of fire fighting equipment than we have." "That commnuity was able to bring a noted chorus to town for two performances; why can't we do it, too?" "We can't let Community Z get ahead of us."

Both among neighboring communities and throughout regions of the United States, there are attempts to "keep up" or "keep ahead." In addition there are those communities with the "wait and see" attitude. Leadership for community development, on the part of individuals, is going to be quite different in each of the above communities. A different type of leadership may be

[2]Paul L. Essert, *Creative Leadership of Adult Education*, New York, Prentice-Hall, Inc., 1951, p. 95.

needed in each. The cultural momentum for growth or stability may be a much greater force to deal with than any single factor or group of factors which could be identified. A community accustomed to keeping up or trying to keep ahead, often provides a task too difficult for a reactionary leader to overcome in his efforts to gain a type of community more fixed and permanent in its goals. By the same principle, a community whose momentum, past and present, has been toward maintaining the status quo, will be a difficult laboratory for a leader or group with objectives calling for major community change. Considerable evidence as to differences among rural communities and among rural neighborhoods, in their acceptance of new ideas, has been shown by sociologists and educators doing research on resistance to change.[3,4,5]

Within neighborhoods, within communities, and even within regions, the effects of tradition determine to a great extent the growth and development that is possible. The fact of cultural momentum should not be used as an excuse by a group, or individuals, seeking change, but rather should be one of the factors given careful consideration.

THE ROLE OF EDUCATION IN COMMUNITY DEVELOPMENT

The leaders of a rural community's educational institutions, organizations, and agencies play a major part in the development of the community. It would be possible to identify objectives for each of the above groups, but it is more practical to use the list of eleven educational needs of rural communities previously identified by Kreitlow and compare this list with the objectives of the schools, and the objectives of other groups. The schools will be considered separately because of their extensive responsibilities in our society. From this base we can see more clearly the responsibility of leaders, from any of the above groups, as they become involved in individual and community development.

---

[3]D. G. Marshall, W. H. Sewell, and A. O. Haller, "Factors Associated with High School Attendance of Wisconsin Farm Youth," *Rural Sociology*, XVIII:3 (Sept., 1953), pp. 257-260.

[4]H. A. Pedersen, "Cultural Differences in the Acceptance of Recommended Practices," *Rural Sociology*, XVI:1 (March, 1951), pp. 37-49.

[5]E. A. Wilkening, "Change in Farm Technology as Related to Familism, Family Decision Making and Family Integration," *American Sociological Review*, XIX:1 (Feb., 1954), pp. 29-37.

OBJECTIVES OF RURAL EDUCATIONAL INSTITUTIONS,
ORGANIZATIONS, AND AGENCIES

The educational needs of rural society identified by Kreitlow are:

1. To develop the ability to use the basic skills effectively.
2. To develop an understanding of one's own community.
3. To develop an understanding of life and living outside the local rural community.
4. To provide the best possible guidance and counseling service for youth.
5. To develop the ability to act in a democratic fashion.
6. To develop an educational program based on the assumption that every child will become a "Class A citizen."
7. To develop an understanding of, and a participation in, a fuller life.
8. To develop a curriculum with the breadth and depth necessary for training in a world society, yet locally oriented.
9. To develop a sound program of adult education.
10. To develop an awareness and understanding of the moral and spiritual values significant in our society.
11. To evaluate continuously the educational programs of the community to see whether needs are being met.[6]

The School and the Objectives. The public school has particular concern for the development of the ability to use the basic skills. This role of the public school has almost complete acceptance in our society. Even for this objective, the school needs the help and cooperation that the other educational groups can give. In addition to its role in teaching the basic skills, the school has a major role to play in developing in youth and adults a sound understanding of their own community, in providing youth with guidance and counsel, and in the development of breadth in the learning experiences of the school-age child. In all other objectives listed, the school has a responsibility, but in many instances the accomplishment of that objective may best be left to some other agency, or to the school in cooperation with some other agency.

---

[6]Burton W. Kreitlow, *Rural Education: Community Backgrounds.* New York, Harper and Brothers, 1954, pp. 126-143

Other Institutions, Organizations, and Agencies; and the Objectives. It is difficult to identify any one of the remaining objectives with any group that has the major responsibility for its accomplishment. The closest is the church's responsibility for meeting the objective dealing with the development of an awareness and understanding of the significant moral and spiritual values in our society. Yet in a rural society as complex as that in the United States, if the church were the only group with concern for this objective, it is unlikely that it could ever be attained. To the rural leader the most important idea to be gained by looking at educational needs and objectives in relation to educational groups is the clear indication that in reaching objectives each group has much to share with the others. In the development of a sound program of adult education, the schools have buildings and facilities, the Cooperative Extension Service has personnel, the farm organizations have local leadership, the churches and libraries have buildings and human resources, and the service clubs have a spirit of service which is most helpful in solving major programs. Community development cannot be overlooked as a means of bringing together the various educational agencies of a community into a voluntarily coordinated team. Leadership and action by twenty agencies and one hundred individuals, each going his own way, may cover a wide range of activities but is not likely to build the foundation for improved community life. Community development is an outcome of group cooperation and coordination.

Need of Education for Community Development

In many ways the rural community is similar to the rural personality. If a person decides to learn, to change, or to act, he can. Over a period of years rural groups have attempted to change the individual rural boy, girl, or adult. These groups have been moderately successful. More recently these same educational groups have entered the field of community development. Instead of looking only at an individual and his goals, they also look at a community and its goals. Just why have these groups begun to look at a community and its goals? Just why have these groups begun to look at community development as a field of their concern? The answer is clear. First, they have accepted the fact that they can change individuals by changing their environment; and second, leaders have recognized that modern rural society and its interrelationship with the total society are so complex that dealing with individuals or groups of individuals is not sufficient to maintain and develop the local community. This recognition is coming after a period of exploration involving community improvement through individual improvement alone. This, though possible, is no longer accepted as an adequate means of community improvement. We must look to ways of encouraging the educational groups to pull together as a team. This represents the need for, and the problem of, community development. There is no formula that can be used; no set of rules which, if followed, will surely lead to better community life, and in turn to improved individuals. Instead, the authors of this volume will suggest basic principles of rural leadership which have proved helpful to other leaders. The cases of leadership and action will show how they have been used; they also will demonstrate the extreme variability of the rural community. It is this variability which makes the suggestion of basic principles a sounder approach than the recommendation of a single pattern of action.

Limitations of Education in Community Development

"There are no limits to what can be accomplished through education." Though this may be true in theory, there are some practical limitations that local citizen leaders and "outside" experts all recognize as delaying and often stopping progress.

Perhaps no team of "experts" has done more work in the field of rural community development than Jean and Jess Ogden. In reporting on five years of experiment in Virginia, they point out the significance of the time factor in a number of ways: Time to get the job started, time to get it done, time to look back and see if the job was accomplished. In the concluding chapter of their book, *These Things We Tried*, they say, "With an extensive program in progress, we cannot conclude, we can only pause to clarify our thinking . . ."[7]

Related to "time" as a limitation, is the need for involvement on the part of most community citizens. *"People in the communities where they live are the group tending to be touched*

---

[7]Jess and Jean Ogden, *These Things We Tried.* University of Virginia, University of Virginia Extension, 1947, p. 404.

only indirectly unless they are consciously included."[8] Consciously to include people is not something which can be accomplished by formula. It takes trial and error and most of all, insight on the part of both "inside" and "outside" leaders. The extent to which people can be involved often determines the extent of the success of a leader's program for action. The ultimate choice as to whether or not an individual or a community change will be made is right in the lap of the individual citizen. This raises a limitation of serious proportion to those leaders and educators who believe in doing things for children, for adults, or for communities. The limitation is not as great (but it is still substantial) if the leader's philosophy of service is "to plan *with* rather than to plan *for.*"

Indifference on the part of communities or individuals is a further limitation. The teacher has been taught to use a variety of tools and techniques to motivate the "indifferent Johnny." The community leader has fared less well in receiving suggestions to motivate the "indifferent Ruralville." With a community, motivation of the "indifferent" appears to be much more complex and discouraging than motivating the indifferent individual. Yet local leadership must do both to be successful. The indifference of both individual and group is often culturally oriented. The Ogdens conclude as follows regarding this slowness to accept new ideas: "Patterns and folkways of communities, as well as habits of individuals, must have time to change."[9]

The process and results of community development are often slow, and just as often discouraging. This limits the enthusiasm of those working toward community goals, and in turn limits the outcomes.

A final limiting factor for leaders to consider is the lack of accepted standards against which to measure community development. People like to be successful; and unless local leaders can see where progress is being made, they tend to become discouraged. Recognition of all the problems of leadership for community development tends to keep some potentially fine leaders from active participation in community development activities. Leaders, more than followers, desire success in group activities. Without an easy measure of progress made, the leader may feel

---

that he has been unsuccessful. An understanding of the limitations and problems involved in community development will give the local leader the courage to begin a program that often takes years to mature.

CONTROVERSY AND COMMUNITY DEVELOPMENT

The period of Community Crisis shown in Figure 1 is the unwanted product of undirected or misdirected ferment and controversy. The controversy of ideas is a major stimulant to community action. Open and honest discussions of community problems are the tools of the effective leader. When problems are controversial in nature, the "discussion treatment" is better than letting them "fester." Better still than treating the symptoms of the controversy is an effort to determine its causes. Effective local leadership learns to use controversy as a means of civic improvement. To educate means to change. In order to make a change there must be some kind of action. The mental, physical, and emotional activity stimulated by critical examination of the facts regarding a community controversy, or an examination of why it came about and the implications of alternative action, all lead to the conclusion that controversy in community affairs can be used as a springboard to positive community growth. Educators and local citizens with a concern for community improvement should take a page from the great developments of the past, and use controversy as a positive step to overcome indifference.

CHAPTER III

Agencies and Organizations
Providing Leadership and Action

This chapter will be concerned with the role of leaders in the following agencies and organizations: the schools, government agencies, farm organizations, business and fraternal organizations, churches and church sponsored groups, and informal and temporary groups of citizens. In these groups there are both professional and citizen leaders who strive to obtain community action on problems of concern. Both citizen and professional leaders should be aware of the ways in which groups concern themselves with community problems. In defining the role of leaders in each group listed above, only the broadest aspects of the role will be considered. There are instances when, for varying lengths of time, the local community situation is such that alternative roles will need to be developed. The following description is designed to serve as a guide to understanding the most common roles of leaders; it is not meant to limit in any way the alternative courses of leadership and action which might be taken.

THE LEADERSHIP OF THE SCHOOL

Community leadership by the public schools is inherent in our system of free public education. A tradition of leadership for community improvement has been built up within the school system itself, in school-related organizations, and in state departments of education. These three foci of leadership will be examined.

Community Schools and Smaller Local Districts. Responsibility for community leadership by the school is vested in the school board, the chief school officer (superintendent or principal), and the classroom teachers and supervisors. Though casual observation of some school systems may lead one to believe that the concern of this group is merely for a finer school plant and

betterment of working conditions for teachers, this is by no means the situation in most communities. Teachers, administrators, and school boards have as their first point of concern the welfare of the boy or girl. Attempts to improve opportunities for the child often lead this group into many associated activities. For example, the administrator in an attempt to provide a broader curriculum for the boys and girls may spend a considerable amount of time working with the Chamber of Commerce. The Chamber of Commerce in turn is attempting to attract new industry into the town. The new industry will provide employment for the partially employed, lead to more money being spent for goods and services from existing business places in town, and finally will add to the total value of property in the town. This additional wealth may be exactly what is needed to add an art supervisor to the school staff or budget a greater amount of school funds to a guidance program for youth in school.

The school's role is one of positive leadership for a better educational opportunity for boys and girls. To this extent the teachers need to play their part in community activities. It is not possible to be positive in a leadership role while spending all one's time in the school plant. If welfare of children is a concern of the teacher, he must show that concern both in and out of the classroom. He must participate actively in those community activities which have as their goal greater educational opportunities.

The school board is very often in a position where it can provide community leadership on such issues as new building programs or school district reorganization. The administrator, with the encouragement of the board, can do much of the preparation of materials to be used by school-related organizations as they assume their role in school improvement.

A related responsibility of the board is to encourage financial support for school service. Though much of this may be done by making sure the product of twelve years of schooling is prepared for the future, there remains the task in most communities of bringing the outcomes of the school to public recognition. The community school, with its high degree of interrelationship between school and community, may be able to accomplish this without additional effort. But most of our public

schools are not that community-oriented, and it takes special efforts on the part of administrator and staff to demonstrate to the public how effectively the school accomplishes its objectives.

The school staff and board need to aid in the provision of opportunities for its graduates. This too may indicate participation in community affairs to the extent that one is able to make his proposals heard. The role of the school at this point extends beyond the traditional twelve years of schooling. It is completely realistic and sound for the school to be concerned with community development in areas that will provide opportunities for those who have been its charge for twelve years. The teacher with concern for the welfare of children and youth cannot cut free that concern on the night of high school graduation. This concern may lead right back to the curriculum of the school. Is the curriculum preparing youth for the right things? Are one-half of the high school graduates leaving the community during their first few years after graduation? Why are they leaving? Should they stay? What needs to be changed in the community to lead them to stay? What needs to be changed in the curriculum to better prepare them for life outside the community? Asking and answering these questions lead a teacher directly into a leadership role in the community. Although not immune to this role, it is one to which many teachers bring little or no preparation. Such a leadership role is primarily one of community stimulation and it is one which may hold important consequences for both school and community.

The final significant role of teachers, administrators, and board is that of developing among students, and all community residents, a belief in and dedication to continuous learning throughout life. It is the belief of the authors of this book that if this dedication is accepted, the leadership problems in rural communities will be greatly reduced. A vigorous pursuit of this goal by school people is needed. It cannot be expected that other groups will take the lead in developing this attitude, although such agencies as the Cooperative Extension Service and the Public Libraries can be of considerable help. In this case, one of the best means of leadership is to do a good job of education during the traditional twelve years of schooling. If learning is deemed desirable for youth, it will be less difficult to show how it can be desirable in later life. A person who is willing to seek

new knowledge and skills is the same person who is willing to look critically at proposals to improve his community.

School Related Organizations. The primary role of such groups as the Parent Teacher Association, Parent Clubs, Mothers' Clubs, and School Boards' Associations is to stimulate the community, or certain groups in the community, to recognize the values of public education and to provide for its development. The focus of these groups is the welfare of children. A P.T.A. may decide that the provision of a complete school lunch program in the school is of real value for children. They may then select a committee to promote a school lunch program. The committee will do everything possible to stimulate school board, administrator, and the general public to provide for the lunch program. This may involve appearances at public meetings, at a meeting of the school board, private conferences with school board members and school staff, preparation of news releases for the weekly paper, or even the distribution of special P.T.A. news releases for children to take home to their parents.

The School Boards' Association in a county or region, together with the School Administrators' Association, may wish to explore ways in which special guidance services could be made available for children in their schools. If the best solution to such a special service as psychiatric counseling is through the county superintendent's office, then the School Boards' Association may need to be the leader in encouraging proper authorities at county level to develop the service.

In many instances, Mothers' Clubs are more effective in stimulating official bodies to provide for the school welfare of children than they are in providing materials or services themselves. A Mothers' Club that attempts to raise funds for a projector and films for a rural school may have a worthy educational objective in mind; yet, if the projector and films are important for the better education of children, then their efforts could better be directed to obtaining such educational equipment through regular school board channels. School related organizations should not reduce their effectiveness by spending effort and money in supplying the direct service or supplies which every good school should have. Instead, they should concentrate on the stimulation of official bodies and the citizen public to provide that which is needed.

A secondary role, yet one which keeps the welfare of the child just as closely in focus, is that of aiding teachers, administrators, and boards in the education of the public. In some instances this may mean helping gain acceptance of a new school offering, such as a guidance and counseling service. In other instances it may mean selling a new idea for school improvement before it is adopted by the school. Other times, aid to the school may be in the form of cooperation in a community survey, or in aiding certain school groups in their "out-of-classroom activities."

The State Department and Intermediate Office of Education. The state department and administrator, supervisors, and special teachers in intermediate or county education offices do not have the local community orientation of previously discussed groups. However, one aspect of their role is similar to that of the other groups. They do have a responsibility to stimulate others to action. In fact, much of their effort to improve education makes stimulation of local administrators, teachers, school boards, and parent groups imperative. They, clearly, have a leadership responsibility for the development of better education. This leadership can be provided in carrying out their duties as outside consultants. Special training, experience, and knowledge are usually necessary for persons to fill these positions; thus their advice and counsel are often sought by local communities. In addition to special counsel and advice on community education problems, they often have certain responsibilities to see that specific educational legislation is carried out in the community. This group can be particularly effective if the emphasis of its leadership is on the constructive aspects of school improvement, rather than on merely carrying out the letter of the law. If the former is accomplished, the latter will often occur without pressure.

Government Agencies

The leadership for community development in other government agencies is clearly recognized. The Cooperative Extension Service, State Colleges and Universities, and Public Libraries have accepted considerable responsibility in leading communities to make desirable changes. In addition to the three which will be studied as examples, there are other government agencies which under certain circumstances are equally effective. Among these are the Soil Conservation Service, State Departments of Agriculture, and State Industrial Commissions.

The Cooperative Extension Service. The Cooperative Extension Service has built a reputation for service to rural people. As it became established, much of its service was on an individual farm basis. As the agency matured, it balanced its emphasis among individuals, the farm family, and the total community. In this latter respect, it has been unusually effective. It has accepted a clear responsibility as the rural agency with the greatest concern for "leader training." By helping individual leaders, the Cooperative Extension Service has in effect extended its help to all groups of the community. A leader must always be helped (educated) in relation to something. In rural communities the Cooperative Extension Service has helped women in connection with leadership in food preparation, better nutrition, child care and training, better town government, and in many other content areas which influence the community both directly and indirectly. Local 4-H Club leaders have been helped by Cooperative Extension Service personnel in group and subject matter techniques and methods; in the development of service projects for the community; and in conservation, health, and safety. These leaders use the knowledge and methods they have learned to make their community more stable and productive. Likewise, the development of leadership to make the family farming enterprise more productive has direct influence on the ability of a community to support its public school program. The helping of local persons for leadership is a major role of the Cooperative Extension Service in its contribution to community development.

An additional task of the Cooperative Extension Service is its aid to and efforts in cooperation with other agencies, organizations, and groups in the community. The staff is well trained in the solution of problems in agriculture, home and family living, and youth activities. The County Extension Agents are called upon as a resource when other agencies or groups of rural farm and village people face problems which they need help to solve. In addition to county extension personnel being available to counsel and advise, they have within their own organization a group of highly trained specialists who can be secured with minimum effort from the state office of the Cooperative Exten-

sion Service. Thus, with both county level and state level personnel available, there are few problems too small or too big for the
Cooperative Extension Service.

A final and developing duty of this agency is that of encouraging discussion of public policy. Policy questions and topics
such as the following are often of concern to the rural community: farm crop subsidy programs, state dairy sanitation
problems, county government, school district reorganization,
foreign policy, and tariff regulations. Though for the most part
the Cooperative Extension Service takes the part of moderator,
stimulator, and educator in matters of public policy, it cannot
encourage discussion of public problems without becoming involved in solutions to such problems. Taking a role of educator,
stimulator, and moderator in the initial phases of public policy
discussion does not eliminate the possibility of the Cooperative
Extension Service being involved in leadership to bring some of
the conclusions and recommendations of the public policy discussion groups to fruition. Thus, through the encouragement of
discussion of public policy, the Cooperative Extension Service
may make two important contributions to community development; first, it may promote public discussion as a forerunner and
basis for sound decisions, and second, as an involved member of
the group, it may aid in carrying out those decisions in the
community.

State Colleges and Universities. The role of state colleges
and universities is primarily that of a consultant to local groups
or individuals. The trained human resources of an institution
of higher learning should be available to both individuals and
communities which support them; this influence must extend far
beyond the college campus and the formally involved student
body. This responsibility of institutions of higher learning has
not been fully developed, even though some universities and state
colleges have organized General Extension Divisions and do provide some new services to all of the people of the state. At the
University of Wisconsin, the statement is often repeated, "The
boundaries of the campus are the boundaries of the state." Even
so, there is much that is yet to be accomplished before its vast
resources can be brought to bear on local community problems.

In addition to consultation and advice, there is a developing
role of action which has been accepted by a few institutions. For

example, the General Extension Divisions of the University of Virginia, Southern Illinois University, and the University of Washington have staff members whose specific task is to work with local groups in the action phase of community development. This means exploring with the citizens and leaders of a community, the present status of that community; the status it seeks; ways and means of getting from where it is to where it ought to be; and finally, helping it to organize and carry out plans of action. This role is not widespread or sufficiently developed at present. Its long-time effectiveness has not been determined. However, the trend toward involvement of colleges and universities in the action of local citizens and leaders is important. The involvement of these institutions in a consultant capacity should never replace the efforts of local organizations; rather it should stimulate local groups to greater efforts on their own behalf.

Libraries. The public libraries have the tradition of being a material resource for use in the solution of individual, group, and community problems. The positive attitude of service expressed in these words, "If we don't have it, we'll get it," is usual in libraries that have developed to a reasonable level of adequacy in rural counties or regions. Through their service in the provision of materials, they contribute to community growth. There are other activities in which they engage that are more direct contributions to development. Good libraries also have human resources who can be effective advisers and consultants to community groups. The leadership in community development and action is, at the present time, a subject of deep concern to many in the library field.

Should the libraries be guardians of the cultural heritage and provide personal reading service to individuals, or should libraries actively engage in working with groups who propose to make changes in our culture? If libraries accept the latter role (and many are beginning to), they have an unusual opportunity to provide community leadership in the consideration of the problems of the day. Their task then becomes one of a stimulator of action and this in turn leads to more effective accomplishment of their service to individuals. When the citizen is engaged in thought and planning he needs help in obtaining pertinent facts, knowledge of traditions involved, programs of other communities, and ideas of contemporary leaders. What better place than the library to seek such help?

The combined role of stimulator and individual reading consultant moves the rural library into the third role of being an advisor and resource for other educational agencies. Where the library has been involved in community activities, it soon is recognized by other agencies as having a unique service to offer to them. Where the library chooses not to participate in community affairs, it is often overlooked as a resource by the other rural agencies.

FARM ORGANIZATIONS

The three farm organizations of greatest influence in the United States are the American Farm Bureau, the Farmer's Union, and the National Grange or Patrons of Husbandry. Others are of significance for special purposes, as cooperatives, or in certain local communities and often over short periods of time. The three major organizations have persisted in their influence since their organization in 1919, 1902, and 1867 respectively. They will be considered as a group rather than individually, since in many respects the responsibilities they take for leadership and action have many characteristics in common.

Being membership organizations, organized with general objectives in mind, they have considerable freedom in their action in local communities. In fact, all three take great pride in the freedom a community or county unit has to do that which it chooses.

The Farm Bureau and the Farmer's Union very clearly accept the role of activator and action agent in community development. The Grange often slips into the same role, though this organization appears to put greater emphasis on the spirited and public policy discussion phase of development than upon the action itself.

All three organizations clearly accept the role of being a stimulator to community action. They each have definite objectives directed toward the education of adults and youth, and the improvement of rural life. They propose to improve rural life through education, and each will try to stimulate individuals to take whatever action is necessary to do this. Participation as a group in community-wide programs is not uncommon. The

Farmer's Union Local, the Local Grange, and the Community Farm Bureau have all said, "This project is worth while, we're for it. Let's get it done." This willingness on the part of these organizations to stimulate members and others to action, and to take an active role in community development, leads other local agencies to seek their help when community development projects are undertaken. Planning with the Cooperative Extension Service on public policy meetings, joint action with local government units on rural zoning changes or weed control, or participation with a village's chamber of commerce on improving town-country relationships are evidences of the broad vision of leadership exhibited by these organizations.

The Farm Bureau, Grange, and Farmer's Union have excelled in an additional task not usually participated in as completely by the other agencies or groups previously mentioned. This is in the active instigation and support of legislation. Most of this support is reserved for legislation directly affecting the farmer; and when the three groups are of the same conviction on a piece of legislation at either state or federal level, they are recognized as a most effective lobby. Local officers and leaders of these organizations have a greater responsibility than most to explore the attitudes and beliefs of those they serve, and to promote those legislative activities which are the concern of their membership. This responsibility carries with it the necessity of an education program on state and national rural problems, so that the membership in these organizations are fully aware of the consequences of the legislation which they and their leaders support.

Often the organizations in the local community find it easier to "parrot" national policy and positions on rural issues than to think for themselves. By so doing, they impair local cooperation. If local leaders accepted the responsibility for policy formation at the "grassroot" level there might be more inter-organization cooperation than we now observe.

Occasionally these three organizations, or two of them, have members in the same county or community. Where this occurs there may be both competition for members and competition of ideas. This competition has in effect tended to strengthen the organizations where it has existed. When there is disagreement on an issue it forces the membership and leaders to be better informed than they otherwise might be. When they support the same point of view their joint efforts are most effective.

BUSINESS AND FRATERNAL ORGANIZATIONS

Lions Clubs, Kiwanis Clubs, Commercial Clubs, Masons, Better Business Committees, and many other groups voluntarily band together for fellowship, business improvement, and community betterment. These groups are in an unusually fine position to stimulate action on and the solution of community problems. Though these groups are composed of many more rural village citizens than of those from the farms, they wield a community influence that is of consequence to both.

The voluntary nature and informal structure of these organizations make it possible for them to emphasize constructive enterprises such as the improvement of athletic fields, a campaign to clean up the trash in the community, or bringing a new industry to town. They may also choose to do nothing, but in these cases the organization is rather short-lived. Those which have positive programs will be considered here.

One of the most significant roles these organizations play is that of being a sounding-board for leaders in the community. The informal good fellowship associated with their activities makes it possible for individuals to test out ideas for community change with a minimum of fear that their ideas will be ruled out of order or ridiculed. Likewise, these groups seek ideas from groups in other communities and often exchange ideas with them through participation in each others' programs or at their district, state, or regional conventions.

A second role pursued by many such organizations is sponsorship and action on a specific community development program. Once such a group is convinced of the value of a particular program or activity they can and do wield an influence often out of proportion to their numbers. The informal atmosphere and spirit of brotherhood in such groups appear to generate an enthusiasm that is most effective in getting the job done.

The third role of consequence particularly suited to such organizations is that of leadership for cooperation on community-wide projects. Instead of attempting to do the job by itself it may be far more desirable to have a united community front at work. The membership of business and fraternal groups is often made up of members who take part in numerous other community agencies and organizations. This gives them an opportunity to determine informally the concern of other groups with particular problems and their willingness to join with others in a cooperative project for their solution. If the informal explorations have been made and cooperation looks possible, the organization will then take definite steps to formalize the joint action of a number of groups and solve the problem. The opportunities to follow this procedure are many because of the relatively small number of communities having official coordinating committees or community councils.

CHURCHES AND CHURCH-SPONSORED GROUPS

One of the greatest influences in the development of rural communities can be that of the churches and church-sponsored organizations. It is easy to underestimate the influence of these institutions and their groups because they often go about their work with a quiet dedication which receives none of the publicity often associated with other community action programs. Their effectiveness can be of particular significance in communities which are made up of predominantly one nationality and religious background. In these instances, practically all community action can emanate from church sources.

The role of the church and church groups varies depending upon the nature and the heterogeneity of the community. One aspect of the work of most churches which is positively identified with community development is their effort in "leadership training." This is accomplished by formal "leader training meetings" and by a variety of church-affiliated groups which give opportunities to young and old to experience leadership responsibilities. In addition, many churches and church groups exhibit an unusual ability to stimulate community action on affairs which are likely to raise the social level of the community citizen. The church may raise its voice on such matters as school segregation, excessive liquor licensing, juvenile delinquency, and corruption in government. The church has established a worthy reputation in many rural communities by being the stimulator of individuals, who in turn will strike out on their own to stimulate the community to engage in the discussion needed to solve many community problems.

In certain situations, and particularly in smaller homogeneous rural communities, the church and church groups become active protagonists on the issues of community change. In communities of a heterogeneous nature the additional hurdle of working with other churches must first be passed. When this is accomplished the various churches are often effective in accomplishing their plans of action, or in cooperating with other community groups on specific programs of change. The action of the church groups is one which is of considerable value in the total growth of the community and their cooperation with other agencies on development projects should be encouraged.

INFORMAL AND TEMPORARY GROUPS

Many times the initial stimulation for community action is not centered in a particular organization, institution, or agency. It comes, instead, from an informal group of community businessmen who may be accustomed to taking a coffee break at ten o'clock every morning, or a group of neighbor women who meet informally as they supervise the play of younger children on a summer's day, or a group of farm women whose informal meetings are via the telephone. Farmers who talk farming and the weather during Wednesday or Friday night shopping in the village, might also comprise such a group. In the above situations, ideas are freely expressed, often rejected, but sometimes accepted as of potential merit. When the latter is the case the group of discussants may say, "Now how can we get others to see this as we do, and do something about it?" And they may add, "I believe we should bring this up at our Commercial Club meeting," or "I'm sure the Farm Bureau would be able to do something about this." The leading role of these informal discussions appears to be that of directing ideas and potential action programs to formal groups that can organize for action.

Occasionally the nature of the problem discussed, and the likelihood that no formal group is equipped to deal with it, will lead to the formation of a temporary organization or committee to stimulate interest in the problem and lead to community-wide action upon it. In this case the committee should be broadly representative of the various facets of community life and should, in effect, act as a coordinator of other agencies for the period of time during which the project is underway.

The two roles of stimulating organized groups or forming a temporary organization for action on a specific problem, have been significant enough in results obtained to give informal and temporary groups full recognition as one of the means by which action is begun. Along with numerous potentials for action presented by the leadership of the schools, government agencies, churches, and other groups, the opportunity for the individual citizen and his neighbor to act informally to promote action could only happen in a democratic society. In fact, the nature of our democratic society makes possible the freedom for both individual and group to raise questions, disagree, finally determine a course of action, and then to pursue that course of action with vigor.

PART **II**

PRINCIPLES AND PRACTICES
OF LEADERSHIP

CHAPTER IV

Dedications of Leaders

INTRODUCTION

"Be Careful What You Want—For You Are Sure to Get It."
—Anon.

One day a vacationing clergyman was travelling along a country road in our great Southern Pine Region. He was approaching a small forest still smouldering from a "grass burn" so common in this area before educators and public opinion combined to recognize forest conservation as a public good. About this time a turpentine worker came running out of the smoke toward the road. He kneeled at the foot of a live oak tree and huddled over the seared and lifeless body of a dog. Alongside were a blackened lunch bucket and the remnants of a jacket, also burned in the fire.

As the traveller stopped to offer help or extend sympathy, the grieving woods worker moaned, "He done it! He done it again, but he ain't gonna do it no more." Then he looked up and saw the stranger. "I tole him to watch m' pail an' jacket. I allus knowed I hadta be keerful what I axed him to do—for he was shore to do it."

The consequences of a leader's suggestions or commands can be equally tragic. In terms of human welfare, the destiny of civilization itself depends on what is in the hearts and minds of leaders as molders of thought and opinion.

The values, dedications, and goals of people are more subtle than the gentlest scent of spring flowers, yet more persistent than the osmotic root pressure formed by the mineral salts that nourished these plants to bloom. Behind every mother's caress, every censor's raised eyebrow or every nervous tapping of a chairman's cigarette are the beliefs which condition and dictate their complex behavior. We cannot escape the daily influence of these personal value systems. We do not want to. They are the auto-gyro compass, and the lodestones for our journey through life.

Dedications and values help individuals to harmonize their lives within a complex society. Lack of these firmly grounded beliefs may cause personal instability or even insanity. Combat troops are known to better withstand pressure when their personal lives are not racked by inner conflict or insecurity. A child fortified with love and useful skills in his growing-up period is not likely to become an anti-social or a "disturbed" adult.

For these same reasons, and others, a leader must look to his personal values and dedications. In addition to himself, a leader bears responsibility for the destiny of others. So as a leader, be careful what you want from others. You are likely to get it.

To illustrate this principle—even authors had better look to their personal dedication. Writers presume to lead with an idea or a thought process. A few years ago we three friends (the authors) first met with the representative of a publishing company to discuss a proposal for this book. Someone asked, "Why is it needed and for whom is it intended?" The publisher-representative said, "There is an important and growing demand for books on leadership. The public appetite for this subject is evidence of real need."

Our senior author said, "College students in leadership, Vo-Ag and Extension courses are asking for an up-to-date text that contains principles and examples that will be applicable in their first jobs."

Another remarked, "Often volunteer leaders of adult and youth clubs and groups are inadequately trained for their opportunities. The professional leaders of these organizations or agencies say they want suggestions on methods and procedures."

"More important to me," said the quiet member of our trio, "is that democracy needs help these days—all the help it can get. I'm for writing a book in such a way that it does the other things too, but first and foremost we should help fulfill the ideal of leadership for democratic life. There are thousands of leaders in rural America who want to be democratic, who want to do what is right. Maybe we can help."

So, that is our dedication and our motivation. If we can share with you in the development of a rural leadership, dedicated to democracy at its best, we will all be richer than princes or kings. We will be happier and have more freedom than the subjects of dictators. We will pass on to the next generation a nation that is productive and satisfying.

WHY BE A LEADER?

Let's assume that if we are going to be leaders, we all want to be *democratic* leaders. Surely, we would not have written and you would not have read this far if such were not the case. But why do we want to be leaders at all? Why not just let others alone and expect them to do the same for us?

Only a fictional Robinson Crusoe could work that deal. Whenever there are two or more persons in the human equation, specialization takes place. When Crusoe's good man Friday appeared, specialization, and consequently leadership, began to emerge. That is reality. The greatest good for all concerned results from diversification and organization of effort. At least we know this is true when all parties to the arrangement are reasonably harmonious and happy in their roles.

It is the harmonizing or the orchestration of individual roles which is the real purpose and challenge of leadership. As in a symphony orchestra, the harmonizing is essential if individuals are to be happy and satisfied in their roles.

In the musical field, orchestration or organizing of individuals for group production is the process whereby an organization of musicians produces a symphony which is greater than the sum of the individual instruments. The piccolo, the tuba, and the violin players are each equally important to the symphonic presentation. And each is himself a creator and a leader of notes in his own field. But the arranger, the conductor, the librarian and the manager are creators of a higher order. They facilitate a group achievement which brings maximum satisfaction to the players as well as to the audience.

Here then is a need and a purpose for a leader—to help release the creative talents of those with whom he works and to aid in recombining these talents in new and higher forms for the maximum satisfaction of all concerned.

MOTIVATIONS OF LEADERS

Two extreme types of motivation may be observed in different leaders. Of course, there are many gradients and combinations in between.

1. A seeking of personal glory or gain.
2. A genuine joy and satisfaction in serving.

Let's consider some symptoms of these types of motivation. Perhaps everyone, in some idle moment of daydreaming, visions himself figuratively "astride a white charger leading a band of warriors into the crusade." Or, what boy has not at some time fancied himself into the honored seat of a shiny black Cadillac riding down Pennsylvania Avenue to the Chief Executive's mansion on Inauguration Day? What red-blooded American girl has not dreamed of becoming a Florence Nightingale or a great movie star?

Such dreams and air castles are a built-in part of our American culture and heritage. They are an expression of what that great anthropologist, Margaret Mead, calls "We third generation Americans." Each new generation of children is expected to climb on the shoulders of their parents to higher and greater heights.

Stark cold reality is very hard on a "third generation" of sons and daughters of highly successful professional or industrial parents. There is no higher rung on the vocational ladder for them. No "next upper" class or caste exists to challenge their efforts toward "true American opportunity" and "upward mobility."

Service to others, however, does exist as an opportunity for satisfaction that is available to all Americans of whatever class or economic group.

Return again to the question of *self-centered* versus *service* motivation of a leader. When Jim Goodfil,[1] the local dentist, permits himself to be "drafted" into the Community Service chairmanship of his Rotary Club, he presumes accurately that this will lead him through a chain of succeeding offices until he is finally the Club President. Also, he knows full well that being community service chairman involves a lot of work and maybe some criticism. And he knows that each of the five or six other chairmanships and offices along the way involve work and sacrifice too. But some will say that Jim was ambitious for fame, at-

---

[1]The examples and stories that follow, in this chapter, are fictitious. The authors considered that the use of real names of persons, clubs or communities in connection with this subject might be embarrassing. Accordingly, these illustrations are drawn from life experiences but are not documented as actual incidents. We believe them to be reasonably typical and therefore admissible for this particular chapter.

tention and perhaps a little indirect advertising for his profession. Maybe he can even make new friends and attract the "gold plate" customers to his office instead of the "porcelain fill" crowd. Is Jim exploiting his leadership opportunity for personal gain? Is this ethical? Let's examine the case.

Jim *is gaining* a lot from his experience. He gains personally in about six ways. (1) He receives a type of human relations experience unequaled by normal day-to-day routine. (2) He makes new friends. (3) He may increase his business (but more likely he sacrifices precious time away from his office). (4) He receives acclaim and recognition from his associates in proportion to their appraisal of his effectiveness as their leader and representative. (5) Perhaps the community thanks him with a news or radio mention. (6) Last, but most important, if Jim Goodfil is normal, he enjoys an inner glow and warmth of satisfaction from feeling useful and needed.

But to say that Jim is unethically exploiting his leadership opportunity is to deny the Golden Rule of human relations. "Service above Self" means hard work and extra hours in Jim's club. And our final criterion which again balances the scales in Jim's favor is that his activities of service to others, even though accompanied by personal rewards, *hurts* no one. It brings only good to others; unless, of course, he has been unkind, dishonest, or damaging in the methods or procedures that he used.

In summary, Jim agreed to work and serve. He hurt or hindered no one in the process. He benefited himself. He aided others. It looks like good leadership and everybody wins.

Let's look at another case. The Happy Corners 4-H Club is searching for a man leader to work with the faithful Mrs. Everyday who has been the only adult leader in the club. The new 4-H manual says there should be an adult man and woman leader in every 4-H Club with parents and others assisting when possible. The club has enjoyed five successful years with Mrs. Everyday and the group is receiving good community cooperation and good parent support. County and district awards and recognitions are beginning to come to the club as well as to the individual 4-H members.

An adult group in the community which helped start the Happy Corners 4-H Club is approached for aid in finding a willing and worthy man leader. It is explained that every 4-H Club *should* have a man and a woman adult leader. Mr. Almostdid is appointed. He protested mildly that he was too busy but he guessed that the club was a good thing and if it didn't involve too much work the president could send his name to the county extension office.

The Extension Office wrote a letter of thanks and welcome to Mr. Almostdid, sent a word of appreciation to the community club and also advised the Happy Corners 4-H group about their new man leader.

Everything was set, but nothing went off. Mr. Almostdid was offered no special help or preparation for his leadership job. He did receive a package of printed bulletins and some mimeographed material in a franked envelope from the County Extension Office. But a lot of other mail comes to him too. He reads most of the first-class and personal letters.

Mrs. Everyday phoned him before each of the next few meetings of the 4-H Club. But it was cultivating and harvest season and Mr. Almostdid had not agreed to sacrifice his own crops so he didn't get into the practice of attending club meetings nor did he attend the quarterly 4-H leader meeting at the County Seat. He did come to the fall Achievement Day and received a pin and a handshake "as one of ten new 4-H leaders in the county this year." In short, Mr. Almostdid became a "leader-in-name-only." He joined the multitude of misguided souls who feebly accept a leader role with a vague notion that their "name only" attached to a good thing somehow will make it even better.

Service! Ethics! Dedications! All of these things and many other conditions were lacking in Mr. Almostdid's leadership experience. Fortunately, the Happy Corners 4-H Club could get along without him. But how much more they could have done if they had found a man as dedicated as Mrs. Everyday!

Both Jim Goodfil and Mr. Almostdid can be classed as earnest, sincere people, willing to serve if wanted. Their motivations would not be considered selfish. Their dedications are "good" in terms of our American culture. While Mr. Almostdid is "sitting on" a leadership job that might better be served by a well-prepared and enthusiastic participant, at worst he is doing no one harm.

The case of Mr. Stirrup provides an interesting variation. When the movement to consolidate one-room country schools into larger administrative units hit his county, Mr. Stirrup "moved in" with it. As frequently happens, the issues surrounding proposals for building new modern structures, establishing bus routes and abandoning existing schools became clouded with emotion and misinformation. Mr. Stirrup offered "to represent the opposition" with his "experienced legal counsel." Working through a group of known skeptics, a citizen's protest meeting was arranged. To this meeting Mr. Stirrup brought impressive-looking volumes of legal rulings and opinions. He had a chart on which was listed the taxes paid by individual landowners in a distant county in 1945 "before" school consolidation and in 1952 "after" school consolidation. No mention was made of a costly county roads improvement program which was undertaken during the same period. It was pointed out that "taxes nearly doubled along with school consolidation."

When the subject of fees arose, Mr. Stirrup magnanimously offered to "organize and represent" the now militant opposition for "only ⅓ the increased tax for just one year that each would bear" under consolidation. The "increased tax" was "computed" on the basis of the alleged 50% tax increase mentioned.

What a subtle scheme! In the spirited discussion about whether ⅓ or ¼ would be a "reasonable fee" for Mr. Stirrup, no one stopped to question the basic assertion that taxes would rise 50%. It is of little comfort here that the 25% fee was agreed to. It netted Mr. Stirrup an average fee of $12.50 from each of 217 aroused taxpayers, or an estimated $2712.50. It netted the community the most serious conflict and split in its history—over an issue that seldom was discussed on its real merits and the actual facts. The alleged 50% tax increase became such a symbol that the school officials finally pleaded for a truce and the proposal was completely dropped, at least for several years.

Mr. Stirrup issued a public statement of "victory" and successfully ran for public office on a platform of "defender of the people's rights" at the next election.

Need one discuss the ethics of this kind of leadership? There was an insidious, or at best, a selfish dedication or motivation behind Mr. Stirrup's activities in opposition to the proposed school consolidation. More than anything else he wanted a "service" fee. Also he may have been ambitious for the public attention which led to an elective office or this could have been an unforeseen windfall. The objective of "personal gain and glory" may have been reached by Mr. Stirrup in the short run. It even may have given him some personal satisfaction (a sizeable fee and a public office).

The words of Abraham Lincoln remind us, "You can fool some of the people all of the time and you can fool all of the people some of the time, but you cannot fool all of the people all of the time." Besides that, we doubt if a man can fool his own "inner self" *any* of the time.

How Do Our Dedications and Value Systems Affect Our Leadership Action?

The actions of a leader are and should be an extension or projection of his inner self. For those who are graphically minded, perhaps Figure 2 will clarify this point. We shall identify four areas or phases of leadership activity or function on the part of an individual leader. Admittedly this is an over-simplification of the process. There are many cross lines and tangential elements that influence a real-life situation but it would be impractical and unimportant to our central thought to inject them here.

It is assumed that some stimulus or situation or *need* enters the figure somewhere before **A**. The actual manner in which this stimulus or impulse is received by the individual is very complex. It may come consciously (perception) or it may be derived from a more intricate thought process like reasoning or emotion. In any case, the critical point in our present discussion is at **A**.

Each of us learns or acquires out of our culture (the environment around us, including family, friends, education, religion, economy, etc.) a set of values, ideals, standards or dedications. These are closely related to what is called conscience. We do not use the term "conscience" here because popular usage of the word frequently includes very minor or short-lived considerations (viz: "My conscience bothers me because I haven't yet written and thanked Aunt Molly for her birthday gift.")

The values, beliefs and dedications at Point **A** serve as a screen or a sifting device. Through them pass (or are inhibited before they pass) all of our impulses toward action or behavior. The stimuli or ideas which are consistent with our dedications and beliefs are allowed to pass through and move along our

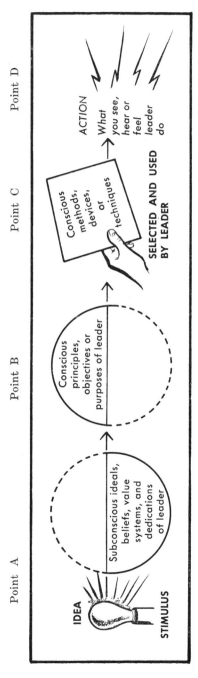

Figure 2. Action as a Projection of the Inner Self

conscious thought stream to station **B.** Here we sort them into types or groups of principles and objectives. This is not a literal process but rather a part of the mind's miraculous power of recall in organized patterns. Frequently a particularly stimulating new idea will generate a new objective or specific goal for us. Those which are both new and difficult to attain may be "held over for another hearing." Some become sidetracked, lost, or forgotten altogether.

You will notice and wonder why we are using the terms "principles" and "objectives" interchangeably in this chapter. As they relate to stage B in Figure 2 we believe this is logical. A principle, as defined and developed more extensively in Chapter V, is a guide line which we use to proceed from one situation or from one foundation to another. An objective is the specific conscious reason or motivation which compels us toward this action. Principles and objectives are at the same level or "station" in the behavior process. Therefore, it is essential to treat the two as a complementary unit in this chapter.

If the stimulus or idea is still strong and perhaps even magnified by combining with other reinforcing ideas or motivations at point **B**, then our conscious thoughts turn to *how* will this idea be carried out. Methods or procedures are selected at **C** and the action or behavior of the leader takes place at **D**.

If, on the other hand, the original idea or stimulus was *not* consistent with and agreeable to our basic values or dedications at **A**, it is likely to be rejected. Or at least we will *want* to reject it and we will resist carrying the idea any further. Sometimes we go through a strange rationalizing process at point **A**. Frequently we are not consciously aware of why some things are acceptable to us and others are unacceptable. We may not realize that this screening is going on. Someone asks us *why* will you not do this. We reply, "Well, I don't know why, but I just don't believe in it."

Or in another situation we may say feebly, "You may be right, but I don't think I am interested."

Before moving on to the subject of significant kinds of values and dedications let's use one example to illustrate the sequence and chain of influences that affect a leader's actions.

One boy, an officer in a high school F.F.A. chapter, clearly becomes guilty of violating one of the chapter's most important rules—good sportsmanship. The chapter advisor places much emphasis on honesty, forthrightness and adherence to established rules. But he has also a strong belief in democratic principles. His emotions and his pedagogical training that punishment should be immediate, or not at all, arouse a desire to reprimand the boy immediately and remove him from chapter office because he violated a chapter rule.

But the instructor's democratic dedication is strong. His belief in the democratic process comes first and he places higher value on letting the chapter handle its own disciplinary problems than he does on satisfying his urge for immediate punishment. This is the subconscious sifting or screening process which was going on for the advisor at point **A** in our diagram. Accordingly, (at point **B**), his objective becomes one of helping the chapter and the boy to learn how the processes of group discipline work. He selects (at point **C**) the method of referring this case to the chapter president for possible consideration by the executive committee. His final observable action (point **C**) is to bring together the offender and the president and to discuss the incident with them. He raises the question whether or not this problem should come before the chapter council since it concerns a chapter rule.

We must not confuse the group of terms "dedications," "values," and "beliefs" with another group of terms—"right and wrong," "legal and illegal," "moral and immoral." The latter are frequently involved in or are a part of the former. But they have a more transitory meaning and importance. Laws and morals and customs change, sometimes rapidly. Basic dedications of individuals are more solidly fixed and enduring. Once firmly established in the minds and hearts of individuals and groups, basic dedications are not easily uprooted. Just as the foundation of a large heavy building is difficult to rebuild or repair, so it is with the value systems of one's character and personality. Also, it pertains that if the dedications and values of an individual are shattered and destroyed without replacement, the person's personality and character fall apart like a building with a crumbling foundation.

At the same time, we must remember that dedications may be "good" or "bad," "socially acceptable" or "socially unacceptable" and "positive" or "negative." It is reported that Al Capone, the infamous Chicago killer and gangster of the 1930's, actually believed himself to be a benefactor of the poor and the weak. At the same time he gave $1000 bills to an aged or suffering old lady in a slums tenement, he was dedicated to maintaining his status as the king of gangsters and U. S. Public Enemy No. 1. Values and dedications, then, can be positive or negative and they predispose an individual or a group toward cooperative action, or against it. So be careful, leader—your dedications are showing!

Some Dedications and Beliefs That Affect Rural Leadership

Agrarianism. The family farm principle provides an interesting example of a basic dedication or value in our American culture. Most of the earliest colonies were founded for mercantilist reasons.[2] It is all the more significant, therefore, that we departed from that philosophy, and settled firmly on a belief that ownership and operation of the land is a right and a responsibility for individual families. Patriots like Jefferson, Franklin, Payne, and Washington established agrarianism as an American policy. Seldom has a prime dedication been more faithfully protected and preserved through two centuries. In virtually every session of Congress, legislation is introduced to promote or protect the family farm. Currently, there exists a sub-committee of the House Committee on Agriculture known as the Family Farm Sub-Committee.

The early Land Ordinances beginning in 1785 and culminating in the Homestead Act of 1862 are prime examples of agrarian policy. Much of our vast public domain was deliberately placed in the hands of family owner-operators at little or no purchase cost. Only settlement and improvement was asked of homesteaders after 1862. This policy was supported by labor groups because it insured plentiful food and an outlet for surplus or dissatisfied industrial workers. Reasonably, one might have expected strong opposition from industrialists. It failed to develop. America believes in this policy.

For over a century these small individual family units were handicapped by inadequate credit for land purchase and production purposes. So a sympathetic U. S. Citizenry, less than a fourth of whom lived on farms, taxed themselves to

[2]M. R. Benidict, *Farm Policies of the U. S., 1870-1950.*

establish a complete system of government-sponsored farm credit that is unique in the world.[3]

There are many institutions seriously dedicated to maintenance of the family farm. One is the American Country Life Association which grew out of the Country Life Commission established by President Theodore Roosevelt at the beginning of this century. There is a Catholic Rural Life Conference and a nationwide Rural Life Sunday (on Rogation Sunday). The Cooperative Extension Service, Vocational Agriculture and virtually the entire Land-Grant College System have the same original dedications. All of the major national farm organizations continuously and diligently guard the "agrarian right" of a single family to own and operate the land for economic gain and family satisfaction.

Our nation's leaders, through at least 200 years, have devoted their lives and cast their votes on particular issues in accordance with whether or not the family farm ideal would be preserved. Do ideals and dedications have an influence on the destiny of men and nations? Here is a prime example.

Faith in God. On the half dollar coin which keeps the notes in front of me from blowing off into the Colorado sun is crested a simple phrase with the highest prestige and status of any collection of words in the English language, "In God We Trust."

Every schoolboy, lodge member, vestryman or legislator knows that our nation was founded in an atmosphere of religious faith and freedom. Our rural culture has been, to an amazing degree, both the incubator and the brooder house for a continuing spiritual dedication.

In our time we have seen the worried and haggard farmers of a drought-parched, mid-west community assemble on a Thursday evening in the Court House square to pray for rain. And we have seen them return again the following week to offer humble thanks—when it did.

Those who would work with rural people should learn well their fundamentals of life. Was it Oliver Cromwell who first

---

[3]The Farm Credit System includes a nationwide system of local Farm Loan Associations for long-term mortgage credit, Production Credit Associations for short-term credit and banks for cooperatives. Also, it includes a Farmers Cooperative Service for educational and research purposes connected with agricultural credit. The system is now autonomous and self-supporting except for the educational and research features of the Farmers Cooperative Service, U.S.D.A.

advised, "Trust in God, and Keep Your Powder Dry"? Today's equivalent of Cromwell's "powder horn" is an ever-increasing body of scientific facts, skills and technical information. "Trust in God" is the leaven which raises man's existence above the sour-dough stage of futility and despair. It is the seed which will always grow—and bear bountiful fruit—when planted in humble soil.

Faith, hope and science are the rural worker's seed, soil and rainfall. Charity and service to others are the rent he pays for space on earth.

The Golden Rule in Human Relations.

"Before you criticize another Indian
Walk in his moccasins for two weeks."—Indian Legend

"There, but for the grace of God, go I."—Anon.

In recent years, research in the social and behavioral sciences has taken tremendous strides forward. This development is timely. It comes as a result of felt needs. The need for more facts, deeper insights and broader principles is still an urgent problem for psychologists, students of human development and cultural anthropologists. As new research and scientific developments came, the popular appetite for more and better gadgets was expanded.

It is common knowledge that our intelligent social usage of these products has not kept pace. The new comforts, leisure time, and increased mobility of our population have created new problems of social and family adjustment even before we were adequately prepared to handle the older ones.

But there is hope. Thrilling, stirring progress is being made. When applied to the problems of human relations, modern science is now finding satisfactory answers. In many areas the skilled hand of the new social scientist is firmly clasped with the experienced hands of the progressive educator and the theologian. Together, this team is developing a rich body of fact, experience, and methods which will shed more light with less heat on the problems of man's relations with other men.

We list here six of the more significant calibrations on the Golden Rule which modern behavioral scientists find are important in human relations. Leaders among rural people will find many of these tenets securely woven into the woof and warp of rural life. Try to measure your own example of "Doing unto others as you would have them do unto you" in the light of these tenets.

1. *Every individual is worthy.* Each is important, necessary in our society and entitled to play a useful and recognized part in the drama of life. Acceptance of each person *for his own self*, regardless of station in life, is the leader's key to complete rapport with all members of the group.

2. *Each individual is unique and different.* Growth and development, learning readiness and social maturation progress in the same sequence but at different rates for every person. A leader must give individual attention and make adjustments for fast, slow, and arrested development.

3. *What a person lives, he becomes.* Personality, character and beliefs are acquired from our culture after birth. Knowledge, skills and attitudes are the learning goals of most educational systems. "We learn what we live, and what we thus learn is through the very process of living built at once into the structure of one's being, there to form the foundation for behavior."[4]

   In the hands of parents, teachers, leaders and our culture lies the welfare and destiny of every individual. There is no such thing as "a self-made man."

4. *The capacity and potential for learning* exists in every individual. The human mind and personality act like an amazingly absorptive sponge. Unlike a regular sponge, however, it can receive, store and share information without loss of the original stock. Sharing knowledge with others has a multiplying rather than a subtracting or dividing effect. Leaders must help develop favorable situations or climate for learning. But individuals must learn for themselves. Learning by doing unlocks many blocks and resistances.

5. *Love is a reality.*[5] It is a potent force for harmony and progress. Cooperation promotes but inter-personal competition many times tends to destroy the basis for human understanding.[6] Empathy and sharing in the problems and goals of others

---

[4]William H. Kilpatrick, *The Community School.* Appleton-Century-Crofts, Inc., 1938, Introductory Chapter.
[5]We speak here of human love and understanding among all persons rather than romantic or exotic love.
[6]Ashley Montague, *On Being Human.* Henry Schuman, Inc., 1950, Chapter 2, pp. 96-102.

are important elements of true love and are the two most useful tools of successful democratic leaders. Love is a magnetism that holds people and groups together. Disintegration, loneliness and despair are the grim reapers of shattered or frustrated love. Love can exist among all persons and within and between groups. It can exist between nations.

Hate is a negative thing. Just as cold is simply the absence of heat, so hate is an absence of love. Hate acts like a centrifuge to tear things into particles of different weights or characteristics. It shatters their composures and cohesiveness. It devastates organization. Hate has no place in the heart of a real leader.

6. *Dedications, ideals and value systems* are the compass and stabilizers for personality. This point is the substance for this entire chapter and by now should be established. It is important only to reaffirm here that the concept has a scientific as well as a practical validity.

Education and Science as Tools for Progress. We are not going to belabor this point. It is obvious that much of what we are and have today is the result of accumulated knowledge, skills and attitudes handed down from earlier generations. That is one function of education—to record and communicate the progress of one generation for the benefit of the next. This ability is the art which distinguishes man from lower animals.

We first learned to chisel crude pictures on the walls of caves only a few thousand years ago. But since that time we have made more progress toward civilization than in the preceding half million years.

Science is the fountain-head of education. The research of industry and of government experiment stations has jumped our country's agricultural development a quarter century ahead of most agrarian nations. Still, though we consider ourselves alert and aggressive, about 10 years elapse between the time a new practice or technique is released and its general adoption into usage throughout the length and breadth of our land. Here is a challenge worthy of our best rural leadership—to help shorten the lapse of time between research discovery and general adoption of better practices—for more abundant living.

When Abraham Lincoln, in 1862, signed the Act of Congress establishing the Land-Grant College System, he resounded a dedi-

cation to the principle of universal education. These public-supported colleges and universities were to bring the opportunities of
a college education to the sons and daughters of farmers and
mechanics. Prior to this time, higher education in the United
States was largely for sons of the wealthy, who could attend
Harvard, Yale or Princeton. Also, of course, there were numerous
church-supported theological seminaries.

Subsequent acts of Congress established the U. S. Department of Agriculture (1862), the experiment stations (1882), the
Cooperative Extension Service (1914), the Vocational Agriculture Program (1917), and numerous other information and
service programs, all dedicated to educational and scientific
assistance for rural people.

Acceptance and use of science and education gives the leader
his most effective weapons against man's most ancient of enemies—ignorance, poverty, disease, indifference and hate.

The Democratic Process. This dedication is of such broad and
deep consequence that it is really the fiber for this entire book,
especially Chapter VI. Therefore, its separate treatment here
would be inadequate and inappropriate. Perhaps this adage
speaks our feeling more clearly than any additional paragraph
would—"What you do speaks so loudly that I cannot hear your
words."

SUMMARY

Leadership is an extension of your inner self to other persons and to groups. What you are and do is conditioned by your
beliefs, dedications and ideals. These you have acquired from
the culture, the people and the experiences that have influenced
you. Development and changes in your dedications usually take
place slowly. But a deeply emotional experience may explode an
ideal into, or out of, your personality with amazing swiftness
and finality. Dedications and value systems may be "good" or
"bad." Either type can have equal but opposite consequences.

All new ideas and stimulations are first screened through
the woof and warp of our dedications, ideals, and value system.
We reject ideas which are not consistent with what we believe.
We tolerate only those which are not threatening to our established concepts. We implement into action those which are con-

sistent with or supporting to our dedications. This implementation and action process is discussed in following chapters.

Specific dedications and value patterns that have withstood the test of time for rural leaders include:

Agrarianism and the Family Farm
Faith in God
The Golden Rule in Human Relations
Education and Science as Tools for Progress
The Democratic Process

The six mistakes of man:

1. The delusion that personal gain is made by crushing others.

2. The tendency to worry about things that cannot be changed or corrected.

3. Insisting that a thing is impossible because we cannot accomplish it.

4. Refusing to set aside trivial preferences.

5. Neglecting development and refinement of the mind, and not acquiring the habit of reading and study.

6. Attempting to compel others to believe and live as we do.

—Cicero

CHAPTER V

Principles of Democratic Leadership

PRINCIPLES AND TECHNIQUES OF LEADERSHIP

We have all been leaders at one time or another. We may not have been deliberate in our attempt to aid or influence other individuals toward the acceptance of some goal, but none-the-less we were the persons responsible. A new idea is presented to our school board, our local 4-H Club, or our business organization; and because of our particular reaction to that idea others may accept it, reject it, or willingly study it for a later decision. The leadership thus exerted, conscious or unconscious, could be one of many kinds. It could be based upon our direct control of others by the nature of our wealth, our social position, or our persuasive tongue. It could be based upon respect for our wisdom on such matters or upon the knowledge that we make no decision in haste where the welfare of the total group is at stake. This informal leadership, exerted in the way described above, could in some cases be democratic and in other cases be more closely related to a leadership of authority; but it is leadership.

Democratic leadership is the means by which one or more persons aid a group in setting and attaining desirable goals. There is real distinction between *democratic leadership* and *leadership in general.* The distinction is sharpest if we observe a highly regarded definition of leadership in general and compare it with that of democratic leadership as stated. Ordway Tead defines leadership thus: *"Leadership is the activity of influencing people to cooperate toward some goal which they come to find desirable."*[1]

The distinction is largely one of *influence.* In democratic leadership the focus is not *to influence* people but *to aid* people. It is the distinction between *my solution* and *our solution.* Democratic leadership puts the *"our"* in focus. Authoritarian leadership puts the *"my"* in focus. Leadership can be either, or at any

---

[1]Ordway Tead, *The Art of Leadership.* New York, McGraw-Hill Book Company, 1935, p. 20.

point in between. The principles of democratic leadership in this book will keep the *"our"* concept in focus.

A principle of democratic leadership is a guide line which we use to proceed from one situation to another. It is a general truth about leadership. It is available to be used as a foundation for our actions. It is the foundation from which stem our techniques and methods. We get a new idea on how to act in a leadership situation; we've never used that idea before and look for some means by which we can judge its worth. The best test of our idea is not a comparison with some other method or technique, but a critical look at our idea in terms of the principle from which it stems. Principles of democratic leadership are most important to the individual when they are a part of his beliefs rather than a crutch to use in a tough situation.

Emerson indicated that "The value of a principle is the number of things it will explain." In one respect, principles are used in leadership as criteria. We select our techniques and methods in terms of the degree to which they meet the criterion of democratic leadership.

Techniques and methods of leadership are the means by which aid is given. A leader can become very skilled in method and technique and yet fail to be successful. Related to every principle are hundreds of methods and techniques that are useful. Specific methods seem to be much more practical in a particular crisis than do principles, and often give the unskilled leader a sense of security. He is able to say, "I really found a method that worked," and then continues to use it in all situations with no further consideration of where it may lead. We do not wish to underestimate the value of techniques and methods in democratic leadership, but neither do we wish to place them above principle.

Mrs. Jones was recognized as an effective leader in a western Montana community. Though effective in getting jobs done, occasionally her efforts were questioned by community groups as being too autocratic. Mrs. Jones' basic beliefs were not autocratic; they were democratic. Her leadership problem was related to her ready acceptance of techniques and methods as the answer to all leadership problems. She would observe someone else using a new film discussion method in a more effective way than she had used it. Because it looked good she would use it the next time she had a chance. It was used without adequate consideration of the group in which it was to be used, or without particular concern for the kind of principles from which it developed. Mrs. Jones thought that all group action was democratic action, not realizing that group activity developed by the leader is not necessarily the same as group action voluntarily initiated and/or accepted by the group.

Just as Mrs. Jones too willingly accepted a technique without proper regard for principle, so many of us tend to become so technique-conscious that we forget the basic guide lines to our philosophy of democratic leadership. Assume for a moment the leadership role that the chairman of a farm organization enjoys. Two principles of democratic leadership that will aid him in making decisions as to methods and techniques to use in leading his unit are the principles of participation and sharing. As will be noted later in this chapter, these relate to man's understanding and support of those things he originates and those decisions in which he shares. Methods to be used by the chairman should be judged not just on their glamour, their effectiveness in some former situation, or their ease of operation, but more significantly on the relationship they have to certain principles of democratic leadership.

It is important to note at this point that making these comparisons and final decisions is no easy task. A particular device or method may be based on a combination of principles, some democratic, others not. Another method may be only vaguely related to our basic operating principles, while still another may be in harmony with them but so technically difficult to accomplish that you, as a leader, will not want to try to use it for fear of making a mistake.

Every leader must be aware of the place of techniques and methods and the place of principles in the total scheme of democratic leadership. There are distinctions between them, with principles being more closely related to the "what" than to the "how." Though both are important, the concern for principles must always be paramount to a reliance on technique. The two are not separate attributes; rather they are coordinated elements needing profound consideration by the leader in a democratic society.

Influence of Varying Situations. The conditions under which leadership aid is offered vary both for different leaders and for the same leader at different times. The aid that a teacher of agriculture can give to a group of adult farmers may be expressed in one way when meeting with this group in a school classroom, but may be expressed in entirely different form when he meets with an adult farmer on his own farm or when he meets one of the group in a coffee shop on main street. A teacher of agriculture in a neighboring community may provide just as effective leadership, but in a completely different pattern, in each of the situations described. Certainly he should!

As rural leaders we must keep in mind that patterns of leadership are far different than blueprints for building a house or different than a pattern for making a dress. The material with which we are working is human material. We recognize that human material is unique in that every individual is different from every other individual. To that extent alone, we are comparable. Just as the individuals differ who make up the groups with whom we work, so do the groups differ. We see this difference in the groups of which we are a part. In fact, each group tends to have a "personality" and "character" of its own.

This difference among groups demands of leaders a flexibility that is equal to or greater than the flexibility and understanding required of a teacher who tries to adjust his teaching to the individual differences of his students. The characteristics which cause variation among groups are the characteristics to which we must adjust our leadership patterns as we attempt to lead. This adjustment made in leadership patterns is more closely related to techniques and methods used than it is to the basic principles and dedications that provide guide lines to our leadership efforts. If we know the key principles of leadership, they will give us the basis for making decisions as to technique and method; a few sound principles will help determine and explain hundreds of techniques. We need not be a human reservoir of knowledge about techniques and methods of leadership if we have in mind key principles to guide our action. More significant still, sound principles give us a basis for creativity in our leadership role. Principles will release the leader from a strait jacket of method. As shown in Figure 3, the use of method without a firm basis in principle often will be ineffective in bringing the efforts of the leader to focus on the goal. This lack of focus on a goal reminds us of the early day politician who, seeing that the time was ripe for action among a group of demonstrators on the capitol steps, left his office, jumped on his horse, and dashed off into the distance. He may have had an effective method, but certain principles of leadership were overlooked. Where leadership situations are as varied as they are in rural communities, it is essential that leaders be aware of basic principles that can be used as guides to their leadership actions. Our basic dedications and our principles for operation establish a line of vision direct to our leadership goal. The methods and techniques used must be within that line of vision to be effective.

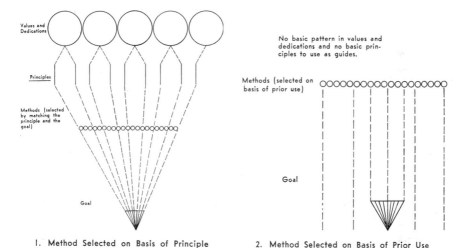

1. Method Selected on Basis of Principle   2. Method Selected on Basis of Prior Use

Figure 3. Two Alternative Means by Which Leadership Methods Are Selected

Adjusting to New Situations. Leading a 4-H Club of twenty boys is not the same as leading a 4-H Club made up of twenty girls, or a club of both boys and girls. Leading this age group is different than providing leadership for an adult farm organization or for a citizens committee interested in making the rural village a better place in which to trade. The basic difference in the above situations is related very specifically to the goals that are established within each group, or by the leader and the group. Referring to Figure 4, we note that a number of alternate goals are found. As the goals change, so does the direction of the leader's efforts. In that change of direction toward the goal, the guide line from principle to goal will indicate other methods that may best be used. Changing situations will have a great deal of influence on the methods and techniques used by a leader, but such temporary adjustments do not affect his dedications and principles. It is clear that in certain situations the goals may be such that we would feel obligated to provide no leadership to reach them. In short, they would be contrary to our values and principles.

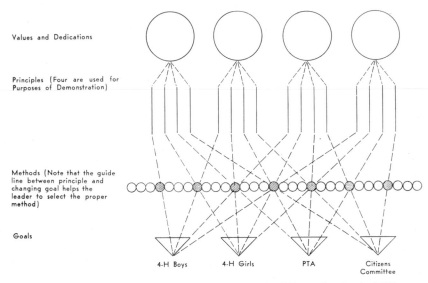

Values and Dedications

Principles (Four are used for Purposes of Demonstration)

Methods (Note that the guide line between principle and changing goal helps the leader to select the proper method)

Goals

4-H Boys   4-H Girls   PTA   Citizens Committee

Figure 4. Selection of Leadership Methods When the Goals Differ

An example in relation to Figure 4 would be a goal so far to the right or left of the figure that a guide line drawn from the values and dedications through the principles could not reach the goal.

To further clarify these three basic elements in leadership, consider your own values and dedications. Are they rooted in our democratic tradition? Do they consider "others" as well as "self"? Consider how you choose the methods you use in your leadership job. Are there any guides (principles) that you use in selecting a method? Are these principles democratic in nature, thus correct for the particular values you hold as basic? *The skilled leader is one who uses basic democratic principles as a key in the selection of methods to use in guiding action toward desirable goals.*

WHY DEMOCRATIC LEADERSHIP?

The production or accomplishment of a number of people working toward common goals is subject to great variation. In some instances where the route to the goal is direct, the efforts of non-democratic leadership may be just as effective as democratic leadership. However, in instances where the goal can be reached only by more complex routes, and where a series of secondary goals must be reached in advance of or along with the primary goal, the method that allows for great flexibility and creativity has decided advantages. The opportunity for free discussion, involvement of all concerned, exchange of ideas, for incorporation of these ideas into the plan to reach the goals, and the opportunity to volunteer one's own special skills where they can be best used are functions of democratic leadership that are superior to other forms of leadership.

A democratic leader of a Homemakers' Club encourages the group to raise questions about the value of lessons brought back from a "leader training" meeting. She encourages others to take the leadership on problems where her own knowledge is limited. She asks persons with special skills to share their ideas with the group. In reality she is an effective democratic leader because she doesn't solve all of the problems herself, nor does she provide all of the leadership. She attempts to pull together the many suggestions made so that all can see how they lead toward the earlier established goals.

The nature of our society, and particularly the nature of the rural community, is such that democratic leadership is a sound choice. It develops people, it is consistent with our way of life, and it works!

The Nature of Our Total Society. Our society is one in which the concept of individual opportunity and individual worth is recognized. Efforts are continually made to maintain that freedom for the individual. The concept of following the majority decision, with a healthy respect for the minority, is just as basic. These two concepts are not opposites nor are they congruent. The hard work of democracy is often made up of efforts to develop harmony between these two concepts. The leaders in

our society are those who have prime responsibility to develop
such harmony. When such is developed, it is often referred to
as an example of good teamwork and sound leadership. The key
idea in these situations is that the leadership action necessary
to balance the rights of the individual with the rights of the
group is democratic.

The flexibility of our total society in both vertical mobility,
which allows a person to rise above or fall below the station in
life into which he was born, and horizontal mobility, which
allows freedom for a person to move from place to place, develops
a situation in which there are almost endless opportunities for the
expression of individual initiative. Much of the stimulation and
impetus for this mobility and initiative is generated or accomplished in groups. The family as a social institution gives the
child his first experience in control by majority rule. The freedom
within the family group, however, usually allows for individual
experimentation by family members. Control in democratic
family life is used judiciously. The analogy can here be made to
other groups in our total society. There is freedom for the child
in our public schools, yet there is control in terms of that which
is valuable for the good of the group. There is freedom for the
adult in his business ventures, yet legislation is developed to
control those individual actions which will lead to hardship for
others. There is freedom for the farmer to own his own land,
but there are restrictions imposed on him by his local government if his lack of weed control infests his neighbor's land.

In the United States we are continually balancing and inter-
balancing the individual and the group. It is in this web of
interrelationship and adjustment that the democratic leader
works.

The Nature of the Rural Community. The relationships
among rural people are more personal and face-to-face than
those in urban society. With close personal relationships the
leader is more involved in the day-to-day activities of his group.
He knows more about the individuals whom he leads. He is a
good deal closer to their motives; thus he has a better knowledge
and understanding of them. He may even be able to recognize
the sources of conflict within the group more readily than can
a leader in a complex urban group. Democratic leadership should
be able to operate most effectively where the motives of indi-

viduals and the rights of groups are easily detected. The nature
of rural society is such that they can be seen. Though no attempt
is being made to prove that it is easier to provide democratic
leadership in rural communities than in urban communities, the
nature of the rural community is such that leadership types can
be more readily identified; also the rural community is an ideal
place for democratic leadership to work. If we can identify the
type of leadership we are providing, it gives us a base point upon
which to operate when change is sought.

Democratic leadership is a "natural" for rural society with
its tradition rooted in free enterprise and the rights of the individual, and its future dependent upon its ability to operate
effectively within our total society.

The Emphasis in the Literature of Leadership. As the educational level of the American citizen has been raised, the need
for a more mature leadership has been required. Though ignorant
masses may have been led by unscrupulous dictators in ancient
times, it becomes more difficult to lead by dictation when the
citizen family is a literate group. The need for a democratic
type leadership has been recognized in the United States for
many years, yet it is only in the past several decades that
emphasis has been placed on it in the professional literature.
The reasons for this increased concern may be many. Among
the reasons are most certainly our increasingly complex society,
our higher standard of living, our increased level of education,
our improved patterns of communication, and our increasing
dependence on each other.

Ordway Tead in 1935 focused an entire book on the translation of leadership capacity into democratic usefulness. He
emphasized the need for understanding the psychologically sound
essentials of leadership and their relationship to democratic
action.[2]

Franklyn Haiman, in a book on leadership, also emphasized
the democratic approach. He wrote, "If the problem of developing effective leaders was of grave concern to Plato and Plutarch
in classical times, how much more so is it today when the complexities of society have increased a millionfold, and when participation in social action has come to include the great masses
of men. It is this latter fact which makes leadership in our day

---

[2]Ordway Tead. *Op. Cit.*, pp. 268-270.

a real problem and a real challenge. As more men become literate and educated, and as social and political participation is extended to an ever-increasing number and variety of such people, leadership must become more widely distributed, more competent, and more democratic. A civilization such as ours cannot long survive with weak and unskilled leadership."[3]

In May, 1952, a new source of help for the many leaders in communities throughout the United States was made available in the form of a journal called *Adult Leadership*. Appearing monthly, except July and August, it is a publication of the Adult Education Association of the United States. A review of the issues of this journal is most convincing as to the extent of today's need and democratic emphasis in the field of leadership.

Recent studies of group behavior have placed considerable importance on the nature of democratic leadership and its relationship to effective action. A number of such studies are reported by Bradford and Gibb in an issue of the *Review of Educational Research*.[4]

Both research and reason have tended to support the democratic approach to leadership problems.[5] However, authoritarian means have not been overlooked. In some instances the emphasis on the rights of the individual have been such that his responsibilities have been neglected. When that happens a kind of anarchistic type of group behavior results with as many weaknesses as those found in autocratic group control. The authors recognize the ease with which a democratic leader can revert to authoritarian methods, how easy it is to drop leadership responsibilities entirely and watch for a "Topsy-like" growth in local groups, and how difficult it sometimes is to have faith in the ability of a group to accept its democratic responsibilities. Even so, we believe that research and experience show the direction we need to go in carrying out leadership responsibilities in

---

[3]Franklyn S. Haiman, *Group Leadership and Democratic Action*. Houghton-Mifflin Company, 1951, pp. 229.

[4]Leland P. Bradford and Jack R. Gibb, "Developments in Group Behavior in Adult Education," *Review of Educational Research*, June, 1953, pp. 233-247.

[5]For those readers who wish to go into the deeper psychological theories of leadership, and to study the results of research into various aspects of this field, we recommend *The Study of Leadership*, edited by Dr. C. G. Browne and Dr. T. S. Cohn, of Wayne State University. The Interstate Printers and Publishers, Inc., Danville, Ill., 1958.

a democratic society. In many respects this conviction rests in an ideal leadership that is steeped in our democratic tradition.

The Ideal of Democratic Leadership

Leadership that is democratic is an ideal for many who accept leadership responsibilities in rural society. Often it is an ideal difficult to approach because of the traditional ways group action has occurred. Yet it is approachable, as examples in the later chapters of this book will show. The ideal of democratic leadership is composed of these important elements: participation, equality (of both opportunity and responsibility), human relationships, individuality, and group authority.

Participation. The opportunity for everyone to take part in the deliberations, interpretations and the actions of the group is a most important part of the ideal. It's an easy point of view for a potential leader to accept, but a difficult one to live up to in practice. Those who aspire to positions of leadership often are themselves "great participators," and because of active participation are interested in and involved in many educational activities. There are many others in rural groups who are not active participators. These are the ones who need encouragement and motivation before their interest is high enough to get them to take active part in group activities. The leader has the task of making opportunities for participation available to all. This demands of the leader a greater knowledge of people and of psychology than is often his. Fortunately, with the help available from professional leaders and educators, this knowledge can be obtained through a variety of in-service education means. Chapters VII and VIII will aid in this regard.

Equality. A second important element in the ideal of democratic leadership is that of equality. Our American tradition emphasizes equality in all group leadership situations. Though emphasized, there are times when would-be-leaders lose sight of that ideal in an effort to gain favor with a group or to hurry through a decision so that immediate action on a project might be taken. The difficulty we have in moving from the ideal to the action is often based on misinterpretations of equality. The strength of democratic participation lies in the fact that different individuals can present different ideas. Some ideas are good, some not so good; but either kind can begin a kind of "chain reaction" which stimulates further thinking and creativity within the group. The most frequent weakness of group activity is a failure to recognize and to use the individual talents and contributions of all members. The fact that the contributions are not of equal value in a given situation does not oppose the concept of equality. It strengthens the emphasis needed on equal opportunity, thus leading to the final product being a "group product" which all can support. That one or two individuals contributed more to a given solution is to their credit, but there is no disapproval of those who in a given situation may have made only minor contributions. Next time their efforts may lead to major developments.

Sound Human Relationships and Individual Respect. The response of individuals to each other can set the tone of any discussion. The respect of one for the other, even though there be differences in opinion, is basic to the democratic ideal. The leader must respect and accept other people before he can himself be respected. The leader must be respected by the group before the give and take of group activity can be on a level that shows an interchange of mutual concern for others. The ideal shows the leader respecting the group and the individuals of the group. The group members respect the leader but also respect each other. This interchange of faith in each other develops a "give and take" in group activity and action that can be described only in terms of human values and individual rights. This respect is the ideal which makes it possible for people to oppose each other's ideas vigorously, but support just as vigorously their right to disagree.

The respect for the individual is such in this ideal situation that free play of the intellect is possible. It combines faith in the individual with faith in the group and recognizes the role of the individual in the group.

Group Authority. The concept of the leader acting with the group or acting for the group has been subject to varying interpretations by leaders and educators. In the democratic ideal the group is the authority while the leader serves the group. When decisions are made by a group it should seek to carry out its plans most efficiently. It is at this point that a leader may become too engrossed in the concept of participation to recognize the need for direct action. When action is to be taken the group may find it most expedient to encourage the leader to act for it, to have the leader direct the action, or to have the leader arrange to get the job done by direct delegation of tasks to outside experts or group members. There is a real difference between the decision stage and the action stage of group activity. If leaders and group members fail to recognize this difference, they may be unable to accomplish any of their specific goals. Lack of achievement is the worst enemy of democratic action. Thus, the role of the leader in accepting the responsibility to act for the group is vital for continued leadership success.

At the same time the group may find, under certain circumstances, it is most effective to act as a total group. Or again the group may delegate one segment to carry through on a suggested solution. It is in these situations that the formal leader must be wise enough to step back and allow for group action. A balance in jobs accomplished by leaders, and those accomplished by committees or the total group, is important if we are to maintain group authority.

In this concept of democratic leadership, the group has the authority which it may delegate at will to the leader. By the same token, it may be retrieved from the leader at will. The delegation of this authority where it can best be used to accomplish its goals is the greatest responsibility of the group.

From Ideal to Action

The adjustments are great which individual leaders make in moving from the democratic ideal to democratic action in specific situations. Things rarely go as planned; some individual takes an unpredictable action, a group changes its mind just as the leader feels that progress has been made, factions within groups arise and compete to the point where concensus is impossible, or the group is not ready or willing to accept a leader's suggestion.

It is when the unforeseen or the unpredictable occurs that leaders show the strength of their democratic ideals. This is the point which determines whether faith in the group and faith in the individual will continue, or whether some other type of leadership will be expressed. This could be by autocratic action or by the leader giving up completely.

The unpredictable actions of groups have numerous causes. For example, the ideal group situation is one where there is mutual respect shown among all members of the group. Such is not always the case, and individuals may become more involved in competing against one another than in producing as a single unit. The same may be true among various groups that make up a total community or county program. Community and county leaders will sometimes find it nearly impossible to get the groups to join hands in an undertaking that can be accomplished only by cooperation.

Groups as well as individuals vary greatly in their experience with democratic participation. Some groups are able to attack and solve difficult community problems, while others are able to deal effectively with only the most simple problems. The combination of different abilities of individuals and groups and various degrees of difficulty in the problems places the leader in a position where faith in the ideal, understanding of the present barriers, and patience may be his most important attributes.

Though the concept of equality of opportunity for all may be readily accepted on a theoretical basis, it is often difficult to carry out in practice. Individuals vary greatly in ability. One person is able to express himself well on a problem under consideration, while another who knows more about the problem is unable to express his ideas in intelligible form. One person is continually finding fault with the suggestions of his colleagues, but offers nothing positive in return, while another in the same group expresses approval of everything, to the point where the leader loses faith in the person's ability to tell good from bad.

Measuring equality of opportunity is not something that can be done with complete accuracy. The leader, instead of dealing with absolutes, is dealing with total situations which include an individual's relative ability, his need as he sees it, his readiness or preparation for participation, and his personal values which affect his attitudes toward both the leader and the problem being considered. In the leadership task it is then essential that there be balance between the concept of equality and the real differences in an individual's ability.

Rural people are cautious in their acceptance of leaders and leadership expression. Their tradition of freedom and individuality cause them to seek "freedom from leadership" at the very same time that they accept "freedom for leadership." This attitude is of considerable aid to the person aspiring to a democratic type of leadership. It tends to thwart any leadership attempt that becomes dogmatic and authoritarian, yet allows for leadership expression and drive on the part of anyone in the group.

In movement from the ideal to the action level of democratic leadership there are times when adjustments and variations from the ideal must be made. These adjustments do not mean that the ideal is changed, only that the real life situation is such that compromise is necessary. For example, a particular rural group may have been accustomed to rather autocratic leadership for many years. When those in positions of leadership leave the group it might be impossible to move directly to a democratic type of group discussion and action. The new leader will have to begin where the group is—in this case within an autocratic type of leadership—and through education and example, and in a step-by-step procedure, move toward the democratic ideal. Also he must be ready to expect frequent reversals to the earlier system.

THE PRINCIPLES

From the personal values and dedications that we hold come the principles that guide our leadership actions. An earlier chapter discusses the over-riding and all-permeating nature and effects of these values and dedications.

No list of principles would cover all situations calling for the exercise of leadership. The most important ones have been selected and will be explained in the remainder of this chapter.

The Principle of Challenge. Anyone who feels a leadership responsibility within a group often feels that responsibility because of the challenge that the group goals have for him. Challenge is stimulating. A challenge stimulates individual activity and it stimulates group activity. Certain difficulties and hurdles are a great challenge to some individuals in a group, while to others alternative courses of action are a stimulant and a challenge. In others the mere opportunity of *freedom of choice* makes any problem-solving situation most exciting. It is through challenge that individual group members and leaders themselves move to the forefront of knowledge and obtain creative ideas for the future. Challenge develops one's enthusiasm, it stimulates thought, it leads to an exchange of ideas and finally to a willingness to try alternative courses of action.

A democratic leader is one who is not afraid of challenge. He is one who is willing to provide challenges and challenging situations both for himself and for his group. One must have faith in both the individuals of a group and in the decisions that they will make as a group.

The Principle of Participation. Man understands and accepts best those actions which he helped originate. The principle of participation is built on the concept of individual faith in oneself. If a person feels that some little thing that he did was responsible in even a small degree for an action taken by a total group, he is much more willing to accept the outcomes of that group action. This psychological bias toward one's own actions is perfectly normal. After all, one lives with himself constantly, and communication and understanding of one's own ideas approaches perfection. Therefore, "If I had a part in it, I agree with it. It has meaning for me." If that is true, if a person feels that group action is his action, the leader has a very important principle to bear in mind.

In addition to understanding group actions related to one's own contributions, it is also very important for the leader to know that the support of such action is often very closely associated with the degree of participation that an individual had in deciding on that action. Even the simple tool of voting on minor decisions of the group provides one with the feeling that he has taken part. It is well to recognize that voting can become meaningless if overdone. When that occurs, one loses the feeling of participation; one feels only that the group is a rubber stamp for the leader's proposals. Often consensus (general agreement), when recognized by a leader and verified by asking for a show of hands, is an effective tool well in line with the guiding principle of participation.

The Principle of Sharing. Leadership is a group phenomenon. One cannot lead unless there are those to be led. The communication of ideas within a group is one of the responsibilities of leadership. This, of course, is true of any type of leadership and is not specific to the democratic concept that is our concern. In democratic leadership, the leadership function itself can be shared as communication among members of the group progresses. A leader must be very willing to share in the results of leadership without insisting that he lose any of the responsibilities of leadership. Democratic group action assumes that there may be many contributors and many leaders in a group before action is taken. A leader who is willing to share the responsibilities of leadership is one who will find that the hard work of getting results can just as readily be shared with those with whom he works. This is considerably different from the type of authoritarian leadership that is characterized by a leader who is the life or the death of group action. One of the most difficult aspects of the sharing of leadership is the willingness for the leader to have others "carry the ball." There may be times in following the principle of sharing when the entire leadership pattern will change. This may mean that you as an individual leader may lose your key leadership role for the major part of the group problem-solving and action period. This suggests that leadership roles exist not for the sake of the leader but for the welfare of the group. Service above self is difficult for some, but tremendously satisfying to the truly democratic leader. An important characteristic of a democratic leader is his ability to lose himself for the benefit of the group.

The Principle of Knowledge. The leader in the democratic society and in a democratic group must know something about something. He is not able to operate as an effective group leader or stimulator of group thought and action merely by technique and method. He must be recognized as having at least average capability or greater in the kind of work which is being discussed or about the problem for which a solution is sought. In addition to knowledge of the subject, the democratic leader must have knowledge of the individuals with whom he works. A leader is lost in his attempt to use any method or technique in accomplishing group goals unless he knows the characteristics of those who are to follow him. The leader, then, must have that characteristic known as "empathy" so that he understands how the other fellow is going to feel about him. He is going to be able to anticipate reactions of others to his own actions, to his own comments, to his own characteristics of leadership, and to his own suggestions for group action. In turn he "feels" or understands the situations or emotions of others in the group. This knowledge of the group and this feeling for the attitudes of others is a key to sound rapport between leader and group. In some situations this rapport seems to be almost to the point of magnetism in which group and leader are attracted to each other. When leaders and groups understand each other, their motives and their feelings, we often characterize the leader as having "the touch." It is well to understand, however, that "the touch" is not just a personality characteristic of the leader which anyone can attain. It is a combination of leader reaction to and understanding of the group, and the group's reaction to and understanding of the leader.

Usually if a group must choose between the qualities of superior factual knowledge and a more understanding empathy in two potential leaders, it will gravitate toward the latter quality. However, in an emergency when unusual competence or factual bases are essential, a group will generally give greater precedence to this kind of knowledge as a desirable quality for its leader.

The principle of knowledge extends not only to subject matter areas, but encompasses the all-important interchange of understanding among leader, individuals in the group, and the group as a dynamic whole.

The Principle of Habit. We tend to do things as we have done them before or as we've seen them done. The Chinese translation of *habit* is "comfortable" or "over and over again." We tend to be comfortable in repeating the way things are done. We do things without thought. It's comfortable that way. The principle of habit is associated with democratic leadership in two ways. The negative aspect of the principle of habit we notice when as leaders we begin to work with a group that is accustomed to making decisions and taking action in ways that represent a different philosophy than ours. For example, a group that has continuously followed the dictates of a leader may be willing to continue under that particular pattern because that is the only pattern it knows. A habit is formed in allowing a leader to take over for the group. In other instances groups may operate very much on a laissez-faire approach, with group action being very difficult to achieve and with little, if any, direction by either individuals or groups of individuals. The positive aspect of the principle of habit deals with the achievement of democratic action by a group of people. If this occurs only one time, it is very unlikely that any established habit pattern will prevail; but if leadership efforts are in line with the other principles of democratic leadership, the group will become accustomed to doing things in that way. Democratic group activities and democratic group actions can be taught. They are habit-forming. They come with repeated experience.

Leaders should not be too concerned if they find little carry-over from one situation to another in their early attempts to provide positive democratic leadership. The important thing to remember is that with sufficient experience, with persistence on the part of leaders, groups will begin to accept the kinds of activities and actions which are inspired by their ideals.

The Principle of the Group Mind. There are a number of things that go on in a group when problems are to be solved. We readily accept the fact that a number of people in a group know more than a single individual in that group. Yet, it has been only recently that we have come to recognize the group process as a chain reaction where ideas are not just added together when a group sits down to discuss a problem and its possible solutions. Instead, one idea may stimulate four, eight, or even a hundred new ideas within the group itself. The recent emphasis in the field of group dynamics stems from this new knowledge regarding the way in which ideas are propagated.[6] The leader, in using the principle of the group mind, does not consider the group mind merely as a reservoir of knowledge added together by pooling the ideas of the individuals in the group, but rather considers the group mind as a place in which ideas can work on each other. Some ideas that people have in the group will be subtracted from the whole because the group recognizes weaknesses in them; other ideas will pass back and forth from pole to pole in a somewhat geometric proportion. To this extent it is possible for one person in a group to present his idea and have that idea mushroom into gigantic proportions by the action and interaction of a number of individuals to the idea.

The Principle of Purpose. We all know that if leaders know where they are going and why they want to get there they can

---

[6]For a detailed treatment of this subject, see *Dynamics of Group Action*, by D. M. Hall. The Interstate Printers and Publishers, Inc., Danville, Ill., 1957.

operate much more efficiently. The same is true for the groups with whom we work. A group will operate more efficiently if it is led to an awareness of its purpose by intelligent leadership. If its decisions for action are made in terms of its purposes and in the direction of its long-time goals, greater progress will result. The principle of purpose in democratic leadership requires that both leader and group be aware of the purposes of its activities and of its actions. Helping the group to become aware of purpose is one of the leadership responsibilities. It is often true that a leader may have his purpose clearly defined in his own mind, and because of an oversight attempt to lead the group toward that purpose before the group has even a partial understanding of the purpose. Often the leader's comment that the group is coming along very fast is related very definitely to the principle of purpose. There is a real distinction in this principle between leadership that is democratic and leadership that is autocratic. We can assume that a group will not move along fast either in making decisions or in taking action if the purposes of such activities are not clearly before them and accepted by the majority of those participating.

The Principle of Process. In democratic leadership the way in which results are accomplished is many times an integral part of the results. In accepting the principle of process there is some danger that a leader will overemphasize the process by which goals are achieved, at the expense of the goals themselves. The means by which goals are achieved are important; yet they must not become more important than the goals. In our leadership and movement toward group goals, much of the democratic nature of the final action could be destroyed by using means and methods in achieving those goals that are in direct opposition to many of our democratic ideals of behavior. On the other hand, the final action may be enhanced by the use of methods in keeping with our ideals. The methods we use may be used by members of the group as they are involved in other leadership jobs. A method which involves all of the group in identifying the problem and reaching a decision will give the group members a feeling that the results are right; the chances of carrying out decisions reached will be improved. By being involved, the group members will develop their own "know-how" on getting community jobs done.

The method used must be examined carefully as to its compatibility with the specific goals of the group and with the ideals of a democratic society.

The Principle of Direction. The leader is in many respects the servant of the group. Because of this he sometimes makes the fatal mistake of waiting for the group to direct him, rather than recognizing that he has important responsibilities for directing it in its deliberations. Leaders should most certainly be aware that group thinking needs some stimulation, that it needs some one or some group of people to help in channeling group activities. Someone needs to ask the question, "Is there a goal that we can agree on?" "Is there a decision we should make?" "Is there anyone who has a further contribution?"

A group also needs some direction in the action stages of problem solution. There is a real need for administration of the action that a group proposes to take. Unless someone (the leader) is willing to assume that he, as a representative of the group, is to do the administering or is to find someone within the group who will do the administering, then the action may never be taken. Any group decision needs action if it is to be accomplished, and any group action needs direction. Certainly there is danger in the principle of direction, because it is here that certain aspects of autocratic leadership may appear and the leader instead of taking responsibility for the direction, which is delegated to him by the group, may go beyond, and direct the group from a more authoritarian point of view.

The Principle of Emulation. It is well for the leader to keep in mind at all times that he becomes an example to other members within his group. "Example is the Best Teacher." Individuals with whom a leader works are likely to copy certain attributes and characteristics and methods used by the leader in working with them. Often in a democratic group situation the development of a number of leaders in a single group is the result of group members attempting to contribute to the group as much as those already in positions of leadership. This characteristic is true in a different sense in more authoritarian forms of leadership. In those instances, group members may be more interested in obtaining leadership power than they are in obtaining group ends. It is particularly important for leaders to remember that their actions are watched by members of the group, that their characteristics which are most desirable in leadership will be copied by other members of the group. The faith that individuals have in their leader and their attempts to equal that leadership, make the responsibility of democratic leadership that much more significant. It is by sincerity to one's ideals and the use of means and methods in line with one's basic principles that an example may be set for others who will help in the leadership jobs that can be done.

The Principle of Learning. Leaders are made, not born. Although certain individuals may have certain characteristics which aid them in their ability to lead, leadership itself is something which can be learned. It is most important for a leader to remember that his particular ability may be very effective in the situation in which he now works, yet in other situations his leadership may be less effective. It may be less effective because of things he does not know about leadership in different kinds of groups or with different kinds of individuals, but these are things which can be learned. The person who is able to operate effectively as a leader in one situation is more likely to be interested in the necessary education which would give him the abilities and understandings to be an effective leader in other situations. In addition to concern for one's self in the principle of learning, there is a more important aspect of this principle in democratic leadership. This aspect deals with the importance of the education of group members for leadership responsibility. It is likely that there are many individuals in a group who strive for opportunities to lead. These people can be taught to lead, though some will not be as effective as others even after considerable learning. They all can be taught and there are times when each individual can make a real leadership contribution. The official and unofficial leaders of group activities in rural America should keep in mind the ideals of democratic action and democratic leadership which encourage over-all development of the group rather than concentration on the development of a single leader.

The Principle of Experience. We are able to learn a lot from watching others. We are able to learn by reading and by listening, yet in the development of over-all leadership ability there's nothing that takes the place of experience and practice. There is no type of group that is better situated to give leadership experience to individuals than is the democratic group. Potential leaders are to be encouraged to try their wings in small leadership tasks. These can be devised in committees, by giving reports, by searching for information to bring to the group, or by acting in assigned capacities for the group with other agencies. The principle of experience is also important for the well-established democratic leader. A problem which is once solved provides the background of experience and confidence that leads to the solution of more complex problems.

Democratic leaders can learn much from both satisfactory and unsatisfactory experiences. Mistakes are sometimes fatal in autocratic group leadership but in democratic leadership, though embarrassing, the group is more than likely to understand that leaders are not infallible. Leaders may well keep in mind that a leadership mistake freely admitted may be freely overcome. Freedom to make mistakes is unique in the democratic leadership pattern. Mahatma Gandhi once said, "Freedom is not worth having if it does not include the freedom to make mistakes."

The Principle of Flexibility. No two leadership situations are exactly alike. This fact has been the downfall of many potential leaders who are unable to adjust to a variety of leadership tasks with groups of different sizes or with groups with different goals. The principle of flexibility is used in different ways by democratic leaders and autocratic leaders. The democratic leader does the adjusting himself, starting where the group is, and through education and through leadership helps lead the group toward its goal. The autocratic leader, on the other hand, is more concerned with the adjustment of the group to where he thinks the group should be. This difference makes the leadership job in the democratic society much more complex and often requires much greater competency. It demands in the leader the ability to transfer those techniques and methods from one situation to another and in the process be accepted as a leader in the new and different group. Certain democratic leaders, aware of the principle of flexibility, realize that they are able to operate within a rather limited range. Their leadership service then is advantageously used if limited to their range of abilities and flexibility. This does not stop them from gaining the necessary education in ways of leading other kinds of groups, but a recognition of their limitations causes them to encourage others who are better able to meet the new situation to take the leadership there. The principle of flexibility thus operates in two directions, one demanding flexibility of the leader to adjust to various situations, and the other demanding that the leader recognize his own limitations and encourage leadership on the part of others when they can do a better job than he can. The leader with the quality of empathy finds it easier to be flexible than a leader who fails to recognize the feelings of those he leads.

In the field of human development we have long recognized the individual difference in the abilities of individuals. We know, for example, that some adults can read well while others are able to read at approximately third- or fourth-grade level. We know that some are able to think and talk on their feet while others may be able to think but are unable to express themselves in front of a group. It is imperative that those who aspire to rural leadership recognize that the differences among groups are just as great if not greater than the differences among individuals. The teacher in our public school attempts to be so flexible that she is able to teach both the dull and the very bright students. There are times, however, when she recognizes her inability to teach some of the brighter students or some of the duller students. It is at this point that others with special capabilities and training are encouraged to take over that very special task. This same need holds true for groups. You as a leader may be able to work effectively with a wide range of groups because of your flexibility and your understanding of group differences. Yet there are times when you would not be an effective leader for a group that has gone beyond the point where you can help them, or a group that is so early in its stages of development that it would be difficult for you to understand the slowness of its progress. In this case, recognition of the role of others who are especially able to handle such situations is a practical application of the principle of flexibility.

The Principle of Integration. Each task which a group accomplishes, each leadership goal achieved, is not an end itself. Look, for example, at the rural community with its twenty, its forty, or its sixty formal and informal groups all seeking goals which are somewhat related to the development of either individuals in the community or development of the community itself. If every leader and if every group worked toward its own goals without consideration of those of other individuals or those of other groups, only limited individual or community progress would result. However, if harmonious relationships among various programs in a community are established and if the groups know what the other groups are doing, if they know the methods that are being used to reach common ends, the results can be additive. In addition to the integration achieved by gaining knowledge of what others are doing, there is a further and more important step of integration at the leadership level which tends to be as dynamic in nature as that of the stimulation of ideas within a group itself. This clearly indicates that if the leadership core is aware of what is being done and how it is being done, if it is encouraged to give freely of its own knowledge to others, if it will accept freely the ideas of others and incorporate them with its own group activity, the results will increase ten and twenty fold. The principle of integration means more than harmonious relationships among the various programs in a rural community. Integration means concern, one group for the other; and willingness to learn, one group from the other.

The Principle of Service. The principle of service is more closely related to the ideal of democratic leadership than are any other of the principles. The principle of service is based on what one can do for the group rather than what one can do for oneself. It is based on one's usefulness to the group and to the community, rather than on self-edification. It means that the leader is sincere in his desire to help others. It indicates that the leader should be willing to step back and allow someone else to gain stature, if by such stepping back the aims and goals of the group are furthered. A democratic leader must be completely honest in his efforts to be of service to others. We can assume if we like that by being of service we ourselves will be served, yet that is not part of the ideal. In the principle of service there's a real distinction between the authoritarian and the democratic leader. It's the distinction between "self" and "service."

The Principle of Leadership Satisfactions. As a final principle of democratic leadership, let's face boldly the fact that the most effective democratic leaders are those who have their greatest satisfaction as leaders in seeing what happens to other people rather than what happens to things or to themselves. They are more concerned about what happens to Mrs. Winter or Mr. Short or Johnny Lind than they are about the objective accomplishment of a special group task. These democratic leaders have their greatest satisfactions in the success that they see in others. The local 4-H Club leader who works with boys and girls for five, ten, or fifteen years may have had average accomplishment as far as the 4-H Club program is concerned in its achievement of awards and prizes at fairs and at county events. Yet, years afterward, as she looks at those with whom she worked and their achievements and their new role as leaders, she thinks back to the time when she gave them a helping hand. To some leaders the development of sound personalities within the group is more satisfying than being responsible for building a new Grange hall or successfully completing a project designed to aid the handicapped. The greatest democratic leadership satisfaction is to help an individual or a group develop to the point where they can accomplish their goals by themselves.

CHAPTER VI

The Leader and the Group

What is it that contributes to the success and productivity of some groups? What is it that contributes to the mediocre success or failure of others? Could the reasons for these variations in success and productivity be in the objectives of the group? Is it in the means through which we seek to achieve these objectives? When a group falls short of its goals, is the leader to blame? When it succeeds, does the group get the credit? Are the variations in the success or failure of a group to be shared jointly by the leader and the members of the group? Whatever the answer to these questions, those factors which influence the success of group activity are of vital concern not only to the group but to the leader as well.

NEED FOR ORGANIZATION AND LEADERSHIP

Man is a social being, and as such craves the fellowship of others. Down through the ages, he has been able to achieve his greatest potential through group activity. During the frontier days, he formed groups primarily for reasons of protection. Later he discovered that it was advantageous to cooperate for economic reasons. As the population increased and skills were developed, families that had previously been economically self-sufficient realized the advantages of exchanging commodities and services. Still later, as society became more complex, man began to specialize in various occupations. In order to protect his economic interests, he soon found it necessary to form occupational groups. Through the efforts of these groups, shorter working hours have been secured, better working conditions have been made possible, and most workers are secure in their jobs as long as they are efficient in the performance of their duties.

People are happier when they have the opportunity to participate in the formulation of policies which govern them. Because of dissatisfaction over the European political procedures, many colonists came to this country. Being aware of the need for participation in law-making, the colonists held town meetings which provided an opportunity for group action on matters of mutual concern.

As the population increased and the territory expanded, it became impossible to use the town meeting as a means of arriving at political decisions. Therefore, policy-making bodies were organized on national, state, and local levels. Frequently, special interest groups were formed in order to influence legislation. Women's temperance leagues have been outspoken in favor of prohibition and in some counties have campaigned successfully against legalizing the selling of alcoholic beverages. The National Association for the Advancement of Colored People has sought legislation which would guarantee certain rights and liberties to minority groups. Many other organizations set up lobbies from time to time which represent them when legislation is being considered which will affect their welfare.

During the early days of American settlement, there was little time and opportunity for social activities due to the pressing demands of protection, livelihood, and government. With the passing of time, man's need for this type of group protection was lessened, the time required to make a living was shortened, and responsibility for formulating policies was delegated to persons representing groups. These developments made it possible for man to enjoy more leisure time, much of which he devoted to social activities. As this change took place, organized groups were formed to provide an outlet for social activities in areas of common interests. Men who liked to hunt and fish just for pleasure organized sportsmen's clubs. Those who liked checkers, cards, dominoes, etc., formed clubs for indoor activities. Women found similar outlets in hobby clubs, garden clubs, homemakers clubs, bridge clubs, and the like.

Although distinct economic, political, and social groups were organized in the beginning, eventually each began to assume some of the functions of the other in order to satisfy the interests and needs of the members of the group. In some instances, groups that started with certain primary objectives made very substantial contributions to its members and to society in other areas of activity. Some of these groups experienced such pleasure in their achievements that they changed the previous objectives of the group. Other groups continued with dual objectives, while still others returned to the exclusive consideration of their original objectives. A young adult club in Little Rock, Arkansas, was organized merely as a social organization to furnish recreation for the members of the group. One club member suggested that they take a carnival to the convalescent center at Jacksonville, Arkansas, for the crippled children housed there. They derived so much pleasure from this civic venture that they revised their objectives to include one charitable project a month.

Group organization has a direct relationship to economic, social, and political development. As group activity increases, the development and complexity of a society increase, which in turn increases the need for further group activity. As a result of this cycle, history shows that the greatest group activity is found in the more highly developed countries where the group contributes to development and vice versa. In the so-called underdeveloped countries, group activity is at a minimum.

The day of isolationism in Amercia has long passed. Not only is the welfare of each rural dweller tied to that of his rural neighbor, but it is inextricably tied to the welfare of his urban brother as well. Never before in the history of mankind has there been as great a need for group action by our rural people as there is today.

This need is being met in a measure through hundreds of organizations in rural communities. They include such agencies as the Extension Service, Soil Conservation Service, Breeder's Association, Farm Bureau, P.T.A., 4-H, F.H.A., N.H.A., F.F.A., N.F.A., and Scouts. These organizations—political, economic, social, civic, and educational—have proved their worth.

The success of these organizations depends in great measure upon the person who provides leadership for the group. Even during the early days of our history, the need for leadership was recognized. As the country grew, and the complexities of society made it necessary for groups to take action in critical situations, it became inevitable that more and more dependence would be placed on leaders. In order that the activities be carried out with intelligence and dispatch, someone had to assume or be assigned the responsibility of guiding the decisions and actions of the group.

Although leadership is transitory, the need for a leader will always remain as long as people meet together with common objectives. Today, the need for good leaders has become recognized to the extent that leadership is provided by and for many rural organizations.

AUTHORITARIAN VERSUS DEMOCRATIC LEADERSHIP

The intensified need for direction of group activities in our present society has been met by an increase in the number of leaders. Some of these leaders have been autocratic while others have been democratic. Some have been able to secure cooperation from groups, while others have only led groups to rebellion. Some have been able to engender inspiration and enthusiasm in the group, while others have only stifled initiative and caused stagnation.

Authoritarian leadership places the making of decisions in the hands of one person or a few persons who act without consulting the members of the group. After decisions have been made, he proceeds to see that the members carry out his plans without question or criticism. In all of his activities with the group, external control is exhibited.

Democratic leadership, as defined in Chapter V, is a means by which one or more persons aid a group in setting and attaining desirable goals. Growing out of the needs of the group, democratic leadership endeavors to help the members arrive at solutions which are adequate and acceptable to them.

Distinguishing Characteristics. Theoretically, authoritarian leadership is vastly different from democratic leadership. However, in practice, one kind of leader sometimes makes use of techniques employed by the other which makes it difficult to label him either authoritarian or democratic. This movement backwards and forwards from one method to the other is sometimes made to deceive the members of the group, while at other times, it is caused by a lack of dedication and knowledge on the part of the leader.

The democratic leader often veers off into autocratic methods intentionally. Sometimes it is done because of insufficient faith in the democratic method. Such is the case with some vocational agriculture teachers in the way they use the problem-solving method. Such teachers may lead students to pose questions for group study, when the questions that will actually be used have already been decided upon by the teacher. They may hope that their predetermined questions are asked. If they are not, these teachers may resort to autocratic means. The same thing holds true when each student is asked to submit five questions in writing with the understanding that examination questions will be selected from them. Again, the autocratic teacher uses his own predetermined questions, with consideration of the questions submitted by the students only if they are the "right ones."

Sometimes the autocratic leader conceals his motives and appears different from what he really is. This is particularly true in America where the standards are set by democratic principles and autocratic action is condemned by public opinion. The leader is aided in this deception by the fact that democratic and autocratic talents of leadership seldom appear in pure form in one individual.

Characteristics by which the two methods of leadership may be distinguished are shown in Table I. Although it is realized that some of these characteristics are more important than

Table I—Distinguishing Characteristics
of
Authoritarian and Democratic Forms of Leadership

Authoritarian	Democratic
1. Based on power over members of the group.	1. Based on power with members of the group.
2. Based on the belief that the leader is superior and knows better than others what should be done and should direct the group accordingly.	2. Based on the belief that the members of the group have the capacity to make their own decisions.
3. Based on devotion to self.	3. Based on devotion to group.
4. Based on the importance of end-results alone.	4. Based on the importance of means as well as end-results.
5. Based on pre-determined plans of the leader.	5. Based on group-determined plans.
6. Based on secrecy of over-all plans.	6. Based on knowledge of over-all plans.
7. Based on manipulation of members of the group.	7. Based on assistance to members of the group.
8. Based on imposed discipline.	8. Based on self-discipline.
9. Based on dependence of members of the group on the leader.	9. Based on interaction among members of the group and between the members of the group and the leader.
10. Based on strict obedience without question.	10. Based on the right of the members of the group to ask questions to help determine the policies and actions.
11. Based on the philosophy that decisions should be formulated by one man.	11. Based on philosophy that policies and decisions should grow out of ideas and suggestions from the group.
12. Based on orders with little consideration for the will of the group.	12. Based on consultations and respect for the will of the group.

others, no effort has been made to rank them in the order of their importance.

ADVANTAGES AND DISADVANTAGES

The distinguishing characteristics listed in Table I lead one to realize that neither method is perfect for all situations. Therefore, it is essential that one understands the strengths and weaknesses of each method.

Advantages of Authoritarian Leadership. A primary advantage of authoritarian leadership is the acceleration of business transactions. A saving of time is realized as the leader makes the decisions and passes them on to the group for execution. This provides an "easy way out," and may be considered a second advantage for the members of the group who are apathetic, lazy, or untrained. They feel more secure when they are told what to do instead of having to make decisions for themselves. This situation exists, for example, when a farmer attends a county extension planning meeting after a full day's work. Because he is tired, and probably sleepy, he often becomes so apathetic that he is quite happy for the leader to make decisions for the group.

A third advantage of authoritarian leadership is that it requires fewer trained and dedicated leaders. This makes it attractive, especially in some rural communities with small populations. If John R. Worker is willing to assume the leadership in most of the community's organized groups, then no other person has to bother about it.

A fourth advantage is that it is amenable to working with large numbers. Size of the group is no problem to the authoritarian. As communication is one-way—from leader to group— the leader always exerts control over the group.

Advantages of Democratic Leadership. Frequently, democratic leadership is accepted and used without proper knowledge, understanding, and appreciation of its inherent values. Many of the advantages lie not only in the end product, but in the processes involved which are interesting and stimulating both to the leader and to the members of the group.

One advantage of this method is that the decisions which grow out of group discussions bring about better results than decisions that are handed down by one man. When many minds are at work and thoughtful consideration is given to problems of mutual concern, there is a continual refinement of ideas in the light of contributions of each participating member.

A second advantage of democratic leadership is that people cooperate more readily in promoting activities which they have participated in formulating. This is due partly to understanding which grows out of participation and partly to a sense of loyalty and devotion which one has for decisions which he comes to feel are his own.

Another advantage of this method is that it draws out individual members of the group and develops leadership. Many a timid person is made to feel that his contributions to the group are worthwhile and appreciated and therefore contributes more and more to the progress of the group. The group members become aware of his capabilities and delegate more and more responsibilities to him which strengthens him and prepares him for roles of leadership in the future.

Then, too, democratic leadership develops clear-thinking, open-minded individuals who are capable of adjusting to new situations brought about by scientific discoveries and inventions.

It has been predicted that more changes will take place in the field of agriculture during the next twenty-five years than in all previous history. The persons best able to use these changes constructively will be those who have had experience in the weighing and analyzing of ideas. This is a vital part of group discussions. It has been found that farmers of the middle third in economic status participate in organized group activity to a greater extent than those in the lower third and they also accept approved farming practices more readily.

Democratic leadership also provides for perpetuation of the group. No one person is indispensable. All members of the group are delegated responsibilities from time to time and are always aware of the objectives and procedures of the organization. This makes it comparatively easy for other members to assume leadership in case the regular leader is missing.

It provides for continual improvement based on the exchange of ideas and opinions of the members of the group. A group which is satisfied with existing conditions and whose leader allows for no dissent from the members eliminates all possibilities of progress.

A final advantage of democratic leadership is that it improves the morale of the group. "Morale," as defined by the

American Association of School Administrators, "is the back-bone of the soul. Morale is the will to carry thru against all obstacles what the heart approves. Morale is faith plus courage plus discipline. Morale is the factor that enables people as individuals or as groups to live up to their highest possibilities; it is the catalyzing agent which steers the soul to work out and keep working out its purpose. Morale is what makes us continue to fight on when courage is gone and faith is only something remembered. Morale is knowing where you want to go and going there. Morale is purpose with vitamins in it. Morale is living with faith gladly or at least relentlessly. Morale is the determination not to let yourself or your comrades down. Morale is sticking to the job for the job's sake. Morale is damning the torpedoes. Morale is being a man. Morale is what keeps you going after your knees give out. Morale is knowing when you're licked, and then you aren't. Morale is one for all and all for one—right thru to the end."[1] This is the kind of morale which is fostered by democratic leadership.

Disadvantages of Authoritarian Leadership. Some disadvantages of authoritarian leadership are:

1. It often leads to dissatisfaction and rebellion.
2. It does not provide for the development of the members of the group.
3. It does not provide for perpetuation of the group.
4. It does not utilize the full resources of the group in arriving at decisions.
5. It often squelches initiative and originality on the part of the members.
6. It is costly and sometimes fatal for the leader to err.
7. It is not acceptable to highly-trained persons.
8. It does not consider the worth and dignity of an individual.
9. It does not usually build morale which is essential for loyalty to the cause.
10. It often selects leaders on the faulty basis of heredity, influence, position in the community, etc., who prove incapable of meeting the demands of leadership.

---

[1] A.A.S.A., "Morale for a Free World," Twenty-Second Yearbook, American Association of School Administrators, 1201 Sixteenth Street, N.W., Washington 6, D.C., p. 27.

Disadvantages of Democratic Leadership. Some disadvantages of democratic leadership are:

1. It might easily lead to the monopolization of the discussions by one or two members of the group.
2. It requires more skill on the part of the leader.
3. It may allow a very vocal minority to dominate a passive majority.
4. It is sometimes difficult for people who are not accustomed to group work to accept the ideas of others, even in the light of evidence, when these ideas are opposed to their own.
5. It is not easily used when large numbers of people are involved.

In spite of the limitations considered above, the authors of this book have abiding faith in the democratic process and believe that democratic leadership is the most efficient means of promoting the best interests of individuals, groups, and society.

THE GROUP AND ITS MEMBERS

The word "group" is an elusive, generic term that is defined in various ways by different people. It may refer to a great number of people or a small number of people. It may refer to a formal or informal gathering, or to an organized or unorganized assemblage. There is no agreement as to the exact form of association to which the term refers. Simply stated, a group may be considered as a number of persons whose relations to each other are sufficiently impressive to influence the thoughts and actions of the members.

Composition of the Group. Each of us, from the beginning of life until death, consciously or unconsciously belongs to innumerable groups. We become members of these groups by birth, compulsion, or choice. They may be classified as primary, secondary, or tertiary.

Primary Groups. Cooley wrote: "By primary groups I mean those characterized by intimate face-to-face association and cooperation. They are primary in several senses, but chiefly in that they are fundamental in forming the social nature and ideals of the individuals. The result of intimate association is a certain fusion of individualities in a common whole, so that one's very self, for many purposes, at least, is the common life and purpose of the group. Perhaps the simplest way of describing this whole-ness is by saying that it is a 'we'; it involves the sort of sympathy and mutual identification for which 'we' is the natural expression."[2]

By birth, one becomes a member of a primary group, the family, which is more or less permanent. The every-day, face-to-face contacts with mother, father, brothers, or sisters, bring about a mutual feeling of love, trust, and dependence. As the child grows and extends his face-to-face contacts beyond the family, he becomes a member of a second primary group, the neighborhood. He becomes a member of a third primary group when his horizons are further broadened to the extent that he is identified with the community.

As a man matures, he has a continuing need for close fellow-ship as exhibited in primary groups. According to Essert, "This does not mean merely getting together with other adults, or finding groups of people with whom one can do things. It means the experience of free expression of natural personalities. It means the experience of associating with others without fear that the associations will be curtailed because of what one says or does. It is the kind of human association found among great families and great friends. In such associations, ostracism and excom-munication are impossible because the association is built upon an inviolable contract, namely, that whatever weaknesses exist in one or the other party will be subordinated to the understanding that all fail 'not seven times but seventy times seven.' "[3]

Although face-to-face contact is necessary to primary groups, it is also essential that there be an underlying feeling of personal interest, devotion, and "oneness" among the members. This type of relationship is more prevalent in rural than in urban areas. At one time, practically all of the farmer's contacts and those of the village resident were primary, but more and more, rural contacts are becoming secondary, and in some instances, tertiary.

Secondary Groups. Secondary groups differ from primary groups in that although face-to-face contact is desirable and generally exists, it is not essential. Examples of such groups are the Farm Bureau, the Farmers Union, and the Grange. These

[2]C. H. Cooley, *Social Organization.* New York, Scribners, 1909, page 23.
[3]Paul L. Essert, *Creative Leadership of Adult Education.* New York, Pren-tice Hall, Inc., 1951, pages 24-25.

groups are joined voluntarily and are quite frequently formally organized with common goals. Many such organizations exist in rural areas and serve a vital function, not only in enriching the lives of the members, but also in fostering policies that will protect the welfare of the community. Many persons who are not members of these organizations are beneficiaries of the activities of such groups. The Farm Bureau and other farm organizations have initiated cooperative action that has resulted in reductions in cost of merchandise and in lower rates on life, property, and liability insurance to their members. Private business concerns competing with such cooperative organizations are frequently forced to lower their rates. Farmers who reside in communities that have such cooperative activity and are not members of these organizations consequently reap great benefits from this competition.

There is no doubt that all farmers have greatly benefited from legislation sponsored by organized farm groups on local, state, and national levels.

Tertiary Groups. Increasingly, rural people are becoming members of tertiary groups which involve an impersonal relationship that is more prevalent in urban than in rural areas. Such relationships exist when people gather in great numbers. It may be to witness concerts, plays, or athletic events. Although you come into close contact with other individuals, you do not know them and may never see them again.

Personality of the Group. Groups acquire personalities as a result of the thinking and actions of the members. One intriguing thing about group association is that although the life of the group is determined by the wishes and interests of its members, yet the purposes and behavior of the group as a group are different from the sum of those of the members who compose it.

As a result of association in a group, a new bond is formed which has its own particular traits that result from the interaction and inter-stimulation among the members of the group. A synthesis of their desires and wishes is created which is better than and different from the sum of the wishes and desires of all the individuals composing it. The group develops its own purposes, ideals, and modes of behavior, which in turn, to a greater or less degree, influence the behavior of each of its members so long as they remain members of the group. So, there is a fusion of individual and group desires. Where individuals have been "tradition-directed," "inner-directed," or "other-directed,"[4] as part of a democratic group, they become "our-directed." The "our-directed" concept is well expressed in the words of Follett:

> When you and I decide on a course of action together and do that thing, you have no power over me nor I over you, but we have power over ourselves together. We have, however, no authority over John Smith. We could try to get "power" over him in a number of ways, and that is what LeDantec would call power, but the only legitimate power we could have in connection with John Smith is what you and John Smith and I could develop together over our three selves.[5]

Group personalities differ according to the objectives of the members. An organization of unmarried ladies is not likely to have the same interests and goals as one composed of married ladies. Therefore, these two organizations may take on completely different aspects. The same would be true with groups of musicians, teachers, businessmen's wives, farmers' wives, and artists. Each would have a different personality.

The personality of a breeders' association is vastly different from that of a bridge club. The former group would be a deliberative body, probably devoting most of its time to the improvement and marketing of their particular breed. The latter group, though often deliberating, would be primarily interested in social, leisure-time activities.

The personality of groups in industrial areas is not the same as that of groups in agricultural areas. The dissimilarity in the interests of the people, their social activities, their resources, their leisure time, and their varied abilities causes the difference in the personality of the two types of groups.

Groups of young people differ in personality from groups of older people. A high school class of vocational agriculture boys, for example, would not have the same personality as a young farmer's class, although the primary objective, to become established in farming, is the same. Normally the members of the younger group are more energetic, more daring, and more idealistic, but on the other hand, they are more dependent, more unstable, more easily discouraged, and less resourceful.

---

[4]David Riesman, *The Lonely Crowd*. New Haven, Yale University Press, 1950, Chapter 1.

[5]Mary P. Follett, *Creative Experience*. New York, Longmans, Green and Company, 1924, p. 186.

Figure 5. Authoritarian Leadership. Under authoritarian leadership, docility pervades the group. The members often are solemn, unhappy, suspicious, suppressed, and tense. A cold atmosphere exists.

Figure 6. Democratic Leadership. Under democratic leadership the members are happy, productive, relaxed, and trusting. A general atmosphere of warmth and "oneness" exists.

Groups are directly influenced by the type of leader they have. The personality of a group under authoritarian leadership certainly is not the same as that of one under democratic leadership.

Just as the personalities of individuals change, so do the personalities of groups change. Some of the factors causing the change are growth, maturing of the individual members, scientific discoveries, inventions, additions in memberships, and fluctuation in the population. Some of the changes are good and some are bad. Because of the nature of democratic procedure which involves the weighing and analyzing of the problem by the group, changes made under democratic leadership are more likely to be desirable ones.

RESPONSIBILITIES OF DEMOCRATIC GROUPS

We have already indicated our faith in the democratic process. In order for groups to be most effective in achieving their purposes, there are certain responsibilities which should be assumed by members of the group. Accepting the following responsibilities and acting in accordance with them will aid in obtaining successful group action:

1. Respect for the personality and dignity of every individual in the group should be maintained at all times.
2. Individual as well as group welfare should be the concern of the group.
3. Provision should be made for a free exchange of ideas in dealing with group affairs.
4. The rights of equality of all members of the group should be protected.
5. Provision should be made for growth of all individuals in the group.
6. A fraternal feeling should exist among the members of the group.
7. Cooperation among the members should be fostered by the group.
8. A continuous quest for information should be maintained by the group.
9. A sense of loyalty should be developed by the group.
10. Wise selection of leaders should be made by the group.

11. Group thinking should be reflected by group action.
12. In selecting projects, the abilities of the members, the resources at hand, and the amount of time required to complete it, should be considered by the group.

GROWTH OF GROUPS

Just as individuals grow and develop over a period of years, so do organizations. Organizations grow in purposes and services, in memberships, in wisdom, in the ability to work together, as well as in achievements. Because organizations are dynamic, not static, they change with environmental situations and they adapt their programs and initiate policies and practices which will benefit the group and society in general. Growth comes about as a result of change and change is largely an outgrowth of needs.

Many farm organizations that gave little attention twenty-five years ago to farm machinery devote a major portion of their time today to farm mechanization. Rural groups in some areas are already giving attention to automation and its possible effects on agriculture. As long as there are technological improvements and scientific discoveries, groups will continue to grow as they adjust to these changes.

As members of groups work together, they acquire the skills and techniques so essential to successful group work. They learn how to give and take. They learn how to subordinate their personal desires in the interest of the group. As a result, they not only amass knowledge and develop appreciation, but gain wisdom as well, which is so vital to group growth.

As people become more aware of the services and functions of organizations which are making worthwhile contributions, more members are added to the group. These new members are aware of the purposes of the organization and bring new ideas into the group which enrich its program.

DEMOCRATIC GROUP LEADERSHIP

Functions of the Leader. Leaders must continually be aware that organized groups are means to ends, but not ends in themselves. People join groups to help them satisfy their own interests, wants, and needs. In democratic groups, the members decide what the goals will be. These goals are achieved through group efforts.

It is necessary to have a leader to help the people in the group achieve their ends through group activity. As such, the leader has certain functions delegated to him. The group will be effective in meeting the interests, wants, and needs of the members, partly in proportion to the degree to which the leader recognizes and carries out his functions. Some of the more important functions of the leader are listed below:[6]

1. *He serves as group executive.* He presides over meetings and sees that the program as decided upon by the group is put into effect and kept in operation as long as the group so desires.

2. *He assists the group in making plans.* He works with members of the group in originating ideas and in initiating programs, giving advice and assistance whenever necessary. He tries to look ahead and anticipate future problems and methods of solving them.

3. *He speaks for the group.* In promoting the best interests of the group, it sometimes becomes necessary to establish contact with other individuals and groups. Upon such occasions, the members of the group often rely upon the leader to speak for them.

4. *He coordinates the activities of the group.* The members of the group, though they agree on common goals, have varied opinions on how to achieve these goals. This would lead to confusion and possible disruption of the group were the leader not able to resolve these differences.

5. *He represents the group ideals.* The leader is often selected because of his keen interests in the welfare of the group and of his devotion and loyalty to its program. People like to identify themselves with individuals whom they like and trust. If the group loses confidence in the leader, he is no longer a leader.

6. *He evaluates the progress of the group.* Continuous evaluation is made of the progress of the group and periodic reports made to the members.

Qualifications of Leaders. Because the success of the group depends to a great extent upon the leader, it is essential that good

---

[6]Functions 1-5 are based on "Functions" as listed by Dwight Sanderson, *Leadership for Rural Life.* New York, Association Press, 1940, pp. 31-34.

leaders be selected. At one time it was believed that good leaders had to be born. Today, however, we believe that we can help develop leaders, (see Chapter VIII). There are certain qualifications which good leaders possess that prepare them for their position of leadership:

1. Knowledge—must be well informed.
2. Pleasing personality—must draw people.
3. Tact—must be able to keep from offending.
4. Courtesy—must be respectful.
5. Initiative—must be able to take the right action at the right time without being told.
6. Impartiality—must have no favorites.
7. Flexibility—must be subject to change.
8. Fearlessness—must have courage.
9. Cheerfulness—must be happy and optimistic.
10. Industrious—must be willing to work hard.
11. Emotional stability—must have poise.
12. Sympathy—must possess a kindred feeling.
13. Enthusiasm—must possess a contagious spirit.
14. Sincerity—must be genuine.
15. Leadership skills—must know how to conduct meetings and guide thinking with ease.
16. Loyalty—must be devoted to the cause.
17. Perseverance—must not give up easily.
18. Versatility—must be able to do more than one thing well.
19. Vision—must have imagination.
20. Integrity—must be honest and upright.
21. Ethics—must have high moral standards.

Rural people are inclined to select their leaders more on the basis of friendships and personal affection than on the basis of the competence of persons as leaders. Although this is not bad, it does at times have a harmful effect upon the progress of the group. Knowing this to be true, rural leaders must develop many qualities that endear them to rural people. Mrs. Edwards, a home demonstration agent in a central Arkansas county, made friends rapidly during her first year of work in the county. When she established home demonstration clubs in the county, many women attended, not because they believed the young lady could teach them anything, but because she was a "nice" young lady and had asked them to come. They wanted to "help her in her new job."

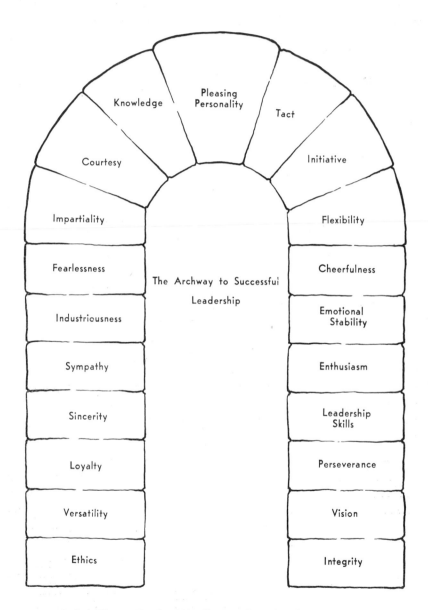

Figure 7. Qualifications of Good Leaders

In two years time the enrollment in her clubs had greatly increased, and members were attending not only because of their affection for her as a person, but primarily to receive the great benefits of her experience and knowledge.

Responsibilities of the Leader. Just as the group has responsibilities, so does the leader. His assumption of these responsibilities not only helps to assure success of the group, but it strengthens him as a leader and a person as well. In order that the leader may best carry out his responsibilities, he must know and understand the members of the group and establish rapport with them. This is important particularly in areas where people are suspicious of others, have firmly imbedded beliefs and habits, and are slow to accept change.

The primary responsibility of the leader is to help the members of the group meet what may be called their socio-psychological needs. The success of the group and of the leader in carrying out his other responsibilities largely depends upon how well this first responsibility is accomplished. Socio-psychological needs have been variously stated by different people. An acceptable list of these needs as seen by the authors includes man's need for a feeling of *belonging, participation, status,* and *security.*

Everybody wants to feel that he or she is liked and accepted by others. We get our greatest joys through association with others who make us feel that we have unity, that we have "oneness," that we are alike. The leader can play a great part in helping new as well as old members have a feeling of belonging.

Participation gives breadth and depth to belonging. The leader endeavors to get full participation not only to meet the psychological needs of the members of the group, but because he feels that full participation increases group knowledge and wisdom. Thus, a person who has participated has both advanced the group progress and met a personal need.

As with belonging, and participation, a person has a need for a feeling of status in any group in which he finds himself. This may be true of a rural child who transfers to an urban school. For a while, he will feel ill-at-ease. He may be looked down upon by the urban youths and be shunned or ridiculed. As he proves his worth, the attitude of the others changes and he becomes a happy, adjusted individual. The same thing might apply were the conditions reversed and an urban youth became a member of a predominantly rural group. The urban youth may then be placed in a position of inferiority because he is not accustomed to thinking and acting in terms so familiar to rural youths.

Finally, everybody needs a feeling of security. A person will feel secure in a group in proportion to the degree that his needs of belonging, participation, and status are met. The group is secure only when a feeling of security has been established within the members.

A second responsibility of the leader is to stimulate thinking on the part of the members of the group. Unless people are motivated to think, they will lose interest and the loss of interest is the first step toward the downfall of the group. To avoid this, the leader must be aware of and make use of every possible means of getting the members to think.

Logical, creative thinking usually results in action. A third responsibility of the leader is to stimulate this action and see that it is directed toward carrying out the program agreed upon by the group.

A fourth responsibility, and one that really facilitates the work of a leader as well as provides for the maximum development of the potentialities of the members, is that of developing leadership in others. The leader is relieved whenever he can find members who are willing and able to accept jobs pertaining to the furtherance of group activities. When the member accepts and carries out the responsibilities assigned to him, he is given an opportunity to do creative thinking and introduce new ideas. Each time that he successfully performs a job, he is encouraged to tackle another one and eventually he might acquire such outstanding leadership skills that he might be in great demand as a leader for other groups that have not developed leadership skills among their members.

INTERACTION OF LEADER AND GROUP

Since leadership is a product of group life and the group benefits from leadership activities, it is clearly recognizable that successful group work depends upon the interaction between the leader and the group. The relation of the leader to the group is quite unique. It is self-perpetuating and cumulative as long as it exists. It is based on a "give-and-take" between the leader and the group. The leader must continually consider the various possible reactions of his followers.

Human beings tend to respond in harmony with the way they are stimulated. If the leader stimulates the group favorably, the group tends to respond favorably. This, in turn, is a favorable stimulation to the leader. Continuous favorable stimulation and response action is conducive to loyalty and respect between the group and the leader and to sound group organization and functioning. On the other hand, an unfavorable stimulation by the leader arouses an unfavorable response in the group, which unfavorably stimulates the leader and a vicious circle is started which undermines the loyalty and respect that the group and leader have for each other and causes poor functioning of the organization.

It has been said that people do not rally around a leader unless the leader needs them. The leader who bases his relationship to the group on a true bond of sympathy and fellowship rather than superiority, authority, prestige, or fear is more likely to elicit the cooperation of the group.

Many seemingly desirable programs have been rejected, at least temporarily, by rural groups because the leader had either no understanding of this basic concept of democratic leadership or no appreciation of it. Such was the case of Mr. Brown, who did not realize that in order to achieve group progress, he had first to be accepted by the group and then start where the group was.

Mr. Brown, an energetic young man with lots of ideas, felt that the local neighborhood school district should be consolidated with the larger community school district located in the village, and he worked toward that end as a member of the local P.T.A., which he joined shortly after moving into the neighborhood. Feeling that he could rejuvenate a "sleeping" people, he hastily began to circulate a petition for the consolidation of the district without the sanction of the P.T.A. The people rejected both the idea and Mr. Brown. He was so discouraged that, at his first opportunity, he moved to another community. It was the feeling of others in the P.T.A. that Mr. Brown's efforts were futile, not so much because the people were against consolidation, but because Mr. Brown was relatively new in the neighborhood and had not allowed himself to be accepted as a member of the group before he assumed the role of leadership.

The interaction that is necessarily a part of democratic leadership clarifies problems, strengthens the leader, promotes advancement of the group, widens the horizons of the group, builds morale, and develops additional leaders.

PROCESS AND PRODUCT

Group thinking and action result in improvement in the cultural, economic, and social life of the members of the group. The ends achieved, however, cannot be considered apart from the means used in achieving them, for the means help determine the ends. What a person or group actually achieves is not necessarily the original goal, but is dependent upon the means used in working toward that goal. A person does not go to school with the intention of failing, but many fail because of the means used. Jails are full of ambitious people who utilized improper means of realizing their ambitions.

Continuous evaluation can be used to guide the means toward the achievement of the ends. Since the process is an integral part of the product, when over-all goals are understood by the group, the progress toward the goals can in some part be evaluated in terms of the means being used. Continuous evaluation will help the members detect shortcomings of the means being used and will provide information which may be useful as a basis for selecting new approaches.

Evaluation not only brings about changes in the means being used to accomplish goals, but makes evident the fact that sometimes the goals themselves need to be redefined. This constant evaluation of process and product leads man to the realization of his desires, wants, and needs through group activity.

CHAPTER VII

Skills of Leadership

To both the volunteer leader and the professional leader, success depends on knowledge and on skills. For purposes of democratic leadership, knowledge without skill is just as futile as skill without knowledge. It is just as absurd to feel that leadership depends on skills alone as it is to feel that knowledge is sufficient unto itself. Individuals are not born with the knowledge nor the skills required for democratic leadership. Both are learned, and they greatly enhance leadership. We grow in the use of these skills by learning from others, by examining the leadership form needed and by experience. Skills of leadership pertain to the ability to use one's knowledge effectively for the welfare of the group. A person who has read and learned well Parliamentary Rules of Order may not have the skill to make practical use of his knowledge in a real leadership situation as is sometimes evidenced by confusion when a motion is being entertained.

There are many skills of leadership that, once learned, may be transferred from one situation to another. These may be considered as general skills applicable in most leadership situations. A proficiency in the use of these general skills will likely aid a person in his development of skills for use in more specific situations. Skills needed in a particular leadership situation vary according to objectives, age, abilities, and knowledge of the members of the group. Leadership in a group that is primarily concerned with the organization of a farmers' cooperative would not at all times require the same skills as it would with a group whose primary concern is Christian elevation through a Bible class. However, we would not want to overemphasize the differences in skills of leadership required in the two groups to the neglect of their similarities as is so easily done. Not only do skills of leadership vary among different groups, but they change from time to time within a single group. These variations are a challenge to leadership which reduces monotony and adds interest and stimulation.

The fact that persons vary in their ability to use skills of leadership is just as natural as it is that one hat will not fit everybody's head nor one shoe everybody's foot. It is also true that one person may have more ability in the use of certain skills than he has in the use of others. When this is recognized by a person, it may result in his effort to strengthen the weaker skills or to enlist the services of other members of the group to perform the leadership skills in which he feels incompetent. Another person who is less dedicated may completely and continually side-step the performance of the skill for which he has undeveloped or limited ability.

Skills must always be in harmony with the basic principles of democratic leadership and the dedications of democratic leaders. Thus the successful leader must try to relate democratic principles to the skills that will be adequate for the great variety of leadership situations that are encountered in rural communities.

Leadership skills are required in both formal and informal groups. The skills to be discussed in this chapter may be considered pertaining largely to leadership in formal groups. Extremely formal groups may be easily distinguished from extremely informal groups. However, in actual operation many rural groups are neither extremely formal nor extremely informal. In such situations it becomes more difficult to distinguish between the two groups. Also, many skills that are required of the successful leader of formal groups are also required of the successful leader of informal groups.

Leadership skills of planning meetings, presiding over meetings, promoting attendance at meetings, securing new members, getting people in the group to work, stimulating and maintaining interest, evaluating new situations, planning discussions and conducting discussions, will be discussed in this chapter. Other skills of leadership such as bringing about a group mind or oneness, reducing obstacles, and solving personality clashes are also important and they receive attention under the above topics.

Both volunteer and professional leaders need help in further developing and improving their skills of leadership. When volunteer and professional leaders work in harmony and with the understanding of the role of each, they can help each other better to learn and use these skills. As we consider these skills, their importance to successful group operation will be made increasingly clearer.

How to Plan a Meeting

Have you ever planned a meeting? If you have, you will agree that a meeting can be no better than the planning that goes into it. The planning is the foundation upon which any meeting is built. We've all been responsible for this planning and know that the efficient, smooth-running meeting is an indication that we've done our job well. Poor planning results in confusion which hinders accomplishment and destroys the enthusiasm of members of the group. Skill in planning meetings is the first step toward successful group operation.

Planning a meeting is a promotional activity which is essential for success. Although aspects of the planning may be delegated and shared by members of the group, the primary responsibility for this activity often rests with a particular leader. He may be called the chairman of the program committee, an officer, a lecturer, or just the person in charge, but he assumes some responsibility for aiding group planning at the same time that he accepts a leadership role under any title.

Successful planning requires knowledge of the group aim, objectives, membership, and previous progress. Just as these qualities vary for different groups and types of meetings, so do the requirements of planning vary. Planning a routine meeting of a bridge club that rotates from house to house among its members certainly would not require the same details as would the planning of a regular monthly meeting of a community council. Similarly, the regular monthly meeting of the community council may not require the same amount of detailed planning as would the annual meeting of the same council at which annual reports of committees may be given, a guest speaker invited, a dinner planned, or preliminary plans for the next year considered.

Although some people have more skill than others in planning meetings, it is not uncommon for three or more hours to be spent in the planning of the average one-hour meeting of a farm organization, and this will be in addition to the continuing long-time planning that is so necessary to success. Although specific planning activities will vary with the different types of meetings, the following considerations will deal with some of the general activities which must be given attention in preparation for most individual meetings.

Check with All Committee Chairmen. The president of many organizations is automatically considered as an ex-officio member of all committees. He meets with these committees when possible in order to keep current on their progress and to contribute whatever help he can to their productive operation. If he is the one who plans the meetings, this knowledge gained from attending the committee sessions will be helpful. In any case, it is very important that the leader who is charged with the task of planning the meetings be aware of the exact duties of each committee and know when each committee is to report to the group. With this information in hand, he reminds the committee chairman of the meeting in which his group is to report. At the time the original committee assignments are made, the committee members, and particularly the chairman, should be thoroughly oriented as to what the committee duties are and when it will be expected to report to the group. This will help the committee have a feeling of security and promote the accurate and satisfactory performance of its job.

The reminder to the committee chairman of the meeting in which his committee report is expected should be after the committee has had time to do some work but sufficiently in advance of the meeting to allow time to complete its report. At the time this reminder is given, the leader should find out who on the committee will give the report; whether the report will be given orally, or mimeographed and passed out; and whether it will be presented narratively or statistically.

Finally, the leader should determine with the chairman of the committee the amount of time necessary to give the report and to entertain discussion of it if necessary. Generally, committee reports should be short, giving only the important details necessary for intelligent action by the group. This keeps the meeting moving rapidly and prevents the monotonous lag that dampens the spirit and enthusiasm of members of the group. To prevent unnecessary "slow down," the leader, with the consent of the committee chairman, should include on his agenda the maximum time to be allotted for the reports.

Observation indicates that leaders in rural organizations can do much to help committee chairmen improve the quality of reports.

Check on Time and Place of Meeting. Making arrangements for the meeting is sometimes delegated to a member of the group or to a committee. However, very often the leader is expected to assume this responsibility. Some rural organizations have a meeting place which they own and a set time for regular meetings. In such cases, "special" or "call" meetings are the main ones that would require special effort of the leader, and then only to arrange a time that is convenient to the members of the group. Most rural organizations do not own their meeting places and have to adjust their meetings to the availability of a place to meet. Making arrangements for meetings of such organizations can be a difficult task particularly in the progressive communities where many organizations exist. To make this easier to do, community councils have been organized in some communities, which may, in addition to other functions, help adjust and regulate time and place of meetings to the needs of groups and availability of meeting places. Some rural organizations have been successful in getting regular meeting rooms assigned to them at the local school. Such was the case in the school at Winneconne, Wisconsin, when a new school was built and a special room assigned to and used by the American Legion until they could afford to purchase a hall of their own.

In planning for the meeting, the responsibility for notifying the members may rest with the president or chairman of the group, the secretary, or some other member. This important function is considered later in the chapter under the heading, "How to Promote Attendance at Meetings," page 115.

Review Activities of Previous Meeting. In preparation for a meeting, the alert leader will review the activities of the previous meeting. The review makes the leader aware of unfinished business that should be considered. He also becomes aware of points omitted during the previous meeting that may need the attention of the members of the group. Often members of a group want and need to refer back to business of the previous meeting. If the leader has reviewed these activities, he is in a position to relate to the letter and the spirit of the last proceedings masterfully and concisely, which saves floundering and confusion, and commands the respect of the members of the group.

Indicate Possible New Business. As part of the planning function of the leader, he is expected to anticipate the new business that should be brought before the meeting. This does not mean that the leader has exclusive rights to present new business, for every member has this right and is expected and encouraged to use it. The leader tries to foresee new business to be sure that nothing of importance is overlooked and to speed up the action as much as possible.

Formulate an Agenda. On the basis of the planning, and as a very important part of it, an agenda should be formulated. The agenda should list title of the organization, time and place of meeting, and activities to take place with suggested time allotments for each. After development, the agenda should be sent to all members of the group in sufficient time for them to be well acquainted with it and to be prepared to contribute to the discussion. Although the time schedule of activities may not be followed precisely, the skilled leader is likely to come very close to allotting appropriate and needed time for each event on the agenda. The ability to do this increases with leadership experience and with knowledge of a particular group.

There is no "trick" in starting and ending meetings on time if they are well planned. At a church meeting recently attended for which an agenda had been formulated, it was surprising how much business was transacted in 45 minutes. "Old" business was concluded within the set time allotment, committee chairmen made reports leaving out unimportant materials, new business was fully discussed in a matter of minutes and the meeting closed on time as expected by the group that had been accustomed to this kind of leadership in that particular church. This is in great contrast to the type of church meetings so prevalent in many rural areas.

How to Preside over a Meeting

Presiding over a meeting is a skill that increases with use. It is one of the most important tasks of the leader and might often determine his success or failure. People who are skillful in this activity often find themselves in great demand for leadership activities in rural areas. Underlying success in this skill are the following important abilities:

Abide by Parliamentary Rules and Procedures. The primary aim of parliamentary rules and procedures is to aid a group to transact business with speed and efficiency, to protect the group from leaders who dictate policies, to protect the rights of each individual in the group, and to insure against unfair play of the leader and members of the group.

Common parliamentary rules have been generally accepted by deliberative bodies as a means for conducting business during the last five centuries because of the efficiency, uniformity, and justice to individuals of the group that they provide. The successful leader of formal groups must be familiar with parliamentary rules and abide by them. However, it should always be remembered that such rules are means to an end and not an end in themselves. Whenever mastery of a skill is accomplished or sought, there is a danger that the means may be mistaken for the ends. When this occurs, the usefulness and efficiency of parliamentary rules is greatly reduced.

The members of many groups are not sufficiently familiar with parliamentary rules and procedures. When such is the case, the leader has the obligation of helping to educate the group in this regard. This requires skill and patience. There are numerous simple books on the subject that may be used as references.[1] Having a leader well equipped in the use of parliamentary rules and a group with no knowledge of them is like having a steam engine backed up to some cars but not linked with them. The engine gets all steamed up but pulls off leaving behind the cars that it is supposed to be pulling.

Some rural organizations are performing a very fine service in the training of rural youth in the use of parliamentary rules. These youth will find the knowledge of parliamentary rules learned in 4-H Clubs and organizations like the F.F.A., F.H.A., and N.F.A. very helpful to them as members and as leaders of rural groups.

Strict adherence to parliamentary rules is not always the best way of arranging a learning-sharing experience. Some group activity can be more informal and highly valuable. A resolution

---

[1]Three inexpensive pamphlets are:

Kenneth Lee Russell, *The How in Parliamentary Procedure*. Danville, Ill., The Interstate, 64 pages, 35¢.

M. Henderson and H. J. Rucker, *Guide to Parliamentary Practices*. Danville, Ill., The Interstate, 32 pages, 20¢.

D. M. Hall, *Dynamics of Group Discussion*. Danville, Ill., The Interstate, 75¢.

Other excellent references for leaders include the following:

Harrison M. Karr, *Now You're Talking*, Danville, Ill., The Interstate, 1955.

Sidney S. Sutherland, *When You Preside*, Danville, Ill., The Interstate, 1956.

or decision is not always needed or desirable. Even when a decision is required, it can often be made without the more formal procedure of a motion or vote. Many decisions can be made simply by noting the "sense of the meeting" after full discussion has reached agreement. Such a method of arriving at decisions is in keeping with democratic procedures and may be considered another skill of leadership.

Have Respect for the Rights and Privileges of Each Individual. Nothing is more basic in democratic groups than having respect for the rights and privileges of others in the group. The leader is fortunate who has this fundamental philosophy; he should adhere to it and should be skilled in educating each individual in the group to appreciate it and abide by it.

Every member has rights and privileges equal to those of every other member. So, every member should have equal opportunity to be heard; to propose solutions and actions and to discuss the pros and cons of an issue. While the leader keeps the group aware of these rights, he also keeps it aware of the responsibilities that accompany each right. Members of the group who accept these responsibilities will only make suggestions and present discussions that are honestly felt to be in the best interests of the group.

While the leader or other members of the group may not agree with the statement of another, they are obligated to respect his contribution so long as it is made in good faith. It is recognized that the value of contributions made by members will vary with the topic being considered. The member whose contribution may be weak or useless on one topic may have an outstanding contribution on another. The leader's role is to keep the opportunity for making contributions open to all.

Keep the Common Goal Constantly before the Group. In the ceremony for opening a meeting of the N.F.A., the president asks the question: "New Farmers, why are we here?" All members of the group then stand and say: "To practice brotherhood, honor rural opportunities and responsibilities, and develop those qualities of leadership which a New Farmer of America should possess."[2] Every rural organization has a goal. Although each member may have individual goals, the organization as a group has a

---

[2]*N. F. A. Guide for New Farmers of America.* Baltimore, The French-Bray Printing Co., 1950, page 45.

common goal. The skilled leader helps the group to be constantly aware of its common goal. With such awareness, fewer conflicts will arise and the real purpose of the group will be more adequately served.

In pursuing the common goal, care must be taken that the main issue is not sidetracked and that only one subject be given attention by the group at one time.When the main issue is sidetracked, members of the group get a feeling of futility. When two or more unrelated subjects are considered by the group at one time, confusion results. This hinders accomplishments. It is no more possible for a group successfully to consider two unrelated subjects at one time than it is for most of us to juggle three apples and play the clarinet simultaneously. Sometimes deliberate efforts to sidetrack a subject are made by certain members of a group. The skilled leader is on the alert for such maneuvers and prevents them with gracefulness and courtesy. He also constantly guards against attempts to consider two or more unrelated subjects at one time.

Resolve Conflicts within the Group. It is almost unavoidable that in a meeting, personality clashes will sometimes occur. They are more apt to occur in newly formed groups than in groups that are older and more established. They will be more frequent in groups that have accomplished very little than in groups that have a record of numerous and outstanding accomplishments, for efficiency and accomplishment go hand in hand with smooth operation and harmony. In younger groups, personality clashes are sometimes due to the efforts of individuals in the group trying to "outshine" others rather than really trying to contribute to progress.

Often, real differences of opinion result in conflicts. Differences of opinion are expected in deliberative meetings, and they are often a healthy sign of democratic progress. They become undesirable only when the leader allows them to get out of hand to the extent that anger among members results, and efforts are directed not toward the best solution but in justifying a particular stand. For example, a conflict could be due to the differences of opinions between the conservative old members and the progressive young members of a group. A balance between the conservative and the progressive elements may have many values for the group in arriving at sound solutions to problems.

The skilled leader needs to be a student of human relations. In resolving conflicts he serves the best interests of the group and at the same time wins the good will and respect of the members. When conflicts arise, individuals are likely to emphasize the points of difference and minimize or overlook the similarities of their points of view. The leader needs to be able to point out the areas of agreement and similarities which will often result in the immediate resolving of conflicts that might otherwise have ended in a stalemate or be long and needlessly drawn out. Conflicts that could have been resolved by skillful leaders have sometimes resulted in untempered arguments that led to the discontinuance of an otherwise healthy and worthwhile group or meeting.

In attempts to resolve conflicts the leader must be clear-headed, sincere, and impartial. Insincerity and partiality will be readily recognized by the members of the group who will lose respect for the leader. When this happens the usefulness of the leader will be greatly lessened if not entirely destroyed.

Contribute Information and Opinions that Will Be Helpful to the Group. The leader is a servant of the group. Some educators feel that a leader should refrain entirely from expressing his ideas, opinions and suggestions. His role, according to them, is to open and close meetings and serve as an avenue for channelling discussion. However, the writers of this book feel that as the servant of the group, the leader is expected to help in any way that he can within the bounds of democratic procedure. In fact, in a group of 20 persons there may be 20 leaders; three with formal roles and 17 with informal roles. On occasions, the formal leader may advise the group on what seems to him to be wise procedure. He may give the group facts that he possesses in order to aid their thinking on points under discussion. Because of the preplanning that he has done, he may have information not generally known to members of the group that will be helpful in focusing group thinking and decision-making. In contributing his information and opinions, the leader should use tact and discretion. He should never be arbitrary or dogmatic. It is not always *what* is said that is important; sometimes, just as important, is *how* and *why* it is said that determines the skill of a leader in contributing information and opinions to the group. The *how* is particularly important in rural groups because of the great sensitiveness of many rural people.

Keep the Meeting Moving. A frequent criticism of meetings of rural groups is that they move along too slowly. This is just as annoying to members of a group as it is to a musician to hear a musical number played in slow tempo that should be played in fast tempo. Keeping the meeting moving depends on how well the leader has planned the meeting as well as on his ability to preside over the meeting.

Although the skilled leader moves through the meeting with dispatch, he does not sacrifice thoroughness for speed. He never permits the meeting to go faster than the size of the group, the degree of controversy, or the understanding of the members of the group will permit. He does not deny the right of members to speak on the topic under consideration. However, he may secure the approval of the group to limit debate if it appears that such debate is likely to be unreasonably drawn out.

Skilled leaders can often sense when there has been sufficient discussion of an issue and continued talk will not reveal new information that will be helpful to the group. At this point the leader may seek general consent to close debate thereby ending needless repetition.

Not only must the leader have skill in presiding over a meeting, but the members of the group should also develop skills in this activity as rapidly as possible. Leadership in a democracy moves from person to person and all rural people should continually prepare themselves for such positions. The leader can do much to help the members of the group attain this goal. Skill in presiding over meetings also helps the members to be better members of any group, and to appreciate and respect skills of leadership in other persons.

How to Promote Attendance at Meetings

Most of us have experienced membership in organizations that had poor attendance at meetings. This poor attendance may be due to a number of factors, many of which the skilled leader will detect and correct. We always had better attendance in the local Farm Bureau of which I was a member than in the local P.T.A., even though the two groups were composed primarily of the same people. This causes one to wonder why the difference. Having a common objective or interest is not always sufficient to insure high attendance at meetings. Attendance may be promoted in a number of ways.

Have a Dynamic Program. A dynamic program is the best insurance that a leader has of consistently getting good attendance at meetings. Nothing sells an organization like its program of activities. Attendance is best insured when the members feel that by missing a meeting something is lost. Members will have such a feeling only when their experience with the group has been pleasant and enjoyable.

The skill of planning and conducting a meeting greatly influences the meeting itself. Just as an efficient farmer plans and designs his utilization of land and resources for each year's crop to insure maximum production returns, so must the leader plan and design each meeting to insure an interesting and challenging program.

Notify Members of Meeting. Sometimes attendance at meetings is low because members forget the time of the meeting. This may be particularly true in rural groups that meet no more than once or twice a month, or that meet at irregular times. Notifying members of the meeting is important as a reminder. It also has a psychological effect, making members feel their own importance.

A number of methods may be used to notify members of meetings. The method best suited to a particular group may not be very adaptable to another group. Also, a variety of methods may be profitably used in a particular group.

The notification should have selling qualities. If written, it should be forceful, interesting and attractive. If oral, it should be persuasive, complete and accurate. Some useful methods of notifying members of meetings are: postcards, personal letters, mimeographed letters, telephone calls, radio announcements, television announcements and personal contacts. Each method has some strong as well as some weak points. By using more than one method the weaknesses of each may be overcome and better results attained.

Make Members Feel Wanted and Needed. To promote attendance at meetings, the skillful leader will make members feel wanted and needed. Rural people like to grant favors. They like to be asked for advice. They like to think that the leader and others in the group are interested in the same things that they are interested in, and their contribution is needed for the success of the group. The leader who is able to capitalize on this characteristic of rural people plays a major role in increasing attendance at meetings. Such leaders develop a sense of pride in and loyalty to the organization within the members. *Esprit de Corps* contributes to the good morale of members. This is necessary to insure their attendance at meetings.

Publicize the Achievements of the Organization. Just as rural people like for others to know about them, they like for others to know about the organizations to which they belong. Good publicity about their organization lends prestige to them as members. Publicity of achievements may be received through many media including the newspaper, magazine, radio, television, and official organs of farm organizations. Material to be used for publicity purposes should be well written, making full and objective use of outstanding achievements of the organization.

Some farm organizations invite reporters and magazine editors to their activities for purposes of securing publicity. People like to be associated with and will attend meetings of organizations that continually make outstanding achievements.

How to Secure New Members

While some rural organizations may not desire to increase their membership, many that want to have not been successful in their efforts to do so. Membership is best increased through deliberate and systematic effort. The skillful leader can play a major role in securing new members. He does this indirectly through working with the group and stimulating group members to be ambassadors for the organization. He also does it through direct contact with persons whom he wishes to induct into the organization.

Conduct a Membership Campaign. Many rural organizations that desire additional members conduct membership campaigns. Generally, such campaigns are conducted once a year for periods varying from one to eight weeks. Membership campaigns should be organized well in advance of the "kick off" date. Appeals may be made through the newspaper, over the radio and by television. Often posters, community and county meetings, personal letters, bulletin boards, fairs and exhibits are used to interest potential members. Probably face-to-face contacts have more appeal to prospective members than any other single method. However, this method, if used alone, is slow and time-consuming and may work an undue hardship on the leader and members of the group.

It has been found that better results are obtained when four or five media are used to advertise an organization or group than when fewer are used. It is important that facts concerning the organization or group are kept before the people constantly during the membership campaign. This publicizing of facts must be well organized to be most effective. An "over-dose" of facts, particularly if poorly timed, is just as harmful to success in getting new members as is an "under-dose." However, a rural group or organization is more likely to be guilty of underselling rather than overselling itself.

Timing of a membership campaign is also important and should be considered when the campaign is being planned. A campaign for membership in a cotton marketing cooperative should be timed to start before cotton is ready to be harvested and end during the early part of the marketing season.

Some county organizations are organized into community or neighborhood groups for purposes of membership campaigns. By so doing, members can solicit new members among persons they are likely to know best. Often this results in wholesome competition among the members. Recognition of some kind is often given to the group and/or individual who brings in the most new members.

In all activities of membership campaigns, the leader has a responsibility for guiding the planning and action. His adequate assumption of these responsibilities means much to the success of the campaign.

Have a Dynamic Program. A dynamic program is an important means of increasing membership as well as of promoting attendance at meetings. In fact, whatever wholesome activity that promotes attendance at meetings will have a desirable effect on getting new members. Our public schools, industry and labor have realized that the best way to sell their organizations is to have a really good program. Members show love and have enthusiasm for organizations and groups that have interesting and worth-while programs. They want their neighbors and friends to know about their pleasant experiences and to participate in them. Their love and enthusiasm for the organization or group is easily apparent to others who get the urge to become members of the group also.

People are generally informed by word of mouth of what is going on in their local communities. They know the organizations and groups with worthy and interesting programs as well as those with dull and uninteresting programs. This is particularly true in rural areas where people have knowledge of each other's business and have been known to pass the time by discussing individuals and groups. The group with a dynamic program is sure to secure more members with less effort than the group whose program is not stimulating.

Make New Members Feel at Ease. Very often the person who will have the most influence in getting new members is the one who himself has not been a member very long. This is true, however, only if the new member has been made to feel at home with the group and if he has enjoyed his brief association within the group.

Sometimes a person who might otherwise desire to join a group, refuses to do so because of a fear or at least a self-consciousness and uneasy feeling about mixing with other persons in the group. The person who has recently joined can probably do more than an older member in getting the prospective member to allay these fears. This condition will not come about if the leader does not see to it that new members are made to feel at ease and comfortable in the group. The leader may do this by words, a smile, a chat with new members, a pat on the back, and by making other members of the group aware of the need for new members to feel at ease and willing to help them become so.

Publicize Achievements of the Organization. Leaders of rural groups must become more sensitive to the need for publicizing the achievements of their organizations and groups. Good publicity results in the good will of others in the community. This good will is the result of an intelligent understanding among the people of the aims, the scope, and the achievements of the group. Out of such understanding grows the desire of people to become members of a group or organization.

Publicity has been very effectively used by industry and labor for some time. Public schools, that once felt this to be unprofessional, have more recently resorted to objective publicity as a means of better informing the public of their activities as well as their needs.

If publicity is to best serve as a means of interesting new members, it should be well planned with consideration given to the following: (1) determine the specific aims to be sought, (2) determine the character of the groups to be influenced, (3) determine the facts to be emphasized, (4) determine the methods and media to be used in the publicity, and (5) determine or evaluate the results.

One of the chief duties of the leader is to help the group enlist new members. Among the things he can do to help obtain them is to conduct membership campaigns, have a dynamic program, make new members feel at ease, and publicize achievements of the organization.

How to Get People in the Group to Work

The group that is most successful is the one in which the members are happily productive. Nonproductivity of members produces stagnation and dissatisfaction, which is destructive to the group. According to its deacons, the success of a very progressive church in rural Alabama is due partly to the ability of the minister to keep challenging work almost constantly before the members. One of the most severe punishments that can be administered to a person is to prevent him from being creatively and productively employed. The skillful leader endeavors to keep the members busy with work that is within their potential ability to do well and enjoy doing. Too often rural leaders do not have sufficient faith in the ability of others. Such leaders, rather than encouraging distribution of the work among the many, try to perform all the tasks themselves for the group. A good motto for leaders to follow is: "I will never perform any task that I can get others in the group to do, if they can do it well, enjoy doing it, and learn while doing it."

Be Aware of Individual Differences among the Members. The leader who adopts the above motto must rely on his knowledge of the potential abilities, likes and dislikes of the members of his group. He must give full recognition to individual differences that exist within the membership. Knowledge of individual differences effectively utilized by the leader provides an outstanding opportunity for getting people to work and for developing the "we" feeling that is often unrealized in rural groups.

Although members of a group have some common abilities and interests, they also have differences that grow out of their innate capacities and environmental acquisitions. Leaders of rural groups have either ignored or made very little use of differences that exist among members of the group. Leaders must increasingly recognize these differences and build upon them. They must utilize these differences in group participation and in assigning work to individuals that will assist each to have status within the group and to contribute his maximum to group achievement in harmony with his particular and peculiar ability and personality. To achieve these ends requires flexibility in the procedures, a sensitiveness to human values, and tact and resourcefulness on the part of the leader in dealing with members of the group.

Be Sensitive to People. As an aid in getting members of the group to work and to improve the welfare of the group, the skillful leader must be sensitive to people. In discussing a leader in adult education, Hewitt and Mather state: ". . . he should be understanding and sympathetic. He must constantly study people of all kinds, so that he will become increasingly accurate in his ability to draw people out. He must know the true meaning of *educo*, and he must have a keen desire to practice it. Leadership is both an art and a science, requiring perception and finesse. A leader is an artist whose materials are human beings. He is a scientist whose field of experiment and research is human nature, infinitely complicated, constantly changing, ever moving, frequently doing the unexpected. His aim is to become constantly more expert in understanding and directing the most powerful forces there are, those locked up in men and women."[3]

Implied in this statement is the necessity for a successful leader continually to grow and to modify his own ideas. The leader who is sensitive to people is constantly aware of the fact that leadership is a process of educational growth that slows or stops when the leader's own education slows or stops.

The rural leader who is sensitive to people not only has

---

[3]Dorothy Hewitt and Kirtley F. Mather, *Adult Education, A Dynamic for Democracy*. New York, D. Appleton-Century Company, Incorporated, 1937, pp. 174-175.

understanding and sympathy *for* others, but he is able to develop these qualities *in* others. He also develops the quality of oneness among the members of the group which is in part an outgrowth of the understanding and sympathy developed. Members of the group get to feel that what affects "you" affects "me" and vice versa. This quality of empathy can seldom if ever be developed in others if the leader himself does not possess it.

Be Tactful in Dealing with People. Tact is often identified with common sense. It is very important in dealing with rural people because they often have numerous suspicions and abundant sensitivity. Tact involves a sense of proportion; it is quiet and reserved when need be, or open and outspoken when the occasion calls for it. Tact effectively used relieves tension, shortens social distance, increases morale, and keeps the leader close to his followers.

The skillful leader is tactful in his talk and actions. He knows the likely reaction of members of the group to a nod of agreement to what they are saying, to the pat on the back, or to a wink of recognition. He knows what to say and when to say it. Also important is *how* something is said. Often it is not as much what to say as it *is* how to say it. Many of us have heard of the farmer who received a letter from his son who was away from home attending college. The farmer, not being able to read, asked a neighbor to read the letter to him. The neighbor who was a rough and grumpy fellow read the letter in his typical gruff voice ignoring periods and commas. "Dear Dad," the letter read, "I lost my job on the school farm last week and have since been unemployed. I have a promise of a job on a nearby farm to start next month. In the meantime, I have run out of money. Please send $25.00 to tide me over until I am again employed. Thank you very much. Your own son, Earnest."

The father was very dissatisfied and disheartened at the tone of the letter and decided not to send the money to a son who spoke so rough to him. After a few days of grieving over his son's letter, he wanted to hear it read to him again and asked a lady in town to read it. She read the same words that the farmer's neighbor had read, but with patience, a kind voice, and proper emphasis. This time the letter sounded entirely different to the farmer and he decided that if his son spoke so nicely to him, he would send him the money requested right away, and he did.

The difference was not in the contents of the letter but in the way it was read. The skillful leader must always measure not only what he says, but how he says it, too.

HOW TO STIMULATE AND MAINTAIN INTEREST

The good leader constantly endeavors to keep members of the group highly interested in group activities. The life and death of the leader and indeed of the group itself largely depends on the interest of the members. In stimulating and maintaining interest nothing takes the place of a dynamic program, as previously discussed.

It has often been said that variety is the spice of life. Certainly if activities are varied, interest is increased. Depending upon the nature of the group, activities may be varied in many ways. Discussions as a means of stimulating interest are successfully used by many groups. Some groups bring in outside speakers as a means of adding variety to their activities and thereby maintaining interest. Generally it is desirable to have planned social activities at least once a year. Even groups that offer minor socialization at each gathering might gain much by having a big annual social activity.

In an effort to vary activities, some groups have occasional movies and planned tours. Such activities, used all too seldom and ineffectively by some rural leaders, are very successfully used by others. Not only are they useful in stimulating and maintaining interest, but they can often increase the knowledge and appreciations of members of the group as well.

Friendly competition within the group and among different groups is also a useful device for stimulating and maintaining interest. As a teacher of vocational agriculture, it was always gratifying to me to observe the added effort and interest that students put into the performance of activities in which they were competing with others in the group.

These are only a few of the many possibilities that a leader with vision and skill may use to vary the activities of a group.

HOW TO EVALUATE NEW SITUATIONS

Successful leadership depends to a great extent on the ability of the leader to adjust to new situations and to adapt his methods of meeting them to the pattern of action and approval of the group. Although a leader should be versatile in his abilities, it is not expected that he can perform with superiority in the many situations in rural areas that require leadership. Versatility in leadership does not mean that a leader can or is expected to adjust satisfactorily to all types of leadership situations. Certainly a successful leader of a rural recreational center may fail entirely as the leader of a band. The two types of activities are entirely different and they call for different aptitudes, knowledge, and abilities. However, many problems of a social and technical nature appear directly in the field of the leadership activity or in related fields that require evaluation and solution. For such problems, the leader is rightfully expected to address himself with accuracy and a minimum of confusion and delay. It is with this type situation that we are primarily concerned at this point.

Experience is of great value in helping the leader successfully to meet new situations. The nursery and kindergarten concentrate on giving their students experiences that will hasten the students' readiness for reading and for all-day attendance at school. The executives of large businesses prepare promising young men for executive positions by having them work up through the ranks, getting experience in and a working knowledge of the various departments and divisions of the business. The wise farmer starts his son on the road to farm management by offering him minor responsibilities while he is young. As he grows older, larger responsibilities are delegated until finally the son has gained experience in all the areas of farm operation including the practical, technical, business and management phases, and is prepared through these experiences to assume complete management of the entire farm.

Most promising young boxers are given experience in the nonprofessional ranks before being guided into the more competitive and rigorous professional class. This experience is needed to help the boxer become ring-wise, alert to various boxing styles, and prepared for the various unexpected conditions that may appear.

As with the boxer, so with the rural leader. Ability to master new situations increases with experience. The leader learns to develop new skills of dealing with people and problems. He learns to anticipate responses to what he says or does, and he learns to accept occasional and momentary defeat gracefully while profiting from the experience.

In evaluating new situations the steps discussed in Chapter IX under the heading "The Scientific Method and Controversy" may be used.

How to Plan a Discussion

Democratic group action is characterized by extensive discussion. To talk a matter over, to get the pros and cons, is as American as is the hot dog or the hybrids of poultry and livestock. The "pot belly" stove around which rural people for years discussed their affairs has largely left the scene, but the discussions linger on, not diminished but increased. Thorndike's observation that "men are never so likely to settle a problem rightly as when they discuss it freely," is just as true in the 1960's as it was when the statement was first made.

Discussion has been variously defined by different people. Most would agree that it may be relatively formal or informal. To be most effective, it should be planned, though planning may not always be necessary. Topics of mutual interest are considered, and the discussion is conducted under the guidance of a leader. A discussion may be considered to be in process when two or more people talk and listen alternately about a topic or subject of mutual interest.

Discussions may be formal or informal depending largely on the size, character and purpose of the group. Groups up to 25 members with purposes that are primarily social and whose members are well acquainted with each other tend to be informal. As the size of the group increases, its activities become more deliberative and less social, and its members are less well acquainted with each other. The group tends to be more formal. Members of informal groups tend to have more freedom of action and unity. The more formal groups are characterized by more restrictions upon their members and sharper division within their ranks.

Due to these distinguishing characteristics, national organizations that operate primarily through local units may tend to be formal at one level of organization and informal at another. The Farm Bureau, for example, takes on informal characteristics in meetings on the community level. County level meetings, though still largely informal, tend to take on moderately formal characteristics. The state level meetings are more formal than the county level meetings but less formal than the national meetings of the Farm Bureau Federation.

Meetings of committees of the Farm Bureau at any level tend to be more informal than are general meetings of that organization at the same level. Also, the smaller the committee, the more informal the meeting tends to be.

Although types of discussions may vary depending to some extent on whether or not they are of a formal or informal nature, skills required of the leader in these discussions are largely the same.

Purposes of a Discussion. The main purpose of a discussion, whether of a formal or informal nature, is primarily the same— to exchange information and ideas on plans or problems and to make recommendations if necessary. These exchanges may be factual or theoretical, practical or speculative. Since in a discussion there must be an exchange of information, it is essential that the participants have some knowledge of the topic to be discussed. A group can no more participate in a discussion of a situation or problem of which they have no knowledge than can an individual return from some place he has never been. As the group knowledge of a situation or problem increases, the ability of the group to engage in fruitful discussion of that particular situation or problem increases. It therefore becomes the responsibility of the leader to help members of the group obtain background information on the topic to be discussed. He may do this by referring members of the group to sources of information such as written materials, lectures, discussions, T.V., movies, individuals, or by furnishing them with information that he himself possesses on the topic.

Exchanging information is basic to the American way of life and it is basic to our belief that in reaching decisions on problems "two heads are better than one." This belief has been implied throughout this book and particularly in Chapter VI where autocratic and democratic leadership are compared.

As a result of exchanging information, difficulties are cleared up, the truth is arrived at, attitudes are formed, decisions are made, and tensions are relieved, all of which are additional purposes for discussion.

Advance Preparation. Probably no other single activity means more to the success of a discussion than does adequate preparation. Auer and Ewbank believe that many discussions fail "not because of what happens during the meeting, but because of what did *not* happen *before* the meeting."[4]

Informal discussions often develop spontaneously as when a group of farmers meet on a street corner in town on Saturday afternoon and chat, or in the church yard on Sunday afternoon immediately following service when friends visit about the sermon or any number of other things. Although no special planning is made for such discussions, some member of the group gives leadership and guidance to the discussion. Most formal and informal discussion, however, requires planning to help assure success when a specific objective is desired to be obtained. The amount and kind of planning required will vary depending on a number of factors including the topic of discussion, size of the group, specific purpose of the discussion, and age of members of the group. However, some general procedures and techniques will apply to the advance preparation necessary for most organized discussions.

No claim is made of listing all of the points for consideration in making preparation for a discussion nor of discussing fully any one of the points that are listed. It is rather intended that the following statements will give some indication of the kind of preparation that leaders should make whether for formal or informal discussion.

The leader should first of all learn all that he can about the members of the group. He should know something about the age level of the group, the area from which they come, their educational background and their socio-economic background. It will also be helpful to the leader to know something about the past experiences of the members of the group, their attitudes, beliefs and ideals. The leader who has for some time been connected with the group will very likely already have this information. Such information is very important for the planning of a discussion. It may help the leader determine the topic to be discussed, the approach to the topic, and the limits of time and depth of the discussion.

Choice of a topic for discussion may be made by the leader or a committee with the consent of the group. Sometimes the

[4]J. Jeffrey Auer and Henry Lee Ewbank, *Handbook for Discussion Leaders.* New York, Harper and Brothers, 1954, p. 25. (Much of the material in this section is based on Chapter 3 of this book.)

group itself decides what the topic for discussion will be. The leader or a committee may poll the membership through questionnaires to determine their desires for a topic of discussion.[5]

Decisions as to the type of discussion must be made during the period of preparation. The type of discussion best suited for the occasion depends on a number of things including the topic itself, how much the members of the group know about the topic, number of persons in the group, the purpose of the meeting, whether a formal or informal atmosphere is desired, how well the members of the group know each other, and the amount of time to be allotted to the discussion. Auer and Ewbank list and discuss ten types of discussions including informal group discussion, cooperative investigation, committee meeting, conference, panel forum, public hearing, symposium forum, lecture forum, debate forum, and combinations of group and public discussions.[6] The first four of these seem appropriate for informal group discussions while the remainder seem appropriate for more formal group discussions.

How to Conduct a Discussion

Skill in leading discussions is very important to the democratic process and to the arrival of the group at best decisions through the integration of ideas of the members. Parliamentary rules of order are often used in general meetings and in discussions. However, it has been pointed out that *Robert's Rules of Order*, which were effective on the basis of what people knew about human behavior in the days that they were written (1878), are no longer the "last word" in the light of modern scientific knowledge of human relations. According to Malcolm Knowles, "Today the human relations problem in group meetings is not seen negatively as the problem of keeping order. It is seen positively as the problem of creating the atmosphere and procedures that help people to work together productively."[7] Mr. Knowles states that *Robert's Rules of Order* ". . . . become positively illogical when we make the modern assumption that formality stands in the way of creating the friendly and exploratory attitudes which good problem solving seems to require."

---

[5]*Ibid*, pages 28-31, gives examples of questionnaires.
[6]*Ibid*, pages 34-46.
[7]Malcolm S. Knowles, "Move Over, Mr. Roberts," *Adult Leadership*, June, 1952.

Certainly a leader who has the skill of conducting a discussion would not allow any system of rules to interfere unduly with the most effective and efficient advancement of the discussion. However, there are some basic principles that the leader should adhere to in conducting a discussion.

Introduce the Topic for Discussion. The tone that will pervade the whole discussion is often set in the opening remarks of the leader. Sometimes a poor start may be overcome but often it results in a poor end. The leader should define the problem or topic, giving its limitations and an explanation of key words that may not have a commonly-accepted meaning. He should introduce consultants, if there are any, giving brief backgrounds of training, experience, and positions that qualify them for their present roles. Care must be taken to prevent making the consultants or members feel ill-at-ease as a result of these introductions. An appropriate joke or comic experience may fit in well at this point to help all relax and feel at home.

In introducing the problem or topic, the leader should explain the procedure of discussion that is to be followed or seek advice of the group on the procedure preferred. He should indicate the importance of the problem. This is done as a means of motivating and stimulating the group. This should be concise and clear, for it sets the pace and style of the discussion that is to follow.

Begin the Discussion. A leader may get the discussion started by asking a question that will evoke response from the group. Some leaders prefer to have a member of the group seed the discussion by asking the first question. In such cases, the leader may have made provision before the meeting to have a member of the group be prepared to ask the first question. He may suggest an appropriate question for the member to ask or he may leave the selection of a question to the member. The idea here, whether the leader himself asks the first question or has some member do it, is to prevent the lull that so often comes after the introduction because no one wants to make the first statement.

In order to get the discussion started promptly, some leaders prepare a list of thought-provoking questions on the problem or topic and circulate them to all the members of the group. To get the discussion underway, he may poll the group to determine the order in which they want the questions discussed, or he may simply ask that some one read the question that he would like discussed first. The system has advantages as well as disadvantages. It does provide some well-thought-out problems that may give a feeling of security to members of the group. On the other hand, the list of questions may have a stifling effect on members of the group, particularly if they get to feel that the list is sacred, not to be attacked, revised, or expanded.

Encourage General Participation. The success of a discussion depends largely on the ability of the leader to get members of the group to participate fully, freely, and frankly. It is through such discussion that groups arrive at sound decisions. If general participation is not obtained, the discussion may become one-sided with only one or a few points of view getting attention on a topic that has many facets. When this occurs, the group is deprived of other points of view, some of which may be superior to those being expressed or at least they may cause members to re-think and revise their previous views. Therein lies the value of discussions in arriving at the best possible answers.

That general participation be encouraged does not mean that every one at the meeting must have something to say. One-hundred-per-cent participation is desirable but not essential to successful discussion. Doggedly to seek 100% participation may embarrass the person who really does not have anything to contribute or does not want to contribute to a particular topic. The democratic process provides that a person has the right to remain silent as well as to talk. It is rare that a leader should single out a person to talk on a particular point. When done, the leader should be positive that the member will not be embarrassed and can adequately perform what is requested of him. The membership in a rural Sunday School class in South Carolina continually dwindled. The leader of the class had a good knowledge of the Bible but he had the habit of calling on whomever he pleased to read from the Bible or to discuss certain points without prior warning. Many of these people read and interpreted the Bible poorly because of low level of schooling. A new leader was later secured for the class and he soon had a high enrollment. Although he maintained good discussions in the class, he never singled out persons to read or talk unless he was sure that the person had ability to do it well.

Keep the Discussion on the Right Track. A high order of skill is needed to keep the discussion on the right track without embarrassing members or stifling participation. To get the discussion back on the track, the leader may pretend that what has been said is not clear to him and may ask that the relationship of the comment to the topic or question be made clear. Or, to use a more direct method, the leader may simply ask for a decision of the group as to whether or not the discussion is still on the subject. Some groups appoint a committee or person who may be called an evaluator to inform the group when the discussion is straying off the point.

Make Occasional Summaries. Occasional summaries are helpful in keeping the discussion on the right track, in bringing needless repetition to the attention of the group, in recognizing areas of agreement or disagreement, and in pointing the direction of further discussion. Summaries should be brief and accurate. They may be made by the leader, the secretary, or an evaluator if one is used. Regardless of who makes the summary, the leader should provide the opportunity for members of the group to make deletions or additions to the report.

Remain in the Background. In conducting a discussion, the skillful leader is like the parent who is happy to remain in the background while her child becomes the center of attention. She gives the child aid and direction only when the child falters or cannot make it by himself. Even then the parent's aid primarily consists of suggestions or questions that give further direction so that the child can again go it alone.

The most effective leaders of discussions are those who are able to get members of the group to share the responsibility of leadership. When this happens, members of the group ask questions for clarification, keep the discussion on the track, summarize, and make transitional statements, all of which are leadership functions. This is an ideal situation that seldom exists in discussions by any group. When it does not, the leader should enter the discussion only to make brief suggestions instead of giving directions or to ask questions instead of answering them.

Conclude the Discussion. It is just as important to end the discussion effectively as it is to get it off to a good start. The discussion should be concluded early enough to give a summary, make recommendations if necessary, and dismiss at the appointed time. If no time has been set for dismissal and no recommendations are to be made by the group, the discussion should be concluded after vital points have been adequately discussed, but before the group becomes weary of the discussion.

The final summary, which may be given by the leader, the secretary, or someone appointed to give it, should be brief, objective, and accurate. Members of the group should have the opportunity to offer suggestions or corrections to the summary.

Finally, recognition should be given to those persons who may have performed special tasks to facilitate the discussion. Also, thanks should be extended to members of the group for their participation.

Figure 8.   New Horizons for Leaders Who Possess Leadership Skills

CHAPTER VIII

Helping Local Leaders

INTRODUCTION

Do you want to be trained? Neither do I! There is something about an invitation to a training meeting that makes me think of lions and dogs. I am motivated strongly to stay at home and play checkers with the family rather than to saunter forth and be a pawn on some agency's human chess board.

That's why we believe the phrase *training* leaders is archaic and should be replaced with a term like *helping* leaders. It sounds more sincere, reflecting the fact we really want to assist the vast army of voluntary leaders toward a happier and more productive experience.

In the abstract, for annual reports or other dull tabulations, terms like leader recruitment, leader training and leader evaluation are all right. They describe sufficiently the goals and processes which are involved. But when we use such terms in this publication we are describing a process of helping leaders to achieve *their* goals. We want no part of manipulating or masterminding a mobilization of rural leaders for a designing and predetermined purpose.

Leader assistance aims at changes in the performance and satisfaction of people who exert influence in some group or agency. We are especially interested here in volunteer leaders; in those who are or will be active in local community programs for action.[1] What help do they want and need? When do they need it? How can we give it to them?

The specific content of the courses or programs designed to assist leaders will vary widely according to community needs and cultural situations, and also according to the present quality of leadership and the resources available. In any case, helping leaders implies an effort to stimulate and encourage the develop-

---

[1]Acknowledgement is made here of an excellent contribution to this subject in the *Adult Leadership* magazine for June, 1953. Part of the material for this chapter is based on ideas or suggestions gleaned from this and other issues of that delightful and informative periodical.

133

ment of knowledge, skills and attitudes that will improve the quality of results and the pleasure and satisfaction that comes from successful leadership performance. Frequently this process requires unlearning old practices and removing blocks to leadership activity as well as stimulating new ideas or procedures.

THE NEED FOR LEADER ASSISTANCE

If there should be any doubt of the need for helping leaders or the size and importance of the job, the annual report of one agriculturally-oriented educational agency[2] gives copious proof. According to the annual report of Cooperative Extension Accomplishments for 1958, a total of 1,281,178 different local leaders were actively engaged in forwarding the Extension program. About 58 per cent were women, 34 per cent men and 8 per cent were older club boys and girls.

The same year these volunteer local leaders held 1,317,787 meetings attended by over 20 million persons without the presence of county extension agents. If this is an average day, local leaders will conduct nearly 4,700 meetings as a part of the Extension programs of our country alone. Add to that the contribution of leaders at meetings of farm organizations, cooperatives, vocational agriculture and other public and private groups and it makes a staggering total. It is an impressive monument to democratic action and self-help; a tribute to rural citizenry and a challenge to all phases of education.

Some indication of the growing importance and magnitude of leader assistance is given in the same report. In 1958 extension agents conducted 174,159 meetings to help local leaders. These meetings had a total attendance of 4,055,262 persons. Of these meetings, 58 per cent were to assist local leaders for adult work and 42 per cent for youth work. Two and a half decades earlier, in 1930, only about 40,000 meetings for leaders were conducted. The recognition and importance of this method of multiplying the effectiveness of professional efforts increased 4½ times in 26 years.

In addition to meetings, many other educational methods are employed by and for local leaders. These include home and office visits, news stories, publications, circular letters, house organs, radio and T.V., along with many others.

[2]Amelia S. Gordy, *Extension Activities and Accomplishments*, 1958, U. S. Dept. of Agriculture, FES-522, July, 1959.

Further evidence of the need for helping leaders is the problem of recruiting them. Virtually all agencies or groups that depend upon volunteers as their basic corps of teachers report recruitment as a problem. If we had more and better leaders results could be multiplied almost without limit! Obviously finding a leader precedes helping or sharing with him. Still, that is not the whole story.

Why do prospects hesitate or refuse to become volunteers? There are many reasons, but one of the most important is a feeling of inadequacy or a fear of failure. Who among us would take on a job as vocational teacher, extension agent, or insurance salesman without some opportunity to learn how to do the job before we met our first "public"?

What does a leader-prospect mean when he says, "Oh, I can't do that, I haven't the time, get Mr. Sykes, he's a schoolteacher"? In all probability he is reflecting the same emotion as a non-swimmer suddenly confronted with a deep body of water. It's not for him! He wants to wade in slowly, gain confidence and learn the strokes first. One of the worst and most frequent tricks perpetrated on human society is to urge leadership on a willing victim without providing at the same time for pre-service and beginning assistance. Volunteers who are left holding a bag of responsibility without the benefit of counsel and support are a sad sight indeed. This practice accounts for the initial hesitancy and early drop-out of many volunteer leaders.

Problems and Difficulties of Leaders. A number of studies furnish information on the jobs or problems with which 4-H Club local leaders have the most difficulty. Those mentioned most frequently are: Training judging teams; training demonstration teams; developing community and parental cooperation; helping members to keep and complete project records; getting and holding the interest of 4-H members; planning the program and making it a year-around one; getting members to plan their own program; planning and attending 4-H events and activities; arranging details, attending, and guiding regular club meetings; dividing responsibilities among other people; getting material and equipment for project work; and lack of time to supervise the program adequately.

In general there are five ways to decrease the difficulties of local leaders:

1. Adjust the program to reduce leaders' difficulties.
2. Redistribute or redefine the function to be performed by local leaders, extension workers, parents, and members.
3. Select leaders whose qualifications are such that they will not encounter difficulty.
4. Prepare leaders so that they will have less difficulty with their work.
5. By appropriate supervision and recognition increase the enthusiasm of local leaders and their desire and interest in overcoming difficulty.

PURPOSES OF LEADER ASSISTANCE

Most important among the reasons why leaders take on or continue a responsibility is a genuine and sincere belief in the worth of the job to be done.[3] Frequently this belief is verbalized only in vague terms like "Saving our soil is important. Yes, I'll help."

"F.F.A. helps boys get started in farming. Sure, I'll let you use my farm for a demonstration."

"Yes, the Grange helps our community. I'll work for the bake sale if you tell me what to bring."

The value of the program as seen through the leader's eyes will condition his attitude toward taking on and continuing a leadership job. Very few will begin or continue a leader's role in a program which in the opinion of themselves and their neighbors is no longer useful. In other words, folks are leaders *for a reason* or for a purpose. Two implications of this are obvious. The purpose should be worthy and it should be clearly understood by the leader. We discussed the first of these points in Chapter IV. The second forms one of the major categories of subject matter for any program of leader-assistance.

The second most important job of leader-assistance is to help the leader *feel* adequate, ready and able to do the assignment. At this point we are assuming that he wants to do the job. He wouldn't be in it otherwise. The assurance of pre-service assistance helped him over this psychological barrier. Now when you give him the initial help it will make his beginning experiences and satisfactions productive and pleasant. It improves his chances for staying with the work over a longer time.

---

[3] Lucinda Crile, *Lay Leadership in the Extension Service.* E.S.C. 428, U. S. Department of Agriculture, 1945.

A new leader is really being asked to change his behavior, his attitude and his relationship to a group of people with whom he may be the closest of neighbors. How will these folks respond? What will they think of him, for permitting himself to be "set above them" as their leader? A paid or professional leader usually begins his career in some field away from home, where he can be a "specialist." Not so with the volunteer. He usually lives in the community and is subject to social pressures, personal jealousies and "facing the consequences" of any mistakes. His past and present are like an open book. His future status and acceptance may be in jeopardy if he "fails" or if he loses the confidence of friends. Why take a chance? He needs strong motivation and reassurance to get past this uncertain stage. Initial assistance and "know how" are essential or he will never make it.

We have said that the leader needs help with clarifying objectives and purposes. He needs to feel qualified to do the job. Next he needs knowledge, facts and supporting materials relating to the teaching or performance job ahead of him. If he is about to become president of a local Farm Bureau unit he needs to know what Farm Bureau is, does and stands for. He may have been a member for 20 years but still not feel that he is secure on some of these fundamentals. He needs to feel that his office is important and he wants to know how to perform his duties.

If Mary Jane Scribe is elected to serve as corresponding secretary for the local Methodist Youth Fellowship she needs the same understanding of objectives plus a knowledge of how much and what kind of participation the Pastor wants from the young people in his church. Without such information neither Mary Jane nor the Farm Bureau president can find the key to success and satisfaction in their leader roles.

The human relations factor haunts every leadership situation. Rare indeed is the leader who doesn't need to consider the eccentricities, temperaments and sensitive inter-personal relations of members in the group. Sometimes it seems that every tongue is undisciplined, every nerve is taut and nothing will work. How does a leader help a group through such crises? Here is another important area for leader assistance—how to harmonize human personalities and harness their creative potentials.

Finally a leader needs perspective and help in learning how to evaluate results. "How am I doing?" is a universal and important concern. All persons and groups crave the reassurance of knowing that their progress is satisfactory. If the facts reveal negative results even this knowledge is better than gnawing uncertainty. Objective evaluation of group results is seldom easy for new leaders. It's a rare talent at best and a leader-assistance program should include generous portions of assistance in the "feel" of it.

Remember, the leader is most likely to judge his own success in terms of the response from members of his group. Clark and Skelton[4] found this in interviews with 510 present and 250 former local 4-H leaders in New York State. There was a direct relationship between satisfaction, success and performance of the leaders. It was noted that the leaders received their greatest satisfaction and rewards from helping members to grow and develop in their educational achievements, including project work, demonstrations, educational trips and group participation. Leaders placed higher value on success of the Club as their own personal reward than they did on such things as recognition pins, certificates or citations. The personal expressions of appreciation from members, parents and Extension agents were highly treasured by most leaders. Those who received such plaudits appeared to be more successful as volunteer leaders.

In summary then, we list five major needs or reasons for helping leaders.

1. He must believe the job is a worthy one.
2. He must feel adequate, able and ready to perform it.
3. He needs basic knowledge about content or "subject matter."
4. Human relations will be his most difficult and worrysome problem.
5. Objective evaluation will be essential to satisfaction and enjoyment of results.

Situations for Helping Leaders

Pre-service Training. Probably the most rewarding efforts in assisting leaders are those which help them solve problems and relieve apprehensions *before they occur*. Here is a place for sharing the results of experience. Of course there is some danger

[4]Robert C. Clark, "Factors Associated with Performance of 4-H Volunteer Leaders in New York State, 1946-48," Doctoral thesis, Cornell University, 1950. W. E. Skelton, "The 4-H Leader," Doctoral thesis, Cornell University, 1950.

in developing set patterns. However, due warnings and precautions can be injected into the educational process.

Here is the one appropriate time for us to use the term *training*. For preparation and schooling is the actual need— advance training for the leader in anticipation of expected requirements. The first four areas of assistance listed above should receive attention in the advance training course. Discussion of over-all principles and objectives will be of more lasting benefit in the pre-service stage than detailed talk about techniques, gadgets and teaching aids.

The Boy Scouts of America staff has long been cited for its effective pre-service training program for executives, unit leaders and volunteers. Detailed manuals are available for every step of the training process. Although some educators have questioned the inflexibility of the training outlines, it is usually found that resourceful teachers will modify the program to fit local needs. Certainly it must be obvious that such training is welcomed and appreciated by adult Scouters. The ratio of adults to youth in the Scouting program is about one to four, well above the record of most youth-serving organizations. More than a million men and women serve voluntarily to help with the Cubs, Boy Scouts and Explorer programs.

A significant example of a pre-service training program for local volunteer 4-H Club leaders has been going on in Onondaga County, New York, since 1946. It is one of very few counties in the United States having a roster of trained, volunteer 4-H leaders *waiting for a club to lead*. What a dream come true for the Extension Agents! Coupled with this, the tenure of leadership and quality of 4-H programs in Onondaga County are well above average. Here is how the county 4-H Club agent describes this pre-service 4-H leader training course:

1. *The Situation and Need.* There are about 90 4-H Clubs in Onondaga County with 270 leaders. This necessarily involves many new leaders each year and the agents here recognize their responsibility to be that of adequately training these leaders so they can operate with confidence and success in their very first year.

2. *Purposes.* The "New Leader Training Course" has become a regular part of the county program in Onondaga County whereby the local club leaders are prepared to carry full responsibility

for their clubs. The agents do not attend local club meetings unless invited for some special purpose by the club leaders. The leaders organize their own clubs, train local club officers and work with the members in planning programs, teach all subject matter, and prepare the members for participation in such county-wide events as Demonstration Days, Dress Revues, Judging Contests and Exhibiting.

3. *How It Was Planned.* The idea of a training course to be held strictly for "new leaders" came about in 1946 after two very capable first-year leaders, in returning from a regional 4-H Leaders Meeting, said, "We came back from these 4-H leader meetings more confused than helped and just have the feeling that we can never do the seemingly efficient job that the experienced leaders speak of. They seem to have all the answers."

Feeling the need to provide training in 4-H Club Organization for "beginners" without the danger of the sessions being dominated by the experienced leaders, the agents planned the first course and invited *only* those leaders about to begin club work, and those who had started within the past year. We have held religiously to that ever since. As we contact new or prospective leaders between our Spring and Fall courses, we tell them of the next "New Leader Training Course" to be held and urge them to wait till they have attended at least the first meeting of the next course before attempting to organize their Club. Their usual reply is "I'd certainly not want to start 4-H work until I have had a chance to come in to such a training program."

4. *How the Course Is Conducted.* All are supper meetings. Attendance is voluntary—all leaders in their first year, and those about to begin leadership, are invited to attend the course. Part of each of the five meetings is group discussion and part is actual practice. The leaders are formed into a hypothetical club and go through all the steps of selecting projects, enrolling, electing officers, conducting meetings, planning programs, keeping secretaries' records and making out reports.

5. *Agents' Evaluation.* The fellowship of these people in the same stage of 4-H leadership is a great morale-builder. At the conclusion of the course both agricultural and homemaking agents know all leaders, and *all leaders*, regardless of type of club, know the agents in both lines of work. Leaders develop only if agents *let them* do the things mentioned in the paragraph

above. As an example—we have from 300 to 325 different individual members giving demonstrations each year at the county level with the leaders doing all the work of helping members select topics and training the demonstrators.

We believe leaders can be taught better through a group process such as this than they can through *direct, individual* face-to-face contact with the agents.

6. *Leaders' Evaluation.* Evaluation sheets are used at the close of each course. Especially after the first one or two courses, we depend upon these heavily to guide us in adjusting future courses to the expressed needs of the leaders.

7. *Rating of Importance of Things Covered in New Leader Training Course by Leaders Completing the Course.*

> 1st. Club Organization
> 2nd. Planning 4-H Club Programs
> 3rd. How to Work with Youth
> 4th. Parliamentary Procedure
> 5th. Keeping the Secretary's Records
> 6th. 4-H Demonstrations
> 7th. Actually elect officers and have them preside
> 8th. 4-H Club Recreation Games
> 9th. 4-H Club Recreation Music
> 10th. Know Your Extension Service
> 11th. 4-H Club Ritual
> 12th. History of 4-H Club Work

The Teachable Moment. When the first egg-laying moth-millers are seen flying out of the clothes-closet or when the first green-gray cutworms start chewing off the stems of young tomato plants there is nothing quite so needed or welcome as a good bulletin on insect control or a well written article in the local paper on the same subject. By the same token, a leader with a problem needs help and usually knows it. Right at the moment of need is the best time to provide assistance. There will not be another time quite so good later. Of course, an even better time would have been before it happened, but the leader would not have been so forcefully motivated as when the problem first comes up.

The principle of learning readiness or the "teachable moment" applies to volunteer leaders as well as to children.

Methods for Helping Leaders. Help for a leader who has a problem must be given in such a way that there is created no feeling of embarrassment or failure. Rather, a climate of impersonal objectivity is needed for free discussion of the principles involved. As sometimes stated, the wise teacher instills trust and confidence with the attitude, "There are no foolish questions and no wrong answers." Each situation, each suggestion and every leader is accepted at face value.

For assisting leaders with their in-service problems there is no limit to the methods and devices that are suitable. Nor is there a problem too big for leaders themselves to solve if they are given help in getting the necessary information and opportunity to study and work out their problems together. All five of the major areas of need listed on page 138 are encountered. The leader who is on the job will know the most urgent problems confronting him. Sympathetic questions and a climate of permissiveness and objective acceptance will soon bring them forth. In this and other chapters we will be discussing methods and techniques for helping leaders with their problems. At this point we wish to caution, however, that problem-solving is not a case of bringing forth a bag of tricks and an assortment of pat answers. If real problems are involved, thorough consideration of each will be essential.

An opportunity to get away from everyday affairs and to share and think objectively about problems provides the finest kind of situation for helping leaders. A weekend leaders camp, a short course at the State College or an outing at a resort hotel provides an ideal setting for leaders to share their successes and their problems. Just as every mother of young children needs at least one hour alone each day for rest and meditation, so also does a leader need an occasional chance to "get up on top of the mountain and see the forest."

A typical "Leadership School" is conducted each year for officers and leaders of the Tennessee Young Farmers' and Homemakers' Clubs. An attractive folder is distributed well in advance. The cost is low and in many cases local groups pay all or part of the cost of sending their group leaders.

An advance promotional folder lists the location, cost, health requirements, what to bring, when to come, where to register, and how to get more information. In addition, the purpose and subject matter content of the school are attractively presented. One glance at the appealing schedule reproduced here speaks for itself. The school has been going for ten years and is exceedingly well attended and conducted.

"Wonderful Opportunities to Learn How to. . .

Be a strong leader in your club
Be a better county and district officer
Plan interesting programs based on membership's needs
Lead recreational activities
Write news stories and do radio programs
Speak in public
Organize a club
Get information to solve problems
Lead group singing
Conduct devotionals

"Methods of Approach. . .

Fundamentals of organizational leadership will be stressed
Panel and group discussions will be used to secure the best of the group's thinking
Small committee groups dealing with the more important problems will be organized
The school will include a suggestive year's program of activities for Young Farmers' and Homemakers' Clubs in a manner which can be duplicated by clubs all over the State
Everyone attending will compile a reference handbook from materials and information provided in the school

"Recreation. . .

An unusually attractive program of recreational activities has been planned for this Leadership School.
The recreation program will be developed in a manner that can be duplicated back in the counties. Explicit data on ideas and methods employed will be furnished.

"Objectives of Young Farmers' and Homemakers' Training School. . .

To train selected young men and women for leadership in their respective counties—particularly in the field of activities and services covered by Tennessee Young Farmers' and Homemakers' Clubs.

To provide an opportunity for rural young men and women from every county of the state to come together and outline activities they believe will be of greatest service to the young people whom they represent."

Individual Leader Needs. Most of the training or assistance given to local leaders will be accomplished in groups or by means of mass media. However, there are some personal problems and needs of leaders that can be met only by individual counsel and assistance. For example, a leader may encounter a health or mental case in his group or club. Or he may be concerned about a moral or social situation or other group problem which is not a concern of other leaders and other groups. This type of problem should not be aired in leader meetings except as they may be impersonalized for clinical discussion.

Another example of an individual leader need may be termed leader morale. Sometimes the whole world appears to topple in cataclysmic fashion around a leader's head. When such needs arise the leader-counselor will do well to give that leader individual assistance or help. Watch out to avoid entanglement in affairs or relationships that are strictly personal and not related to the leadership job. But if a volunteer leader comes to his counselor with a genuine problem, here is a chance to demonstrate the sincerity and skill of both. Sad, indeed, is the case where a volunteer leader rides many miles at his own expense to share a problem with an area counselor only to receive a cold shoulder or an indifferent shrug. Listen carefully and with understanding. You may not be ready with a pat answer to the problem but the very process of sitting down and listening, analyzing and organizing the facts will be a great help and comfort to the leader. No single formula will always work or help in such cases. But the steps to follow in approaching a solution are time-worn and logical:

1. Listen carefully. Lay the situation or problem face up on the table. Outline it on paper if much detail is involved. A confidential record may be important later. Be sure to get all of the facts on both sides of the question. Observe the strictest

of ethics in receiving personal or confidential information. Never betray a faith or trust given to you in confidence.

2. Analyze or organize these available facts. Put them in logical sequence or in order of importance. Discuss each item to be sure it is accurate and as complete as possible. This often clarifies the problem and helps the leader sift important facts apart from gossip or emotional bias.

3. Bring new facts or evidence. Get all viewpoints. Draw on other resources. An on-the-spot phone call often clears up cloudy points. Other persons may have additional needed information.

4. Write down several hunches or possible explanations. This should be done as calmly as possible. Tenseness and emotion are serious blocks to reason and sound logic.

5. Consider alternative solutions. Take plenty of time for this. Often additional time helps work things out and brings new facts and better choices. Remember, you are helping the leader to reach his own conclusion and solution, not spoon-feeding him with yours.

6. If action is appropriate it should be taken only in concert with all persons or groups concerned.

7. Follow through to harmonize and evaluate the results.

SUMMARY OF METHODS OR TECHNIQUES FOR HELPING LEADERS

A description of all the ways of helping leaders would require an entire book. Indeed, such references are available. For that reason we are simply listing, as reminders, a few of the time-tested methods that work. This is by way of summarizing ideas and suggestions that appear elsewhere.

A. Helping Leaders in Groups

1. Pre-service meetings for prospective leaders
2. Meetings for new leaders
3. Problem clinics, based on actual or simulated cases
4. Subject matter institutes
5. Demonstrations by experienced leaders or members
6. Special parent-leader meetings to discuss needs of youth and the community
7. Tours and educational trips

8. Symposium by several authorities on objectives or philosophy
9. Work sessions to practice skills of teaching
10. Construction, procurement or use of visual aids
11. Child study groups
12. Achievement events, fairs, exhibits
13. Recognition events and special awards
14. Buzz sessions, brainstorming, discussions
15. Socio-drama, pageants, puppet shows
16. Luncheon or dinner seminars and chalk talks
17. Discussion and analysis of research or study projects

B. Helping Leaders through Mass Communication

1. Leader-letter or house organ
2. News, magazine, radio and TV features
3. Circular letters, bulletins, books
4. Public exhibits, movies, recordings, signboards
5. Leader manuals, teaching materials

C. Helping Leaders in Other Ways

1. Personal visits, letters, telephone calls and office calls
2. Visits to the leader's group or activity
3. Participation in evaluation or study projects
4. Praise and recognition of progress and accomplishment
5. Providing needed materials, organization or assistance on time and in a usable way
6. Understanding and counsel on special problems
7. Inspiration, enthusiasm and good example

****

"—— but he that is greatest among you, let him be as the younger; and he that is chief, as he that doth serve."

St. Luke XXII, 26

CHAPTER IX

Controversy in the Community

Just as my thoughts are being organized on how controversy should be faced by leaders in the community, the telephone rings. The call is from a superintendent of schools who is seeking help on a problem he has never faced before. He describes a controversy in his community and (with but few minor variations) it sounds like hundreds of others. He explains that four small community high schools have been considering the formation of a single school district. The issue has been "red hot" for some time, but a solution was arrived at and a referendum of the voters taken. "Yes, the referendum passed, but" — and here's the controversy he faces today — "In my community and in one other the majority vote was favorable enough to pass the referendum in spite of a minority of favorable votes in the two other small communities." Though a vote was taken, this superintendent knows that controversy still exists. He also knows that without controversy the vote would not have been taken. The communities would have conformed to past school district structure and made no study of their school problems.

The situation described by this superintendent of schools provides an example of the kind of controversy faced by thousands of professional and volunteer leaders in rural communities. Even after a vote, a controversy is not settled. Yet, up to this point in the four communities, we find after further exploration that controversy brought more information about schools and education to the people than had ever reached them before. The new controversy can again be used to educate—to aid the community—to get them thinking—to lead to intelligent decisions. It can also disrupt the community for years to come. This is why the authors believe that leaders should recognize controversy as a community situation in which effective leadership can occur. In fact, effective leadership must occur when there is controversy if communities and the people in them are to improve.

147

The Curve of Controversy

Figure 9 pictures controversy in the community as a normal curve. Note, for example, how important an honest search for solutions is to the leader. The majority of people in the community who are shown by this area of the curve are the ones where the most fruitful results can be achieved from leadership efforts on your part. Note also that complete conformity and total conflict are pictured at opposite ends of the scale with equal proportions of the curve assigned to them. The extreme left of the curve (Point 1) would be a state of complete lack of controversy. The citizens of a community in this situation would be enslaved. On the extreme right of the curve (Point 7) the situ-

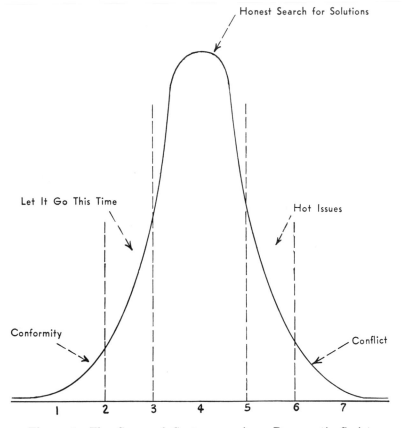

Figure 9. The Curve of Controversy in a Democratic Society

ation would be one of conflict so great that physical violence would occur. Both extremes on the curve are to be avoided in so far as possible. The curve suggests that leaders should be concerned with leading from both extremes toward an "honest search for solutions." It is important to keep those involved in "hot issues" looking critically and honestly at the facts necessary for problem solution. Just as important is a leader's help to those who would be willing to "let it go this time" when in effect this would delay an "honest search for solutions." The curve of controversy can be identified in most communities because people haven't learned to search for solutions in a democratic way. They may lack information, they may not have learned how to communicate with each other, or they simply have no motivations to do better. Democratic leadership makes it possible for a community to have most of its people searching for solutions to whatever problems arise.

What kinds of controversies have you experienced in your community? Have you observed the process of a rural village installing a water and sewer system? The most significant part to watch is not the digging of the mains and laying of the pipes, but is the decision-making that goes on before the first dirt is turned.

Have you ever experienced the process rural church members engage in when a proposal is made to move an open country church congregation to a larger church in a nearby village? Or even the discussion of a problem of declining open country church membership before anyone makes such a proposal?

Have you participated in discussions of the award system for 4-H club work at county fairs?

Have you listened to town boards, county boards, or library boards discuss the proposal to support new bookmobile service to people living in the open country?

Have you attended hearings on the municipal budget? Annual school meetings? Legislative hearings on establishing new taxes? A street corner discussion on a resolution passed by the Farmers' Union? Or a local meeting of the Farm Bureau which is considering sending a wire on farm problems to the Secretary of Agriculture?

If you've experienced any of these or anything resembling these, you know that controversy exists. If you give it careful thought, you'll recognize that controversy has been responsible for many important changes in your community.

The recognition that controversy exists in a democratic society was apparent to a group of Wisconsin community leaders who met for two days in April, 1955, to take part in a series of meetings titled *Conference on Methods of Handling Controversial Issues*. It was the responsibility of this writer to summarize what we learned at this conference. Six factors were listed. They are:

1. We learned that we must get the facts to handle controversial issues intelligently. Without facts the major issue may be missed. With facts the major issue may disappear. Knowing what is behind an issue, its present status, and potential outcomes if no solution is found will help the community and its leaders focus on the issue rather than on the people involved.

2. We learned that handling controversial issues is a step-by-step logical process, yet often charged with emotions that get in the way of an orderly procedure. Solutions to problems come when sufficient understanding of them is reached. Often this understanding can't come until steps have been taken to build background knowledge, remove the issue from the persons involved, and see that a start can be made on resolving it.

3. We learned that we should look for alternative courses of action to those initially proposed. The first ideas are not necessarily the best. In fact, each idea for solution can be a stimulator of other ideas. When alternative actions are looked at in terms of value to the community or its citizens, the alternative selected is likely to be one developed as a result of building on to those suggested early in the controversy.

4. We learned that it is also desirable to secure the participation of persons other than those directly involved. The person standing on the outside of the ring often has a better sense of perspective than those inside. Alternatives can be more objectively weighed. Those not directly involved often see aspects of the controversy which the direct participants see only after they have been pointed out.

5. We learned the necessity of keeping our channels of communications open to the total community. Without clear communication an issue may never really be solved. Some communities have attempted to resolve the same issue nu-

merous times because no one knew that the first, second, or third attempt was made. You don't settle problems in a communications vacuum.

6. We learned that controversy can challenge people to learn. The reaction "something has to be done" is the first stage of seeking an answer to "what can be done?"

Yes, there is controversy in the community and the wise leader uses it to improve the community and its citizens. But how should controversies be approached? How should they be used for progress?

Actually, we can see leaders who react differently to the challenge of controversy. Some would use a "strong hand" and use controversy as an excuse to control. Returning to Figure 9 we can see how this method would lead to either conflict or conformity.

Other leaders would treat the controversy as if it didn't exist. They would try to ignore it. This action on their part would tend to favor a society of conformists. It is also possible that if an issue is ignored too long, and the situation causing it is genuine, sharp movement toward the conflict end of the scale in Figure 9 will be the only way it will get leadership attention.

You can see from the outcome of these two alternatives that the leader in a democratic society should choose another course of action. This course leads to democratic action by an informed citizenry. It can occur when the leader (local or professional, formal or informal) believes in and encourages democratic action by the citizens!

The Scientific Method and Controversy

Following the guidelines of the scientific method the leader can focus on a logical approach to the solution of community problems which are the basis of the controversy. How do you solve such problems? Let's look at each of the important elements of this kind of problem solution, keeping in mind that overcoming our own bias and emotion is important at every stage of solution.

First, we need to *define the problem*. Something caused the controversy. What is it? What is behind the way people are reacting? What is the real issue that the community is talking about?

After finding that, we can *get the facts* about the problem. What do we know about it already? Where can we get other facts about the problem? What have other communities done about this problem? Are there any experts who can help us on this one?

Once the facts are available to the community, it becomes necessary to *organize and analyze* the facts. What do they mean? How do they fit together? To what part of the problem do they relate? Do the facts mean the same thing to all of us? If not, what different meanings are given to them?

It is after this has been done that *a number of alternative solutions to the problem should be suggested.* What solution would this group propose? What solution would that group propose? What would be best for the taxpayer? What would be best for the children? What would be best in terms of our relationships with other communities? What would be the solution suggested by the experts? In the search for solutions the leader should be more of a catalyst than the authority. The leader can be most effective at this stage in bringing the proposed solutions clearly to the attention of the group, thus making it easier for the group to select the best or to develop a better solution by putting several of the ideas together.

After looking carefully at the alternative solutions, it is necessary to *choose a course of action.* There may well be considerable compromise among groups and among individuals at this point, but if the problem is to be solved, one solution must be tried. It should be the solution arrived at by the best thinking of the group. It isn't always the alternative you favored originally, but seeing merit in proposals of others is one of the qualities of an effective leader.

It is most important in using the scientific method in community problem-solving that we *evaluate the course of action we choose.* At each step along the way we have been checking facts carefully, looking at proposals in terms of our own and community objectives. We cannot stop our evaluation here. It must include a continuing examination of the new actions we take. In fact, the very next problem may arise because we do look at and we do evaluate the past actions. This is the factor which makes community progress possible in a democracy. We don't wait for a dictator to order the change. With the help of leaders, we do our own changing.

CONTROVERSY—DESIRABLE OR UNDESIRABLE

An examination of the nature of controversy and a recognition that issues may be used as a means to challenge a citizen to act, calls for more study of controversy. What determines controversy in the community? When is it desirable? When is it undesirable?

Most issues about which there are differences of opinion in the community stem from changes going on around us. There would be few issues arising out of the consolidation of open country churches with village churches if our transportation system was dependent upon horses and dirt roads. There would be few issues on school consolidation if six years of schooling was all society expected for its youth. There would be few issues on increased taxes if our concept of government had not changed. There would be few issues on parity prices for farmers if production per farmer were as low today as it was in 1860. There would be fewer controversies among 4-H club leaders as to whether to organize 4-H clubs in cities if the farm popuation had not dropped to twelve percent of the people in the United States.

Even with obvious changes going on around us people will interpret these changes differently. Research has shown that some of us resist new ideas and proposals for change more vigorously than do others. For example, in a Wisconsin study it was found that people living in rural neighborhoods, with most of the families belonging to the same church and having the same nationality background, resist new ideas in farming, organizations, and schools to a significantly greater degree than people living in neighborhoods that are mixed in their religious and nationality background.[1]

Often the unavailability of facts to one group causes the initial arguments which are symptomatic of the beginning of controversy. If leaders are alert to these arguments and use the scientific method in approaching them, they may find that no problem really exists—or that making the facts available solves a minor problem before it ever gets controversial. Ignorance of the facts is not as great a cause of real controversy as is poor interpretation of the facts. In the interpretation of facts the

[1]Burton W. Kreitlow and James A. Duncan, *Farmer Acceptance of Educational Changes*. Bulletin 525, University of Wisconsin, College of Agriculture, July, 1956, p. 3.

scientific method and the democratic method aid in overcoming this obstacle. Yet, it is no guarantee that an easy solution is possible. There are times each of us can remember when leaders with democratic dedications who had followed through on the scientific method still found themselves unalterably opposed to each other on the selection of a course of action. Each may have thought the other ignorant. The fact was that they interpreted the potential outcome of proposed solutions quite differently. This possibility of difference in interpretation by intelligent people should be understood. This difference may stem from a number of factors. The dedications a person has and the values he holds dear cause him to interpret in a somewhat different perspective the proposals made by a person with differing values and dedications.

The cultural background of the people concerned may also be responsible for these differences. Using the very same facts, we who have been reared in rural communities may disagree in our interpretation with those reared in an urban environment. The influence of cultural background is easiest to see if we compare interpretations of those in the community who immigrated to the United States from some foreign country and those who were born and reared in a family which has spent several generations in our community.

There are other determinants of controversy which should be recognized, too. Though they aren't the cause of many real controversies, they are difficult ones with which leaders must deal. The vested interests of individuals or groups often lead to controversy. The mere fact that Mr. Jones made a proposal for a change in the by-laws of the farm organization leads Mr. Smith to suspect that it has something to do with giving Mr. Jones a stronger hand in controlling the program of the organization. As soon as Mr. Smith raises questions to try to clarify the issue Mr. Jones thinks to himself, "Now what's he after? Is he trying to take over?"

Conflicts of personality are often misinterpreted as controversy over ideas. Leaders should examine carefully the basis of controversy to make sure it is not a symptom stemming from a clash of personalities. The community leader with democratic dedication accepts each person as he is, and together they search for the facts behind controversy. To waste time in petty bickering, in "I won't take part if she's in it" activities, in riding rough-shod over people you don't like, has never built a base for community improvement. The first brick in the foundation of community development is the acceptance of each person as he is.

The controversy which begins with vested interests or personal animosities may well be ignored if it is not vital to the progress of the community or group. On the other hand, some controversies which begin this way do lead to major complications. They must then be attacked with the same dispatch and vigor as if they grew out of change affecting everyone in the community. We must even admit that occasionally an undesirable type of beginning to a community controversy may lead to desirable end-results. In spite of this, it is not a recommended way of making progress.

When Is Controversy Desirable? Accepting controversy as inevitable is one thing, using it effectively and creatively is another. The leader in the community must make personal decisions on whether it will aid the community to move toward settlement of a controversy at this time. Will the results justify the time spent? Are the potential outcomes such that it's worth the effort of the many community citizens who might get involved? Are there so many dangers of possible conflict in this controversy that it should be delayed for the present? Would we get further behind the times if we let this budding controversy alone now? Would it merely be a means of conforming? (Take a look at Figure 9 again.)

Decision-making for effective use of controversy is a big job for any leader, local or professional. It means weighing potential outcome, looking for potential disrupting influences, recognizing whether or not the controversy will develop without your influence, distinguishing between controversy and healthy skepticism, seeing if you could stop a potentially-dangerous controversy from developing, and finally selecting a time to attempt to solve the controversy when the most positive results are likely to occur. A controversy is desirable when it helps to build the community and its citizens.

When Is Controversy Undesirable? It must be remembered that the solution of any community problem, the outcome of a community controversy, always carries with it the potential of being undesirable for someone or some group. The same can be said for that which forestalls controversy, thus forestalling action. This conformity to things past or present also has the potential of being undesirable.

A controversy is undesirable to the extent that as a result of its development the likely outcomes would be less desirable to the community than maintaining the status quo. A controversy without the possibility of a creative solution to the problem carries with it too many dangers of disrupting community life. There are times when it doesn't pay off in community or individual development.

Undesirable controversies are those begun over little things. Some people like to "pick gnats" in public in an effort to "start a good fight." The democratic leader sees through this and either ignores the effort of these people or sets the stage for an early examination of the facts of the case. A leader has no business getting involved with problems that lead to mere argument or haranguing without a potential solution at the community level or with only unacceptable solutions. Controversies without good alternative solutions are often the most difficult to stop. It is to the advantage of the community to have leaders who stop them before they start.

Controversies are undesirable when there is in the potential solutions no opportunity to strengthen the community. They are undesirable when they are artificial and used for selfish and personal goals.

The Leader and Controversy

George B. DeHuszar in his book, *Practical Applications of Democracy,*[2] places considerable emphasis on what he calls "do-democracy." As a leader with values and dedications containing strong democratic overtones his words are most meaningful. He states: "Do-democracy is not based on listening or talking, nor on counting noses." *It is based on participation, facing problems together.* Creative participation by intelligent beings in the on-going process of society is essential to the general welfare. Thus the problem of democracy is not merely how to obtain consent, but also how to create opportunities for participation and a

---

[2]George B. DeHuszar, *Practical Applications of Democracy.* New York, Harper and Brothers, 1945, pp. 12-13.

determination to participate. Many of the great improvements in rural communities have come about through controversy and the creative leadership of some of its members. The authors of this volume do not wish to overemphasize controversy but neither do we wish to scorn or fear its use. We're aware that there can be little change in any community or in any one of us without challenge. An intelligent use of controversy by leaders supplies that challenge. This was pointed out by G. Aubrey Young. In writing about controversy in religion he stated, "To the acquiescent and complacent, controversy comes as a blessing in disguise. It disturbs and disrupts, but in the process it makes dead minds come alive."[3]

Leaders may be able to recognize in some of their own experiences the effects of other leaders on them. Controversy can be used as a stimulant to the mind. Have you ever made a casual statement as to an action a group should take and then have another person say, "I don't think it will work," or "perhaps we should do it this way instead"? Your reaction to statements of this nature that are made in good faith gives a small example of the challenge of controversy.

In dealing with problems that are or have the potential of being controversial the rural leader should consider the principles of democratic leadership identified in Chapter V and select methods and techniques accordingly. The *principle of challenge* is almost inherent in this kind of a problem. The *principle of the group mind* is an essential consideration when alternative solutions are sought. The *principle of knowledge* if followed may save a great deal of the community's time. If we know what the problem is and the facts concerning it, the basis for interpretation is present. The *principles of process, flexibility,* and *service* have implications for dealing with controversy that should not be overlooked.

All of this asks much of the democratic leader. We are sure your kind of leadership was considered by Professor Fellman at the Wisconsin Conference on Methods of Handling Controversial Issues, when he said:

> "Where there is much desire to learn," John Milton once said, "there of necessity will be much arguing, much writing, many opinions." Those who put an especially high premium on

[3] G. Aubrey Young, "The Role of Controversy in Religion," *Adult Leadership*, Volume 6, No. 3, September, 1957, p. 77.

mental peace and psychic security are often disturbed by the never-ending din, but the din cannot be avoided, for to silence it, as James Madison once suggested, involves the substitution of a remedy which is worse than the disease. Life in a noisy society is infinitely preferable to life in a nice quiet penitentiary.

Nevertheless, it must be clear that democratic government is government the hard way, for those in power must stand up under the constant strain of criticism and opposition. A successful democratic politician needs the hide of a rhinoceros. It takes a certain toughness of mind and spirit to remain faithful to the methods of democracy. A democrat must face the facts of life, the unpleasant as well as the pleasant. In contrast, dictatorship has no faith in man's intellect, and denies his capacity for self control; it is basically escapist in character. Dictatorship has been called, appropriately enough, "the emotional air-raid shelter of moral cowards."

A system which is a standing invitation to controversy asks much of people in many ways. With its reliance upon reason and persuasion, it asks people to think. Indeed, it asks them to think a great deal about difficult public questions. Every educator knows how very painful thinking really is, both for himself and for his students. It is undeniable that a great many people find a considerable measure of satisfaction in dictatorship because it releases them from the irksome obligation of thinking. Democracy also asks us to be tolerant of those with whom we may be in sharpest disagreement. In the immortal words of Justice Holmes:

> "If there is any principle of the Constitution that more imperatively calls for attachment than any other it is the principle of free thought—not free thought for those who agree with us, but freedom for the thought that we hate."[4]

There is a tendency for many people (leaders included) to fear controversy. This may be because they feel insecure, they see no point to change, they are afraid of getting involved in a problem that is too complex, they lack the knowledge to react to it and don't wish to get involved, they associate it with argument and have been taught as children that arguments are bad, or they just prefer to escape being bothered. Looking at controversy in the community leads the authors to conclude that there are many things to be feared more than controversy. For example, we fear more the stillness of thought that would occur if no one was willing to face up squarely to the problems of our day. It is better to maintain the tradition of solving our community problems by putting them to the test of study and discussion than it is to be a conforming slave.

---

[4]David Fellman, *The Role of Controversy in a Democracy*, in a report of the Conference on Methods of Handling Controversial Issues and published by the Governor's Commission on Human Rights. Madison, Wisconsin, 1955, pp. 8-9.

Controversy can be looked at as being both desirable and inevitable in a democratic society. Where there is the potential of change there is the potential of controversy. A democratic society accepts first and foremost the conviction that change is inescapable. Community leadership that is democratic will just as inescapably face controversy if the community is to remain democratic.

Under these conditions, the balance arrived at after controversy is over is not a final truth but a tentative plateau that embodies some of the elements of truth. It is the best solution in this community at this time. In fact, our democratic society, controversy, the scientific method, and democratic leadership are partners in rural community progress.

CHAPTER X

Working Together in the Community

In the rural family there are various levels of cooperation and conflict. We often point with pride to families where the spirit of working together is exemplified by major family accomplishments. In most of these instances the family members do cooperate. They do coordinate the activities of one family member with those of another and with those of the family unit. Most participation in rural family life is in working together as a family group. Yet, there are times in rural families when individuals strike out on their own, and such independent action is often encouraged by family groups. Indeed, such independent action is looked on as a sign of individual maturity. Also there are times when conflict among family members occurs. This may be of minor consequence or it may lead to disruption of the family unit.

The rural community is in many respects analogous to the rural family. There are evidences of working together, of cooperation and coordination among community groups, organizations, and agencies. There are examples of independent action by one or more of these, and there are instances when there is considerable conflict among these groups. Unlike the family, most action of community groups is independent action; and though it is essential and desirable that it be so, this independence of action is the basis of many of the competitions and conflicts which occur. It is in cases where two or more groups seek identical goals that competition is first noted. When the objective is of such a broad nature that no one group could hope to attain it completely, it is unlikely that great competition among groups would occur. In this case it may be possible for all groups to accomplish the objective only if joint effort were brought to bear. When the objective is clear and readily attainable by a single group, and then if three or four groups try to attain it the same year, competition is almost sure to arise. Often conflict will begin over who is to do the job and receive the credit for its accomplishment. There are certain community problems which demand that community groups work together to achieve reasonable solutions. This is likewise true of family problems and their solution.

The process of working together will be called coordination. *Coordination among groups in the community is the process of working together to establish goals and take action on specific community problems.* As we observe rural communities and families we can see evidences of competition, conflict, cooperation, and coordination. Vogt, in describing rural families on the frontier, indicates that often they interact rather than cooperate; and that this interaction has a "feudin' tone" to it, except in the case of a community crisis when cooperation is evident.[1] Coordination with its harmony and reciprocity is not noted. T. Lynn Smith identifies institutional competition as one of the types of competition in the rural community.[2] Though we may want to consider both family and community as normal when they are coordinating their various abilities and efforts, the authors believe it is realistic to point out that in many rural communities coordination is more of a hoped-for potential than a goal already achieved. It is from this belief that the process of working together in the community will be examined. Consideration will be given to the need for coordination, the methods of coordination, and the leadership for coordination.

NEED FOR COORDINATION

Lake Mills is a midwestern community with 2,500 people living in the village center and 3,500 in the farm service area. At one of their meetings, a group of Lake Mills citizens began discussing the various agencies, groups, and organizations to which people could belong in their community. They listed these groups and were astonished to count eighty-seven, ranging from the homemakers' club and a birthday club to a commercial club and a card club. There were formally organized groups like the Young Farmers who met sixteen times a year with the teacher of agriculture in the high school, and the Lions Club which met every Tuesday for lunch. There were less formal groups like a birthday club in one of the farm neighborhoods which met whenever one of the group remembered that some one else had a birthday. It was noted that most of the eighty-seven groups had made at least sporadic attempts to improve the community.

[1] Evon Z. Vogt, *Modern Homesteaders.* Cambridge, The Belknap Press, 1955, p. 140.
[2] T. Lynn Smith, *The Sociology of Rural Life.* New York, Harper and Brothers, 1947, p. 457.

After this informative session and the shock of learning how many groups were trying in a general way to do the same thing, this group of Lake Mills citizens realized that an effort should be made to work together in an attempt to solve the many problems in the community. Coordination may not have been considered, yet it tends to follow successful cooperative efforts. In the instance of Lake Mills, the sheer weight of numbers of groups was sufficient to convince those listing them that something should be done.

Another evidence of the need for efforts to coordinate community groups is the recognized lack of cooperation within communities throughout the United States. Occasionally *the evidence of conflict underlines the need for change.* This conflict is observed as community groups attempt to reach common goals. One should not be too concerned when there is competition among groups in certain projects. This is particularly true in situations where the results are of secondary importance, or where the goal is so large that there is room for effort by different groups. Actually competition, if legitimate, can be a fine stimulation to groups that are taking different approaches to the same large community project. Good competition may even lead to cooperation and coordination at the later stages of development.

The leader within a community group may well ask himself, "On which of our undertakings could we have worked jointly with other groups?" or "Which other community groups are now working on community activities that we could help on?" The answers to both questions usually indicate a number of community activities and programs which need cooperative efforts to be accomplished effectively. For example, cooperation is very often needed and welcomed by groups attempting to conduct highway safety campaigns, to establish an adequate village-farm fire protection system, to bring a number of cultural enterprises to the community, or to campaign for better school facilities. In some villages there is a reluctance to seek cooperation from farm groups, and in other instances farm groups hesitate to seek cooperation from those in the village. In reality the climate for effective cooperation in community development comes from the experience of working together. To obtain this experience—to get started working together, is the responsibility of the community's leadership.

Coordination should never be a goal in itself. Rather, it is the means by which community objectives are reached. The actual working together for community good, though it demands leadership skills and ability to accomplish, can only be effective in so far as the goals for community betterment are sound. Coordination of action on a community level can be developed only when a number of leaders see the wisdom of joint action as a means of reaching a common goal.

The part individual leadership plays in community action is that of clarifying goals and identifying ways of reaching them. The person who attempts to get other leaders to assist his organization in a program must first and foremost be able to explain the goals of joint action in such a way that others can understand them and see the value to themselves or to their group. Other leaders must be able to see their responsibility, and the responsibility of their group, on any project which may be pursued jointly. To be able to clarify these responsibilities so that cooperation rather than conflict occurs is a most difficult task for the person attempting to encourage joint action. Of particular concern here is the fact that the objectives of one's own organization are often evident to others. If they are also the focus of the proposed joint action it may appear to be a selfish effort and the objectives become the stumbling block to the cooperation of leaders. In some ways, leadership for coordination must be able to lose some of its loyalty to the parent group for the benefit of the total community. When this can be done in good faith and can be understood by the group one represents as well as by the groups who are to work together, the first major hurdle to community action is passed.

Coordination takes leadership because groups, like people, tend to be comfortable doing things over and over again in the same way. To change direction, to rise above one's present status, takes either the jolt of crisis or the persistent tugs of a leader. The leader in the community recognizes that he needs to tug and be tugged. A community action program provides the setting in which both can occur.

METHODS OF COORDINATION

Informal coordination, coordination through the use of temporary committees, and formally organized community councils or coordinating committees are the three most common methods of rural community coordination that are employed. Each will be described and consideration given to the community situations in which each is most likely to be successful. In addition, combinations of the three will be discussed.

Informal Coordination. Doing things together without rules, regulations, and charter is typical of American rural society. In referring to informal cooperation among individuals Nelson says, "In the history of rural life voluntary acts of helpfulness to achieve a common end are characteristic."[3] As voluntary cooperation among individuals was typical, so was voluntary cooperation among groups. The fact of social change has made certain adjustments necessary; one of these is the greater specialization of rural society, individual, and group activities. With this specialization has come less opportunity for voluntary cooperation by any of these. The "noncontractual cooperation" as described by Smith[4] and associated with the "neighbor assisting neighbor" attitude, is not as readily accepted as it once was. The trend in rural communities is toward the more contractual cooperation which is more closely associated with urban societies, specified rules, and a stricter adherence to rules and regulations.

In spite of the decreasing opportunities for informal cooperation, the rural leaders should not overlook opportunities where it is possible to help each other within the spirit of our historical neighborliness. Individual initiative to promote informal cooperation and coordination is a legitimate role of the community leader and should be exercised whenever possible. One need not be concerned with the label of being "traditional" if he makes efforts to effect informal cooperative action. In fact, rural people respect the leader who can get things done in "the good old fashioned way." They also recognize more clearly than ever the need for more formal lines of cooperation when informal activities are not adequate.

In many rural communities there is a core of leadership of from ten to twenty persons who have leadership roles in most of the major organizations, agencies, or groups. Here the opportunity for informal cooperation is excellent. In effect, the com-

---

[3]Lowry Nelson, *Rural Sociology*. New York, American Book Company, 1948, p. 173.
[4]Smith, *Op. Cit.*, pp. 480-481.

munity has a system of interlocking directorships maintained by the active participation of a limited number of leaders. Though this may aid in the informal cooperation possible, it has a serious hindrance in terms of the limited leadership-development opportunities it provides.

Temporary Committees. Temporary committees come into being when leaders recognize that informal cooperation cannot be relied upon to get a specific job done in satisfactory time. To get it done, the temporary committee is organized for the job. It is assumed from the start that when the job is accomplished the committee will cease to function. Matthews, in writing on organizing for service, explains that:

> "Cooperative action can hardly be avoided by groups with active programs. Many projects cannot be undertaken with the personnel and financial resources of one organization alone. Others require the cooperation of a municipal body such as a board of health, board of education, or a park commission. Some involve activities that overlap or touch on areas that lie within the interest of other organizations.
>
> "Arrangements for planning, organizing and directing a cooperative project; and the kind and degree of participation and responsibility by each organization vary as widely as the projects themselves. The formation of an intergroup committee with an equal sharing of work and responsibility by all major community groups, represent the logical development of cooperation in broad service programs or in particular fields such as health, education, and recreation."[5]

By taking action and forming committees for specific projects a community's leadership may develop the habit of working together. This habit can lead either of two directions or remain stationary. It may develop such fine acquaintanceship and understanding of each other and of each other's programs that tasks requiring cooperation will be accomplished on an informal basis and no additional temporary committees will be needed. On the other hand the effectiveness of the experience of working on temporary committees may be so positive that the leaders may be encouraged to organize on a more permanent basis with some form of a community coordinating council. Also possible is the continuation of the use of temporary committees as the need arises.

There are communities in which the only time groups join hands in action is during times of crisis. At other times they

[5]Mark S. Matthews, *Guide to Community Action*. New York, Harper and Brothers, 1954, pp. 99-100.

largely ignore each other. The leader with vision will take advantage of a crisis by helping others develop a pattern of successful cooperation. Instead of moving from crisis to crisis, the cooperation developed may make it possible for a community to avoid crisis. This is done by making necessary adjustments in advance.

Community Councils. More formal in organization than the above means of cooperation is the community council. Morgan writes that the scope of the council should be much greater than just determining how to intermesh the activities of several agencies—"nothing less in fact, than the development of every phase of community life in good proportion to every other."[6]

Matthews indicates that the formation of temporary committees often leads to a more permanent council structure. He describes this as follows: "A council usually consists of representatives of all major interests, organized on a permanent basis to work for a common purpose. Some councils are concerned only with determining needs to be met by appropriate agencies or organizations. Some serve as coordinating agencies. Others carry out programs with the help of cooperating groups. Important contributions to the solution of broad area problems are being made by such organizations."[7]

Sanderson and Polson refer to community councils as an indirect means of community organization. (Direct action involves all members of a community assembling to take direct action.) They describe a council as being composed of representatives of all groups concerned with community welfare and a certain number of members selected at large.[8]

That there is considerable confusion as to the purposes, organization, and actions of community councils has been pointed out by many authorities who have studied councils. The Ogdens raise many questions about the community council of which the following are examples: "Should it be made up of professional workers who feel the need for a clearinghouse? Or should it go a step further and include, along with the professional workers, heads of organizations such as local service clubs, parent-teacher organizations, and women's clubs? Or should it be

[6]Arthur E. Morgan, *The Small Community, Foundation of Democratic Life.* New York, Harper and Brothers, 1942, pp. 152-153.
[7]Matthews, *Op. Cit.*, p. 100.
[8]Dwight Sanderson and Robert A. Polson, *Rural Community Organization.* New York, John Wiley and Sons, Inc., 1939, p. 166.

a citizen's council, which may take responsibility for planning; for mobilizing the resources of the various agencies—local, state, and national; and for helping carry out plans—including, perhaps, professionals and officials either as citizens or as representatives of agencies?"[9] They further indicate that there is evidence of confusion among people within the same community as well as among communities. In a more recent publication Hoiberg states that: "Scores of illustrations could be given, for example, of localities where community councils function superbly as planning agencies; but there are others in which they do not seem to be effective."[10]

Recognizing the unanswered questions and the variety of attitudes relating to community councils, representatives of fifteen organizations and agencies in Wisconsin determined to study community councils and prepare a bulletin to be used by local citizens who sought community action by means of community councils. It was also meant for those who had questions about how to organize a community council and get it functioning. One of the authors of this book served as chairman of this study group during the production of the bulletin. The committee preparing it recognized that it was dealing with but one way to solve community problems. But because it represents one of the most careful analyses of councils ever published it will be printed here with only minor changes.[11]

What Is a Community Council?

A Community Council is one type of organization for voluntary effort to solve problems of common concern in a community.

It is *"voluntary."* Participation is not compulsory. The council's actions do not have the force of law, but only the power of public opinion.

"Common concern" means concern with those problems of community life beyond the ability of the individual citizen, family, or single organization to solve alone.

---

[9]Jean and Jess Ogden, *These Things We Tried.* University of Virginia, University of Virginia Extension, 1947, p. 88.
[10]Otto G. Hoiberg, *Exploring the Small Community.* Lincoln, University of Nebraska Press, 1955, p. 24.
[11]Reprinted from *Teamwork in the Community,* by Wisconsin Community Organization Committee. By permission of the Wisconsin Community Organization Committee.

And what is a community? For our purposes here, a community is an area—any area—in which people are willing and ready to work together on a cooperative basis, to get what they want. This may be a neighborhood, a town and country community, a school district, a village or city, or any combination of these.

Who Belongs to a Community Council?

The membership of a community council as shown in Figure 10 usually includes (1) delegates or representatives of civic, professional, educational, religious, agricultural, labor, and business organizations; (2) delegates or representatives of public and voluntary community service agencies; and (3) individual members chosen for their interest, knowledge, or competence in civic affairs and not representing any particular organization.

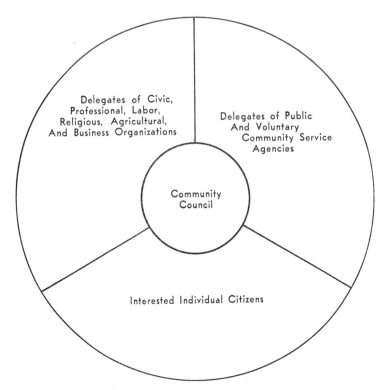

Figure 10. The Membership of a Community Council

All economic and social groups, as well as geographic areas, should be urged to participate. A community council cannot get results if it leaves out groups which have a genuine interest in community improvement and direct lines of communication to citizens. The main idea, when it comes to membership, is to *get* participation, not to *limit* it.

A community council needs youth for its own sake and for the sake of youth. In return for receiving new ideas and fresh enthusiasm it will give youth a training ground for future responsible leadership.

While it is important to include the professional staff of member agencies, the success of a community council in winning community support will depend most upon strong citizen participation.

What Does a Community Council Do?

No two community councils will be exactly alike in program, but they share the general purpose of improving all phases of community life. The most vital part of a community council's job is to study problems and needs and to plan cooperatively to meet them. It does this by:

1. Encouraging informed citizen participation
2. Fact-finding
3. Developing public understanding and support
4. Coordinating community activities and services
5. Cooperative action

Encouraging Informed Citizen Participation. Citizen participation in community life is the foundation of a strong democracy. But an active citizen must be a well-informed citizen. A truly representative community council educates for civic leadership.

Illustrations:

—Through a fact-finding committee to study needs and resources of a community.

—Through a radio panel about recreational services.

—Through directing a poll of youth and adult employment opportunities.

Fact-Finding. One of the most valuable things a community council can do is continually and carefully to gather facts about its community—its health, human relations, education, recreation, religious, economic, and welfare needs —and to agree on how these needs can best be met. If a council does nothing more than to study such facts and present them fairly and completely, it has proved its worth.

A council will find it advantageous to call in consultants from outside the community to direct or assist in making fact-finding studies.

Illustrations:

—A study to find out how widely boys and girls are participating in the program of youth agencies. Such a study might result in the discovery that certain age or racial groups are not being served, or that some areas have more than enough youth agencies, while others have too few.

—A study of zoning problems in relation to adequate housing. This might result in improved living conditions for families.

Developing Public Understanding and Support. A community council stimulates public awareness of community problems, develops an understanding of how the community deals with these problems, and gains support for the necessary services and programs. How? By sponsoring public meetings and forums; maintaining speakers' bureaus; distributing studies and reports; and getting publicity through the press and radio. Community understanding of needs and services develops through council delegates' reports to their own organizations.

Illustrations:

—Publishing a directory of the community's health, welfare, education, and recreation resources.

—Arranging for newspaper articles or radio programs of an informational or educational nature.

—Providing up-to-date information on business, industry, and employment opportunities.

Coordinating Community Activities and Services. Community councils provide a meeting ground for people from different public or voluntary agencies or organizations to come together, share their experiences, understand each others' viewpoints, and agree on some definite plans. By working voluntarily on joint projects, community leaders learn to lift their eyes from their own specialized interests and take a look at the whole community. When advisable, they assign parts of the total job to suitable organizations so that people will receive the best possible services with the least duplication of effort, time, and money.

A community council also coordinates by bringing old and new services into proper balance. By its understanding of all the facts it is more likely to reflect the best judgement of all concerned.

Councils often provide some common service to member organizations unable to achieve it alone.

Illustrations:

—Arranging meetings at which each organization can describe its purpose and program to other organizations.

—Getting out a calendar of future events and meetings to help individual organizations avoid conflicts in dates.

—Developing a cooperative developmental program for volunteer leaders of all leisure-time organizations.

Cooperative Action. After considering the facts and agreeing upon a logical course of action, the council takes steps to carry out its plans. This may require modifying an existing service or developing an entirely new one. In any case, interested citizens and organizations arrive at a joint decision.

Council action may mean conference and negotiation with officials administering the services. It may mean consultation with the group which appropriates funds such as the Community Chest, or county, village, or town boards or the city council.

Councils should not generally operate community services directly, though they may do so occasionally on a temporary demonstration basis.

Illustrations:

> —Negotiating with two existing agencies or organizations for a merger of their services or projects.
>
> —Holding conferences with school authorities to work out plans for use of school buildings for summer recreation.
>
> —Presenting to the city council recommendations for improvement of a swimming beach or pool.

What Kind of Organization Structure Is Necessary?

The council should develop its own pattern of organization and not attempt to adopt that of another community. The success of a council does not depend upon a fixed pattern but rather upon its ability to deal with its own community needs. It is well to keep the organization simple and flexible, with an executive committee or board, necessary officers, and committees as needed to carry out specific tasks or projects. Particularly in a small council it is unwise to develop too many standing committees.

Figure 11 is an example of the structure of a community council.

While it is important that a council adopt a constitution and by-laws, overemphasis upon this in the developmental stage, to the neglect of a program based upon community needs, may result in loss of interest on the part of the membership.

Leadership. The success of a council depends on several things, but perhaps most important of all is the quality of its leadership. The council able to arrange for some paid staff service, even if only part-time, is fortunate.

Selection or election of officers, directors, and committee chairmen must be more than a haphazard process. A nominating committee is one way of getting good results. Council leadership should meet the following qualifications:

> —Have sincere faith in people.
>
> —Have broad vision and a community point of view.

—Have ability to get people to work together in a democratic way.

—Command wide respect in the community.

—Give enough time to do the job required.

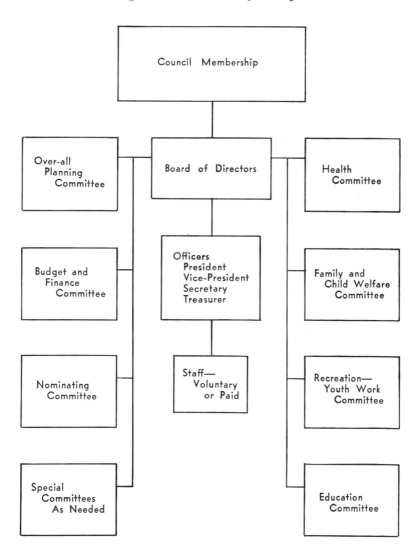

Figure 11. The Structure of a Community Council

How Does the Council Get Results?

It is unwise to attempt too large a program in the beginning. It is better to select one or two projects where a definite problem exists and where the chance of success is reasonably sure.

Public confidence in a community council brings positive community action on its recommendations. Such community action springs from wide participation in the planning by citizens and officials. But sometimes the proposed improvement will depend upon action by persons not participating or concurring with the majority opinion. What does the council do then? The answer is that the council *educates*. It does not *compel*. It must rely upon public opinion, public understanding, and the power of facts. This is the reason why fact-finding must be objective and thorough; participation in planning must be broad and representative; and leadership must be devoted and able. But even these may not be enough. Sometimes there must be much patient negotiation, persuasion, and a meeting of the minds based on the logic of the situation before the proposed improvement becomes an accomplished fact.

The council has no authority over any of its organization members or representatives. Each organization is autonomous and administers its own affairs. Actually the council does not plan for organizations; rather it is the medium through which member organizations agree to plan and work together. The most solid successes may come from changes that have occurred in the attitudes of the people as they have participated in the planning process.

Do You Need a Council in Your Community?

Organizing a community council just because somebody thinks it is a good idea is not solid planning. Like any other organization, to be effective it must have a purpose. Ask yourself questions such as these:

> —Do we have any problems in our community that citizens and organizations recognize as needing some community action?
>
> —Do we need a library service in our town?

—Does the presence of migratory workers point up
a need to improve their conditions?

—Is there a need for better grade and high
schools? Vocational and adult programs?

—Is lack of jobs for young people a problem?

—Does our community need better health services?

—Is juvenile delinquency a problem?

—What about leisure time and recreation needs of
our young people and adults?

—Is there adequate enforcement of laws governing places of commercial recreation?

—Does our community need more industrial and
business development?

If your community has any one of these or other similar
problems, a community council is one method of treating
those of foremost concern. Instead of organizing a youth
committee to meet a problem this time and a health council
or committee to meet another one next time, or a welfare
or human relations council, a library council or recreation
council—it may be more practical to set up one good community council to give attention to any of these problems as
they arise, or to coordinate the activities of existing special
interest councils.

Tips on How to Organize

There is no set pattern for organizing a community
council. Each community will develop its own plans according to its own circumstances. The following suggestions,
however, may help to guide a local community:

Any individual or organization can take the initiative.

Be sure there is a community need or problem about which
the community is or should be concerned. Do not organize
until there is a real need for doing so. The more urgent
the need the more likely people will respond to a request
for cooperation.

Call upon the services of local, county, and state departments, colleges, or universities. Study available literature.

Discuss the idea with other groups and individuals and
get their reactions. Provide them with literature on com-

munity councils. Take ample time to allow these groups and individuals to understand the council idea in relation to their problems.

Extend invitation to interested leaders and groups to meet and discuss the needs and plans for a council and to determine the next steps. They may serve as a committee to work toward development of a community council or they may select such a committee from leaders in various community groups. For chairman, get a person who is well known and accepted in the community.

Find a suitable time and place for an organization meeting. The invitations should be sent out over the signature of the steering committee.

Get someone to explain a community council, its purpose, how it will operate, the kind of community problems with which it will deal, and how much such a council will mean to the community. Allow time for discussion.

Hand out a brief statement explaining the purpose of a community council and the problems in the community needing attention. People can take this home for study and use it for discussion within their organizations.

If the group favors establishing a council, one of several courses may be taken, including the following:

Request each representative to present the plan to his group and arrange for appointment of a delegate or representative.

Elect or appoint a committee to make further plans and arrange for a future meeting.

Elect temporary officers and elect or appoint a nominating committee and any other committees necessary to deal with any urgent community problems until the permanent organization is developed.

Use of Outside Resources

The community council should make use of all available information and resources in achieving its purpose. In the local community there are individuals whose interests, skills, and specialized knowledge would be helpful. At the county level there are county superintendents of schools, county nurses, county extension agents, and county welfare directors interested in the community.

Also, there are consultants and specialists from colleges, universities, private organizations, and state departments and agencies in the fields of community planning, health, education, vocational education, recreation, youth problems, and social and civic problems. If called upon, these people will be glad to assist the council to carry out its purposes.

Combining Several Methods. In the final analysis, organizing for community action has no established pattern. It must be planned more in terms of a careful analysis of each community situation than by a prescribed formula. Because the pattern to achieve action is so varied, local leadership should not overlook the possibility of using two or three methods in combination. In substance those making recommendations on the potential of any of the methods suggested do so with a number of reservations as to when the methods would be effective.

The determination of when informal coordination, a temporary committee, or a community council is best to use at a particular time is dependent on the local leadership of a community. Thus the leaders of several organizations or leaders of certain segments of community life may be working together informally on coordination of their efforts to improve the health of the community. They may have been responsible for, or may have encouraged the formation of a committee to study the provision of more wholesome recreation for youth; and they may be the group suggesting the organization of a community council to aid the community in gaining the kind of cooperation and coordination of agencies that they envision as the ideal.

Although both temporary committees and community councils lead to informal as well as to formal coordination, we can be quite sure that unless coordination has been effective informally its chance of being effective when formally organized will be slight.

Figure 12 shows the relationship among the three types of coordination. In the center is Informal Cooperation which is essential before any other type is possible and which is strengthened by the presence of community councils shown by lines **A,** or by temporary committees shown by lines **B.** In addition lines **C**

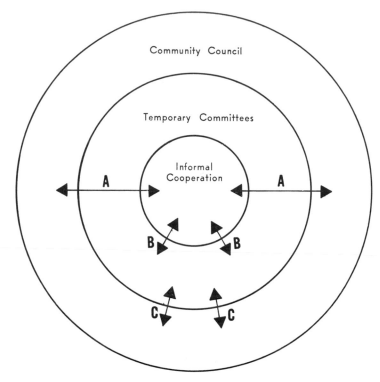

Figure 12. The Relationships Among Three Types of Community Coordination

show the interchange and strength building potential of Temporary Committees and Community Councils. Each helps develop the other and the exchange increases a leader's contribution. They get to know each other well enough to take action through informal rather than through formal methods. In larger communities more formal organization is often necessary, but in most rural communities leaders can very easily see a potential for action on the basis of informal cooperation.

PRINCIPLES OF LEADERSHIP AND COMMUNITY COORDINATION

There are certain of the principles of democratic leadership which are of real significance to any person or organization taking the leadership responsibility necessary to start a program of community coordination. These are the principles of knowledge, participation, sharing, group mind, purpose, direction, experience, and the principle of integration. *The principle of integration* is the key principle in any effort toward community coordination.

Because these principles are comprehensively described in Chapter V, only brief statements as to their role in coordination will be made here.

The principle of knowledge is in this case of considerable import because coordination is very dependent upon the best informed local leadership. If the person making the suggestion for cooperative effort is recognized for his "know-how" the chances are that his suggestion will be given more positive consideration.

The individual leader who does not take advantage of the knowledge inherent in the groups with which he works is missing a strong force for success. In problems of coordination where scientific knowledge is still very meager, the ideas and suggestions of the group are often of much more consequence than the ideas of the leader. Full advantage of the knowledge of the group should be taken. Skillful leadership in bringing this knowledge to the surface is a responsibility of the individual leader or leaders who propose steps for community development through coordination.

The experience of participation and sharing that has occurred within a group or a community in its efforts toward self-improvement will be of great positive support when suggestions are made which will lead to a more comprehensive integration of community resources. Most citizens can readily see the value of coordinating physical resources, but may overlook the necessity for getting the human resources to the position where coordination will be possible. Participation and sharing within individual organizations and informal groups is essential to such participation and sharing on a community scale.

It may be assumed that the leader suggesting cooperative efforts is aware of the purposes behind his suggestions. It cannot be assumed that all individuals and groups are aware of these purposes. Thus, it is essential in leadership efforts for coordination that the basic purposes of such coordination be understood by those involved. Telling them what the leader thinks the purposes are, is not the most effective way. It is far wiser for the leader to help set up the kinds of experiences in the group or among groups where the individuals can determine the purposes for themselves. When the purposes are clear the direction can be charted.

Some person or key group must be charged with the responsibility of directing the traffic of ideas and action as progress toward the goal is attempted. This may be the individual or group which was first responsible for getting the community to think about coordination. It must of necessity be those whom the various groups are willing to trust with the direction of this effort to build the community. Efforts for coordination cannot be left to chance; someone must take charge.

Examples cited earlier show that community coordination, both informal and formal, thrives on successful experience. It is essential that the leadership group keep this in mind in aiding projects involving community coordination. Early success is important when community groups are working together. A simple accomplishment after three months of cooperative effort is conducive to greater accomplishment. If all efforts are made toward a major accomplishment that takes three years to reach, the leaders may discover that interest will wane after the first year and the goal may never be reached.

Community coordination is built upon integration. Integration of ideas, of physical resources, of human resources, and of outcomes is necessary before any coordinated effort is truly effective. Though other principles of leadership are involved they will be ineffective unless the necessity for integration of goal, effort, and outcome is recognized and understood by the leaders. This integration is among the agencies, among the leaders, between leader and group, between leader and nonorganized segments of the community, and between those directly involved in cooperative efforts and those who may share only in the accomplishments.

Integration of community resources for the benefit of the citizen is the goal as well as the principle, the outcome as well as the method, the problem as well as the solution.

PART **III**

Programs of Action

CHAPTER XI

Carley's Corners Started a Farmers' Cooperative

This is a story of success and defeat. It's an example of what a rural neighborhood can do and of what it often fails to do. It's a story in which the leadership is almost completely local. No outside experts are doing the work for the local group. They are used as a resource for information only. In this story they may have been used too little or they may have encouraged, where to discourage would have been sounder advice. Local leaders in a very informal setting seemed to achieve considerable success; as the formality increased, the success of the venture decreased.

What is it that provides the basis for success or failure in a neighborhood cooperative project? How democratic was the leadership of those involved at Carley's Corners? Was the necessary leadership of any type consistent enough to bring success? As this story is read, keep in mind that the person contributing it to this book was involved as a cooperator in one of the families providing part of the leadership. The glow of success and the disappointment of defeat that is expressed in the story could come only from one writing from such a vantage point. As readers of his story, we can look for reasons for the unsuccessful ending to the story: the type of leadership and participation involved, the financial aspects of this type of a community project, and the enthusiam that can be aroused in a rural neighborhood.

The Carley's Corners Venture[1]

Background of Carley's Corners. Carley's Corners is a small farming neighborhood in Eastern Ontario. In all, about twenty farmers and their families are included in the Carley's Corners neighborhood. We call it a community and it stretches for three

---

[1]This story was contributed by Mr. Harold Baker of Merrickville, Ontario, Canada and is used with his permission. The names of persons in this description are fictitious.

miles along a paved country road. It also includes one gravel side road two miles long. It varies little from hundreds of other surrounding neighborhoods in the rather infertile area in Eastern Ontario pinched between the Ottawa and St. Lawrence Rivers. One thing made it different to me; it was my home community.

This story begins in 1940. At that time I was a Carley's Corners teenager and lived what I considered to be a normal life in the country. I attended the grey-brick, one-room grade school at the corner where the gravel side road met the paved road— Carley's Corners. Along with the twenty other pupils in all eight grades, I enjoyed the simple games we played at school. On rainy days we got permission from our teachers to play in the church shed, the only other building on the corner.

It would be unwise to say that the people in Carley's Corners were not progressive. I was one of them. Very early in life I learned from the mistakes and triumphs of my five older brothers and sisters the advantages of organizations like 4-H and Junior Farmer Clubs. For one thing, it was the best way we had to get the family car. Most of my school chums didn't bother with such organizations, but being the youngest in my family, I somehow developed an independence which was an advantage. My parents approved of my membership in the organizations supervised by the County Extension Office.

Carley's Corners was a very quiet neighborhood. The average farm was 125 acres of hungry soil, quite unproductive unless heavily fertilized. Dairying, with some hogs, was the mainstay of its agriculture. Drainage was a severe problem, but few took advantage of the provincial aid offered. Electricity had just recently reached the neighborhood, but central heating, running water, and other conveniences were luxuries to be desired but not essential. No one had a very large income, and many had mortgages on their farms. The average educational level was Grade IX, the first year in high school. No one in Carley's Corners had attended college. All of these people were neighborly and proud of their church, school, neighbors, the conduct of their youth, and the cooperation of everyone. The neighborhood had no outstanding leaders. Other than the church and school, only one organization united folks. In 1939, a Community Club was organized for the sole purpose of getting families together, with education as its primary purpose.

Carley's Corners was within the Merrickville Community where everyone shopped. Merrickville was three miles down the paved road from Carley's Corners. I bicycled to high school in Merrickville and my best chum rode horseback. My father, like other farmers, went to Merrickville at least once a week for groceries and household needs. With our little farm truck, he took the grain we grew to be ground and bought concentrated and starter feeds.

The Development of the Project. Now, two decades later and one thousand miles away, it is interesting to recall what happened. When my father went to town (Merrickville), he paid $1.50 for a 100-pound bag of salt at the feed store. Forty miles away at Winchester, it would have cost $1.10. Other farmers had the same experience. This and this alone started a heated discussion at our Community Club meeting. I recall the question and statements:

"What can we do?"

"If he had some opposition he'd lower his prices."

"We should send a truck to Winchester and get it for $1.10."

"That's not the only thing he's high on."

Mr. Scott was from Scotland and had this to offer: "In Scotland the farmers have cooperatives and handle their own supplies."

Slowly the idea caught on. It took two or three meetings and a couple of months, but that was the beginning. Yes, we had arguments and opposition, but Mr. Scott, Mr. Campbell, Mr. Johnston, and Mr. Boyd were well respected citizens and they were for it. The initial cooperation and interest came quickly; the cooperative came slowly.

Someone had heard of the United Farmers Cooperative of Ontario: "Why couldn't we get our salt directly from them?"

Without any formal organization the farmers ordered a carload of salt and preorders were filled at the car on the rail. I remember being one of the four who helped unload it. That was probably my main contribution. It took just one day to dispose of forty-five tons. We sold it to members of the Carley's Corners Community Club for $1.00 per bag and put 28¢ of it in the club funds. Outsiders bought it for $1.10. Three weeks later another car came along. The price of salt at the feed store dropped to $1.20. It worked! The next move was to buy a car of binder twine on a similar basis. Later, eight carloads of feed were purchased and unloaded at the rail. Then the first major problem arose. Everyone was out of feed and waiting for the next car to come in. Since we had no storage space, the car had to be on time or feed would have to be purchased elsewhere.

Up to this point, we had been successful and, as a result, enthusiastic about the future. Now direction was needed. Mr. Boyd, who had taken a short course given by Extension, knew of a fieldman employed by the United Farmers Cooperative of Ontario.

"Let's ask him to speak at our next meeting." He came and at this point we realized how small Carley's Corners was. We had to go beyond our neighborhood, and all districts around Merrickville were invited to attend the next meeting. Shares in a cooperative were sold the next week. It took only six weeks to raise sufficient capital to buy the old Knapp mill in Merrickville. It was quite obsolete. It had no grain bins, and facilities for grinding and mixing feed were poor. Publicity and word of mouth started a booming business. The Carley's Corners Community Club sat back with a deep sense of satisfaction. This had been a banner year. They had started the "Merrickville Farmers Cooperative." In the process they had worked themselves out of a job. Mr. Boyd was hired as manager at a low salary. The others were no longer directly involved except as members.

For a number of years everything went well. Business expanded from feeds and milling to hardware, an egg grading station and chick hatchery. During these years, patronage dividends built up to $6,000.00.

In 1949, the Directors decided to build a new, modern mill, and a delegation of four Directors and the Manager were appointed to visit a few of the newest cooperative mills in Western Ontario. After this inspection of several mills, the Directors and Manager, along with a representative of United Cooperatives, drew up plans for a new building for the Merrickville Cooperative. The building was to have space for a general hardware store and office in the front, an egg grading station, hatchery, grain bins for six carloads of whole grain, and storage space for several cars of bagged feed, along with necessary machinery for the manufacturing of prepared feeds.

Before the building was started a canvass of all members was made for loans to finance the project. Along with this, a loan of $10,000.00 was applied for and received from the Government. The yearly volume of business had grown to $130,-000.00 and it was thought that with the new facilities, it should increase to $200,000.00. This, however, was one point where we failed to reach our objective, and the volume of business which we could manage under former circumstances with lower overhead was not sufficient to carry the increased costs of overhead, including considerable interest.

Everyone took a great deal of interest in the building project, so much so that the business may have been neglected. We had 200 members. If they had done even a large proportion of their business with their Cooperative, the objective of $200,-000.00 business volume could easily have been reached.

I was proud of my community. An economic situation had created an even greater integration of effort in the community than was previously present. The Merrickville Cooperative Association, its Manager and Directors, were providing a service to the community. But it was in a period of post-war prosperity! After the new plant was constructed the overhead cut into profits. No dividends were declared and members began buying elsewhere.

The Results. Efforts of leadership may not always be repaid by continuous success. It was Christmas, 1955, and with great disappointment it was learned that the Merrickville Cooperative Association had gone bankrupt; Mr. Boyd had resigned as manager; and the shareholders, all 192 of them, had their money invested in a "dead" business and couldn't get it out. The feed store in Merrickville once more was able to set its prices without effective local competition.

Why failure after years of success? Is it because a cooperative requires cooperation as well as a strong farming area to support its business? Does it require directors and members who will buy feed at the cooperative even though they could go elsewhere to save a few cents? Do these same people forget the value of dividends to them, and the value of trade to *their* business? Does the test of their loyalty come in a price slump? Those who should know say that the trouble at Merrickville rests in the "yes" answers to the above questions.

Who was to blame for the lack of business? Was it the members, the directors, the manager, or the fieldman? What was missing in the leadership? What kind of leadership is needed now?

ANALYSIS OF THE CARLEY'S CORNERS VENTURE

This is the time to review the principles of leadership described in Chapter V. They have an application to Carley's Corners. Perhaps you have already recognized how certain methods used in establishing the cooperative were selected on the basis of the principles described. You may have wondered whether or not other methods were selected from expediency instead, or because they were the only methods known to the leaders. Perhaps you have said to yourself, "I would have done that differently!"

The analysis which follows will be made in terms of the principles of democratic leadership that were *used* and those that were *omitted*. *Alternative actions* will also be suggested. It is well to remember in reading this analysis that other types of analyses could be made. For example, the entire venture could be examined in terms of the economics of a cooperative, in terms of the contributions of a cooperative to community life, or on the basis of a number of other criteria.

Democratic Principles Used. It took a problem to get people thinking. With the problem came a *challenge* to do something about it. In this instance the challenge was on the basis of an economic problem. Everyone who bought feed products in Merrickville, and knew the price he paid and what he would have to pay forty miles farther down the road, saw the problem clearly. All that was needed to turn this simple bit of *knowledge* into a *challenge* was a chance for the citizens to compare their feelings on this *knowledge*. This opportunity was provided by the Community Club. Although on a very informal basis, perhaps even unaware that they were providing leadership, those farmers who began discussing the economics of feed buying at their Community Club meeting were using the principle of *challenge* in one of its most effective ways. A minimum number of important facts, a problem that all can see, and a simple question "What can we do?" got them going. The principle of *challenge* was used effectively in the initial stage of this cooperative venture.

Nearly every farm family in Carley's Corners *participated* in the initial discussion of the problem and its proposed solutions. Informal cooperation was so positive that certain business transactions were made without a formal organization being established. Up to this point the principle of *participation* was used effectively. From the beginning of the more formal aspects of the project until its unsuccessful conclusion it appears that less and less emphasis was placed on *participation* and more and more on *direction* without understanding.

The principle of *sharing* was used at two levels in Carley's Corners. The first was very effective and was closely allied to the *participation* of everyone in the early stages of the cooperative's development. The second was a financial sharing which soon became divorced from the actual sharing of the operation of the cooperative venture. The *sharing* was delegated to the directors and manager. The principle of *sharing* cannot be delegated. Once it is, the ties are lost and the project becomes just another alternative. In this case it was one of several places to trade. The economic share in the cooperative does not assure *sharing* in the way it is described in Chapter V.

The principle of *knowledge* was recognized clearly by those informal leaders in whom the initiation of the project rested. They had some facts, they wanted more. They wondered about the organization of a Farmer's Cooperative and sought an outside resource to help them with its initial organization. Although the organization was begun on very limited *knowledge*, it was a logical development from the knowledge they had. Again it appears from this story that once the venture moved from informal to formal action, the type of leadership changed with it. No longer was the principle of *knowledge* recognized by those whose leadership counted. The change of leadership appears to be more by default than by design. These leaders knew how to lead and work in the informal atmosphere of Carley's Corners; they didn't know how in a community-wide cooperative. Thus the leadership role was neglected. The principle of *knowledge* was forgotten on two counts. First, by the formal leaders themselves and, second, by those sharing in the cooperative.

The best examples of the use of the principle of the *group mind* and the principle of *purpose* are found in the opportunity provided by the Community Club for the farmers to talk over their problems. Out of these discussions came ideas and plans bigger than any one person's idea, more purposeful than the separate ideas of Carley's Corners individual farmers. When the planning for the cooperative enterprise was turned over to the directors and the manager, the loss was apparent almost immediately. To those members who later began purchasing their feed elsewhere, one of the major *purposes* of the cooperative was lost, as well as the contributions those farmers might have made to the conduct of the enterprise.

Direction and *participation* require a knife-edge balance. Both are necessary in democratic leadership and certain ingredients of each must be present at the same time. The informal leaders of Carley's Corners recognized that someone had to be in charge; they recognized the need for further *knowledge;* but they seemed to overlook the balance between the two or were unable to provide the democratic leadership necessary to establish that balance. This loss of balance may be the critical factor which changed the outcome of this venture from success to failure.

The small group of farmers and their leaders in the Community Club who got the idea for a cooperative realized the need for *training* of those who were to lead their new venture. However, when it became apparent that the cooperative had to cover the entire Merrickville community, the leadership traded *training* for enthusiasm. The six-week period used to sell sufficient shares in the cooperative to buy the old mill was undoubtedly considered a great success by the leaders. Yet it was done more on enthusiasm than on *training* for the real role of the cooperative which lay ahead. It may have been better to have taken longer to sell shares but to have *trained* leaders for the job of maintaining business in the cooperative after the mill was purchased.

The early success of the informal effort to buy salt and feed by the carload did provide a fine *experience* for those who participated and those leaders who were responsible. In fact, it was the key to their enthusiastic support of formal organization. Those who became members and leaders at a later date did not have this successful *experience* on which to draw. After formal organization the leaders may have become too far removed from the objectives of those who established the cooperative. The early leadership *experiences* were in accomplishing simple objectives— cheaper salt, cheaper feed, and cheaper binder twine. The later objectives added hardware supplies, egg grading, hatchery, grain storage, and feed preparation and manufacturing. Both leaders and members needed *training* to make this big change possible. No one took the responsibility to provide it.

Principles Omitted. An examination of the leadership pattern during the Carley's Corners experiences with the cooperative shows a very interesting change. This change in leadership occurred as the cooperative venture became more formalized. Until the Merrickville Cooperative was organized, the leadership was informal, but in its informality, certain democratic principles were used much more effectively than they were later. The use of the principles of *challenge, participation, sharing, knowledge, group mind, purpose, direction,* and *experience* were evident in the way local leaders carried out their plans. There was a sharp decline in the use of these principles following the formal organization of the cooperative. It may have been the result of a feeling that "now our job is done, the cooperative will run itself," or purely the result of neglect. The use of the above principles was even less noticeable after the big building project in 1949. Yet, in the process of raising money to finance this building, the leadership was successful. This gives the reader a hint that the leadership in the Merrickville Cooperative was more adept at accomplishing short-term, very specific projects where an appeal to emotion and loyalty was possible, than they were at long-time projects where continuing interest of the members was necessary. The neglect of a number of the vital principles after formal organization bears out this suggestion.

In addition to the change in the use of the principles above, there were several which were neglected throughout the enterprise. The story showed little evidence that the leadership tried to develop the *habit* of buying at the cooperative, either by themselves or by the members. The *habit* was never established.

The *process* of leading seemed to unfold more by chance than by design. There is no evidence showing any concern for the methods used to accomplish necessary tasks. While the organization was informal, it was successful because the opportunity to *integrate* ideas and points of view was naturally present. Following formal organization, the leadership needed to understand and use the processes essential to democratic leadership. This, they did not do.

The entire leadership process showed lack of *flexibility*. Leadership was much the same even if the situation changed. Sometimes it worked, sometimes it didn't; it didn't become critical until the cooperative failed. It is possible that those in leadership positions did not at any time recognize their leadership responsibilities. Though a cooperative is basically a democratic venture, this example showed little democratic planning and control. It is more typical of a laissez-faire type of enterprise lacking responsible direction. With the basic concern of the venture being the purchase of feeds for farm stock at lower prices, the opportunities for leadership to recognize the principles of *service* and *leadership satisfactions* were limited. The limitations in the objective of the venture limited the opportunities for leadership.

Alternative Actions. What would have made the Merrickville Cooperative a successful rather than an unsuccessful venture? The three alternative actions suggested are not necessarily the only alternatives that could be made. These are the ones identified by considering the principles of democratic leadership as the criterion. With another criterion, other suggestions could be made. An examination of this case from a purely economic point of view would be enlightening. With democratic principles as a base, however, the alternatives are these: a less rapid change from the informal to a formal organization; an attempt to develop the cooperative habit and continuous education of members; and less emphasis on beating the Merrickville Feed Store and more on a high level of service.

Less rapid change from the informal to the formal organization. Carley's Corners was a neighborhood where many activities, both social and economic, were very informal. People knew each other well and they trusted each other. They knew how to cooperate informally if a neighbor needed help. They were even able to join forces to purchase, sell, and unload a carload of salt when it was cheaper than buying it at their usual place of business. All of this was usual and natural for them. Too suddenly, the informal atmosphere of "getting together" to save some money became the formal atmosphere of directors and a manager who operated under a formal charter. The decisions were no longer made over lunch after a Community Club meeting. The area participating in the venture was not just Carley's Corners but the entire Merrickville community of which Carley's Corners was but a small part. The gap between Carley's Corners and Merrickville, and the gap between informal cooperation and formal cooperation, was too great. There was a loss of contact and a loss of interest. There was an opportunity to use effectively the intense interest of many citizens in a cooperative as it was being organized. Instead, it was formed rapidly with this same interest and then almost immediately became something which was no closer to them than any other feed store. By making the change from informal to formal too rapidly, the entire meaning of the cooperative was lost to the would-be participants and supporters.

An attempt to develop the cooperative habit and continuous education of the members. Closely related to the first alternative is the emphasis that leaders should have placed on establishing the habit of buying cooperatively. As it worked out, this was left purely to chance. The Merrickville community farmers bought cooperatively only as long as they saw that the list price on feed was at least one cent per hundred-weight under that of the feed store. The old habit was that of buying where the marked price was lowest. The experience of the cooperative as recorded indicates little, if any, emphasis on educating the membership to the merits of a cooperative enterprise. This may have been difficult to accomplish, yet with the Community Club as a resource with educational objectives, it would have been possible. It appears that member education on cooperative matters—both purpose and process—was left to chance. Cooperatives, or any other business, just don't work that way. One only has to be reminded of the extensive advertising campaigns waged by business and industry to recognize that developing an awareness of what, when, and how to buy is in itself a continuing educational process. The Merrickville Cooperative would have had greater chances of success if it had made more vigorous efforts to develop the cooperative habit by a vigorous and continuing program of member education.

Greater emphasis on high level service. The foundation of both the informal cooperative to buy salt and feed and the formal organization of the Merrickville Cooperative was to buy for less. This was indeed a narrow foundation. From the experience of the cooperative we note that it was also the foundation for the failure of the cooperative. When profits were needed to pay accrued debts; when dividends were no longer issued; and finally, when prices went up to the Merrickville Feed Store levels, the Cooperative failed. An alternative action would have placed service to customers at just as high a status as price. A customer who gets what he pays for plus faster service, friendlier service, and a conviction of a high quality product is more likely to remain a customer. The cooperative idea cannot sell a long-time program on price alone as the Carley's Corners citizens now know.

Will a cooperative ever be successful in Merrickville? In a community as small as Merrickville, there are advantages and disadvantages to such a venture. To be successful, greater attention will need to be paid to the alternative actions suggested here. Before any attempt is made to begin again, the potential members must be made aware of their stake in the venture, the potentials for success and defeat, and the necessity for continuous participation in the activities of their organization. After such consideration, a decision to organize a cooperative would not be based on emotion generated by saving 40¢ on a hundred pounds of salt, but on the facts of a venture to be begun only if it looked sound for years to come.

CHAPTER XII

Leadership in a Homemakers' Club

The dimensions of time and change add many interesting facets to leadership needs and problems. This chapter analyzes part of the leadership dynamics of a community during its transition from a rural to a suburban landscape.

The Alpha community is now a thickly settled suburb close to one of the large Metropolitan cities of our Eastern seaboard. Until World War II it was primarily rural and there were numerous dairy farms scattered throughout the area. Now all of these have been overrun by housing developments, military research institutions or educational centers. There is no heavy industry or commercial activity of importance nearby.

In early colonial days this area was contained in large and productive estates or free-holdings. Competition from the western prairie lands closed off the plantation era after the Civil War. The only reminder of that period are the names of roads or communities and the long unused "slave fences," field boundaries and stone piles to be found in the second-growth timbered tracts.

Most of the present residents of Alpha have moved in from near and far during the past fifteen years or so. Many have built or enlarged their own homes by the do-it-yourself process. However, a scattering of the old families remain, like deep-rooted forest giants, spreading their somewhat tattered branches protectively over the new-growth saplings. Every season brings new families, new schools and new services.

The old established families observe this encroachment with a resigned bewilderment. There are few if any signs of resentment. Many of the long-time residents have extended their hands far enough to accept the contract settlements of the hungry real estate developers for their acreage at greatly inflated prices.

The Longs are such a family.[1] Mr. and Mrs. George Long live in an old two-story, white frame house in the heart of the

---

[1] The names and places in this case example have been changed to protect their anonymity. The situation and incidents are essentially real, however.

Alpha community. In earlier years they were farmers in this same location. Their married son and daughter have settled close by in modest one-story brick and asbestos shingle ranch-type cottages, each on a half-acre lot. A real estate agent provided these homes in the settlement when he contracted to buy the remaining 44 acres of the farm in 1946.

George Long is retired but does some light carpentry and repair work in the area. The son, George, Jr., works in the city ten miles away. He shares rides in a car pool with three other fellows. His wife, Mary, teaches in one of the new elementary schools of the area. The daughter is married to Jim Guber and they now have three children. The Guber-Long romance developed while Jim was stationed at one of the military units nearby, in 1944.

Mrs. George Long is about 60. She is conservative, hard working and frugal. The loss of her older son during the Anzio Campaign of World War II in Italy was a staggering blow. She undertook some Red Cross work to help cover up the empty feeling but every bandage she rolled was a cruel reminder of her lost son. She continued to do a little church work and added a moderate amount of Red Cross nutrition and sewing to her experience after the war. She is a good homemaker.

Mrs. George Long's first leadership step came in March, 1950. The county home demonstration agent asked her if she would be willing to call together a small group of her neighbor women to discuss Extension education work.

Mrs. Long invited six of her friends and her daughter, Martha. They had coffee and cakes and listened to Miss Ryan, the home demonstration agent, describe what other home-makers were doing and learning in 30 home demonstration clubs throughout Beta County. In the discussion period that followed, Mrs. Long led with an opinion that the program sounded interesting. Following her leadership the others concurred.

The idea of forming an Alpha Homemakers' Club was suggested by Miss Ryan. Mrs. Long approved and others agreed that it seemed a logical thing to do. There were only eight prospective members at Mrs. Long's that afternoon. So Miss Ryan suggested that the eight might spread the word and call another meeting later. Mrs. Long offered her home for the second meeting. Miss Ryan said that it would be an imposition to use her hospitality again so soon. However, Mrs. Long preferred it that way.

The next gathering was an outdoor picnic supper at Mrs. George Long's in June. A secretary's book for the club was started sometime later. It indicates that 37 ladies attended this picnic. The Alpha Homemakers' Club was actually organized with officers on November 6, 1950. The record indicates that 27 attended this November meeting at Mrs. Long's home. She served as president and was a very helpful figure in the meeting, since she had belonged to a homemakers' club before. Her daughter, Martha, was chairman of one committee. Nearly every item of business was initiated or announced by Mrs. Long. Miss Ryan was not present.

The purpose of this chapter is to describe the transitional roles of leadership that took place in the development of a successful homemakers' club. For that reason it is appropriate to hesitate at this point and say a few words about key individuals in the club. Although Miss Ryan made the first suggestions on organizing a club, the responsible local volunteer organizer was Mrs. George Long.

It is probable that Mrs. Long wanted to be and felt that she was a very democratic person. By inviting the group repeatedly to her home she doubtless felt she was doing an important community service. By persisting in this over-extension of hospitality, she was actually creating the opposite effect. By accepting the first presidency and directing every action of the club, she deepened the impression that this was Mrs. Long's club. Soon all of the members, including many of her long-time friends, were simply "going along for the ride." She remained in the club's top office for two and a half years.

Mrs. Carter, the first vice president, was a home economics graduate of a midwest college. She was about 50 years of age and had four children, including twin sons about 30 years old, who were successfully launched on careers. She was alert, attractive and efficient. Soon after she was selected as vice president, Mrs. Carter reluctantly agreed to manage the school cafeteria as a sideline to her homemaking.

Within the Alpha Homemakers, Mrs. Carter was a person of many ideas. However, because she worked nearly full time away from home she seldom offered to help carry out the projects or ideas she suggested. She had a broad knowledge of good homemaking practices and some appreciation of how an organization should be conducted. She soon became impatient and critical of Mrs. Long's conservatism and lack of parliamentary knowledge. She was especially intolerant of Mrs. Long's almost complete domination of meetings during the first year. Mrs. Carter spoke up for a plan of having subject-matter leaders from the club attend the county leader training meetings. Mrs. Long failed to see the possibilities of this, however, so she continued to attend all the county meetings herself. Mrs. Carter did not hold office in the club during its second year.

Mrs. Ball was the club's first secretary. She had been an office secretary before she married Tom Ball and came to Alpha. She and Tom had several very young children and they preoccupied much of her time. Frequently she was unable to attend meetings. There are voids in the club's secretary book indicating that her efforts in the club's behalf were somewhat sporadic. A new secretary chosen the second year was even less efficient. Volunteers provided most of the minutes and records for the club's second year and a half.

Mrs. William Hale was the club's first treasurer and she was elevated to the vice presidency the second year. She is about 50, quiet, dependable and a member of one of the long established families. She was supportive of Mrs. Long and faithful to her wishes, although she seldom expressed her own. Her selection as the vice president the second year is an indication of her closeness to Mrs. Long and her good status in the community.

The first set of officers was selected by acclamation or concensus. Everyone just assumed that Mrs. Long would be president. It was equally obvious that the treasurer should be a dependable and trusted member of a stable family, like Mrs. Hale. The secretary should be someone who could write well and keep records so Mrs. Ball filled that role as a former stenographer. Since it was to be a home economics type of club, it was logical that Mrs. Carter be selected vice president because she had a college degree in that field.

Interestingly, the club membership rejected the aggressive ambitions of Mrs. Renz. She was a noisy young newcomer from a nearby state. She boasted about how she had been a home demonstration agent before marriage and she loved to talk about how a club should be conducted and what it could do, if—. Actually she had been an assistant agent and this only for about nine months.

There was a time when Mrs. Renz took on the genial and beloved Miss Ryan for an argument about the club's constitution and by-laws. This set most of the other members against her. She did not give up trying for a club office, but except for committee work she did not rise above the membership level. Not many persons in Beta county would want or attempt to correct or cross Miss Ryan. She had been an Extension agent there for nearly 30 years. Her easy-going manner annoyed some of the more officious "club women types." But by and large, she was well liked and not one to be flustered or threatened by any young Johnny-Come-Lately. The Alpha Homemakers were not about to be flustered either.

The secretary's minutes show that monthly meetings during the club's first year were occupied mostly with routine announcements or reports of county meetings by Mrs. Long. She faithfully represented the club at county home economics affairs. But she did so with a martyrish attitude evidenced by remarks like, "I couldn't get any one else to go, so I went to Miss Ryan's office for the home nursing meeting, January 9." Members commented among themselves that she asked no one to go and wanted to do it herself. The secretary's records fail to list any very vital programs this first year. The club's meetings were shallow and superficial.

Attendance at the monthly club meetings dwindled gradually from a good start with 27 in November, 1950 to 13 and 15 in the closing months of 1952. Little wonder, for those who did attend were likely to sit through such sessions as the following, which was reported for October, 1951:

> The October meeting was called to order at 8:15 by Mrs. Long at the home of Mrs. Doe. The treasurer's and secretary's reports were read.
>
> Mrs. Long gave instructions for the plant sale at the County Fair. (Some short-hand characters written in by the Secretary at this point indicate Mrs. Long did not expect the sale to amount to very much.) Two persons volunteered to learn to operate the motion picture machine at the library. (It was reported later in November that Mrs. Long attended the library meeting since no one else could go.) Also it was announced that two persons were invited to the Electric Company

> to view the Christmas decorations and special lighting. (Mrs.
> Long and Mrs. Hale attended.)
>   The Beta county fair was discussed (by Mrs. Long) and then
> the meeting was turned over to the refreshments committee
> after which we adjourned.

Other meetings during the year 1951 ran on in about the
same manner. There were occasional lessons in flower arrangement, ceramics, craft and other handiwork subjects given by the
president or members of the club.

Because of a change in the county home demonstration
planning procedures, the 1952 club year, which began in July,
1951, was extended to 18 months, ending in December, 1952.
Beginning early in the year 1952, several members were becoming restive and pushed for more participation and involvement
of all the club's membership. One of these was Mrs. W. D. Oakley. She had enjoyed home economics extension work in several
residential areas elsewhere. She currently was serving as secretary of the County Homemakers' Council and in many other
ways had access to and experience with Extension work. She
attended the same county meetings as Mrs. Long and in addition worked closely with the county home demonstration agents,
state specialists and others on numerous homemaking activities.
During meetings of the Alpha Club, Mrs. Oakley increasingly
became a source of information and ideas. The club minutes
show much evidence of her growing in group leadership even
though she held no office in the community club at that time.
Members of the club began to look to Mrs. Oakley for ideas and
stimulation. Illustrative of this is the January, 1952, meeting
summary, reproduced below:

> The meeting was called to order at 8:15 at the home of Mrs.
> Dilter with (13) members present. The secretary's report was
> read and approved as read. The treasury showed a balance on
> hand of $53.01.
>   Ways and means for raising funds for the fire company
> were discussed. (Mrs. Long was extremely committed to the
> club's fire company pledge and had practically exclusively
> handled the club's pledge. It was usually discussed by her in
> one manner or another at every meeting.) A square dance was
> tentatively decided upon and Mrs. Rivers was elected chair-
> man of the committee and Mrs. George Long, Jr., Mrs. Murphy
> and Mrs. Carter were selected to help in the planning of the
> square dance in the near future.
>   Following Mrs. Oakley's suggestion of the last meeting it
> was decided that address booklets should be compiled. Green
> was selected as the cover sheet, decorated with the State
> flower.

Members volunteered to meet Tuesday evenings to work on the welfare project. The first meeting will be held January 15 at the home of Mrs. Oakley.

Mrs. Oakley made the following announcements:

1. Mrs. Fare, president of the Gamma Club, who is a registered nurse, has been appointed county health chairman.
2. A discussion on family relations will be held January 14 at 10 o'clock in Miss Ryan's office.
3. A class in stenciling will be held January 16 at 10 o'clock in Miss Ryan's office.
4. Mr. Wood will conduct a class on the care of house plants January 29 at Miss Ryan's office.
5. A class in Chinese cookery will be held January 25 in Miss Ryan's office at 10 o'clock.
6. Instructions in care of sewing machines will be announced soon.
7. The county has changed the home demonstration year to correspond with the calendar year and local clubs are asked to do likewise.

The February meeting will be held at the home of Mrs. Magnuson. Meeting adjourned at 10:15 with refreshments.

> June C. Miner
> Secretary pro-tem

Normal procedure of home demonstration club work would call for election or appointment of one or two subject matter leaders to represent the club at some or all of the training meetings described by Mrs. Oakley. This is a matter which Mrs. Long consistently ignored. She attended many of the county meetings herself and sometimes brought back reports but this did not satisfy the membership. Mrs. Oakley knew how the system *should* work. She, Mrs. Carter and a few others, were becoming dissatisfied and murmuring about the ineffectiveness of Mrs. Long as president, as early as January 1952.

As the club year 1952 progressed, members gained more experience and confidence in organizational affairs. They also gained wider appreciation and understanding of things that the club could do if its president would let some of the other members help. Members like Mrs. Carter, Mrs. Oakley and even the fussy Mrs. Renz were respectful toward Mrs. Long but they nevertheless were anxious for the club to move on toward broader horizons and more democratic procedures. There was outright resentment against her dictatorial methods for handling the club's treasury. For example the March 1952 minutes indicate:

Mrs. Long stated "we are going to give $10 as a gift to Miss Ryan." (The secretary's shorthand insert indicates the club had no opportunity for discussion or action.)

The April minutes add further evidence:

> Mrs. Carter asked that the matter of a gift for Miss Ryan be discussed. She moved that the club send $5 to the county treasurer for this gift. After discussion the motion was approved.

In other ways and at other meetings there was growing rebellion against undemocratic procedures during 1952.

The November minutes reveal that one of the younger members suggested the need for a nominating committee to prepare a slate of officers for consideration at the annual meeting in December. Mrs. Long said she didn't think this was necessary. One member commented that a committee would make certain that election was properly done in the December meeting. After discussion it was agreed that Mrs. Long should appoint a nominating committee.

The nominating committee brought in the following slate which was approved by the club for 1953:

Mrs. W. D. Oakley—President
Mrs. William Hale—Vice President
Mrs. Joe Carter—Secretary
Mrs. George Long, Jr.—Treasurer

From the first meetings of 1953 there is evidence that the new officers began to make significant changes in both procedures and programs. Among many other accomplishments that year the following appear significant, in terms of this analysis of their leadership.

1. The club voted Mrs. Long a strong expression of thanks for her leadership and gave her an honorary pin as past president. She continued to take some part in meeting discussions but from this point on her leadership influence waned.

2. A rather impressive array of committees began to function on program, by-laws, hospitality, membership and several other projects of temporary nature.

3. Membership increased to 30 and attendance almost doubled to a usual 25-27 at most meetings.

4. The secretary's records grew in length and substance. In 1951-52 they usually covered a half page and included about 5 to 10 items. In 1953 they averaged a page and a half and frequently included 20 or more items.

5. The treasury balance stayed at about the same average level, $50 to $75, but about five times as much money was handled each year by the club, indicating that there was more program and activity.

6. Subject matter or special program leaders began to function. The minutes show that nearly every meeting included some type of demonstration, report or action by the club's educational leaders. Every member served as a leader of at least one of these sessions during the year. There was frequent mention of subject matter leaders and alternates both attending training meetings.

7. The club participated actively in a great many county activities and sent a group of five to the state rural women's short course.

8. Several times toward the close of the year 1953 the minutes indicated that more women wanted to join than could be accepted unless a larger meeting place was found.

9. The club sponsored the establishment of a girl's 4-H club and found a leader for it. They attempted to start a boy's 4-H club but no man leader could be found.

10. Money and assistance were given to numerous causes like Red Cross, Christmas fund, fire and rescue squads.

11. The club appears to have enjoyed a very active and successful year. Mrs. Oakley soon became very popular. She exhibited great friendliness and alertness to group interests and concerns. There was some resistance from the "old guard" during the first few months of 1953. When this appeared, Mrs. Oakley calmly and methodically found new responsibilities for each recalcitrant. Before the year's end the grumbling was replaced by a busy buzzing resulting from productive participation in activity.

The same president was re-elected for 1954, along with a new vice president, secretary and treasurer. The veep was moved up from secretary. Especially notable in the 1954 minutes is the dispersion of leadership. Mrs. Oakley appears to have worked hard at involving all of the members in the club's program of work. Her own name seldom appears in the secretary's record, except as she chaired the meeting or reported on county organizational matters. The minutes for 1954 are crammed with brief mentions of special study meetings, planning committees, exhibits, sympathies and courtesies extended, special parties and picnics, along with a rather impressive schedule of educational subject matter programs.

In the year 1954 there was discussion of more women who wanted to join the club and it was finally decided to limit membership to 30 so they could meet in the homes most of the time. Some work meetings were scheduled in a newly completed hall on the edge of Alpha. Finally another club was started in the Alpha area by Miss Ryan and members of the Alpha club in October, 1954.

One problem seems to have developed in 1955. Many of the working wives and younger women with babies preferred to meet evenings. The older women who could more easily get away from home preferred day meetings. On one vote the group split 12 to 13 on this issue. It was a clear-cut conflict of interest. Instead of deciding the issue by vote, however, the club continued to discuss alternatives and a trial plan was developed. The group held some evening meetings on subjects of prime interest to young mothers. Their husbands did the baby-sitting and homework these nights. Daytime meetings were arranged on the more general subjects. As the information and records available to the author drew toward a close, it was obvious that the meeting problem was still vexatious. In one respect it was indication of unity, however. The club did not want to accept the obvious solution of dividing its membership. They had become a close-knit, enthusiastic team and liked to pull together.

With the close of the year 1954 our record and information about the Alpha Club tapers off. From one of the County Council officers we learned that the Alpha Club was still exceedingly active in 1957. Mrs. Fare succeeded Mrs. Oakley as president and was in turn replaced by the former vice president, Mrs. Carter, each for terms of one year. The "old guard" completely disappeared. An amazing unity and homogeneity took its place. Esprit de corps continued good and the club was both educationally and socially active. It is quite apparent that during the years 1953 and 1954 a very effective teamwork relationship evolved. Several new competent leaders were "discovered." The entire membership grew in organizational stature and competence. As a result the club developed a wealth of talent and leadership available for any worthy purpose.

Analysis of the Leadership in Alpha Homemakers' Club. The purpose in describing the Alpha Club is for use as a case history to illustrate the principles of leadership. If you will now review quickly the 13 principles discussed in Chapter V it will make the following analysis more meaningful. You will observe that not all of the principles apply to this example. But most of them do.

APPLICATION OF THE PRINCIPLES OF DEMOCRATIC LEADER-
SHIP TO THE ALPHA HOMEMAKERS' CLUB

1. Knowledge

About subject matter. It may be assumed that few of the Alpha homemakers had expert competence in home economics when the club started in 1950. Under these circumstances one might normally expect the president, Mrs. Long, to exert every effort to extend and expand the members' opportunities to gain such knowledge. Instead she kept the leadership training opportunity herself and failed to develop member growth and initiative.

As soon as Mrs. Oakley became president this situation changed and the whole complexion of the club changed for the better.

About group techniques. For some reason Mrs. Long failed to recognize and utilize the power and potential in her group membership. Probably her personal need for status and prestige was so great that she could not share it with other members. Possibly also her knowledge of techniques was so limited that she *did not know how* to utilize the human resources and talents in her group.

Whatever the cause of Mrs. Long's deficiency, it seems quite apparent that Mrs. Oakley possessed the ability to spark a sharing attitude, with resulting increase in club activity, spirit and accomplishments. It appears that she knew and used successful techniques immediately, including a successful program planning process which she used at her first meeting and which is discussed later in this chapter.

2. Participation and Sharing

This principle, more than any other single factor indicated in the club minutes, is responsible for the spurt of growth and success that began in 1953. Clearly the members were being starved of their rightful opportunities by Mrs. Long and the "old guard." If there was any "magic" in the leadership of Mrs. Oakley it possibly was her ability to involve all of the club members in group planning, discussion, action and evaluation.

Mrs. Oakley reported later to this writer that she could trace the group's "new look" to the first meeting of 1953. The executive committee of officers had met to plan the new year's program of meetings. But it was agreed, instead, to devote the entire January meeting of the club to this process. Every member participated.

Five buzz groups of about six members each worked on five different aspects of the club's plan of work for 1953. Each member of the executive committee except Mrs. Oakley chaired a group. Then all five groups reported and the whole club hammered out its plan of work on the anvil of discussion.

What a change from the "hand out" procedures of the two previous years. Even Mrs. Long enjoyed it immensely!

Except for the usual duties of president, Mrs. Oakley took over none of the club's leadership functions. She was seldom mentioned in the minutes. Yet it is certain that she helped to establish some of the situations and opportunities which provided growth for dozens of the club's members.

Possibly the two-year "starvation period" when members shared few, if any, leadership opportunities may have stimulated their determination to grab every available assignment when the new regime came in. Possibly, also, there may have been a normal growth or incubation period for group leadership to evolve. At any rate the Mrs. Oakley regime of 1953-54 capitalized on the available situation and talent, tapping both by well organized involvement of all members in club affairs.

3. Service

We have little or no clear-cut evidence of a difference in the ideals and attitudes of service as between Mrs. Long and Mrs. Oakley. Probably both had a strong desire to help other people but the manner and means selected were distinctly different.

4. **The Group Mind or Purpose**

Probably in the early days of the Alpha Club there were *two group minds*. It seems clear that the "old guard," with Mrs. Long as their leader, was one group. They were united in several purposes: (A) to tap the educational offerings of the county extension service, (B) to hold the club offices and control its destinies, (C) to demonstrate their status in the community, and (D) to assist the newcomers to become established in Alpha.

Probably the group of younger newcomers to Alpha did not share all of these same four objectives. They probably shared the educational objective plus one unique purpose of their own—to find a place and become accepted and established in community affairs.

Seemingly there did evolve a single set of group objectives during the following year, 1953. There was an initial period of reorganization, regrouping and clarification early in 1953. After that a unified but many-threaded group mind or group purpose evolved as the club members began to participate more freely and fully. A group mind evolved out of group activity and individual participation.

5. **Process**

Process and skills of leadership appear to have been all important in the Alpha Club. We have evidence that the process followed by Mrs. Long was effective only during an early, initial period of the Club's existence. It is possible that a dictatorial or "limited skills" leader such as Mrs. Long may serve an important function as a stimulator and a legitimizer in community affairs. It is probable, too, that her limited knowledge of good club procedures was not a serious hindrance in the club's first year or two of life. If her regime had continued indefinitely the wavering interest, dwindling attendance and shallow program probably would have fostered acute problems and serious limitations or even a disbandment of the club.

We have little evidence of how and *by what process* Mrs. Oakley was able to stimulate and maintain group interest. More evidence is needed on that. But we can guess that she used many skills effectively.

6. Direction and Challenge

Mrs. Long relied strongly on the principle of direction. In this respect she was a leader of "the old school." Being a person of distinction and status she felt that her support and presence were enough to motivate group action.

Contrasted to this, Mrs. Carter, Mrs. Oakley and others, were "idea" women. They came forth with challenges or ideas and permitted the natural and normal forces of inquiring minds to generate and motivate action. It worked, too.

In our free democratic society, a challenge or a good idea will win every time over a command or dictatorial approach. Of course, it must be recognized that not all situations in America are free and democratic. But the Alpha Homemakers' Club was!

Another aspect of the principle of challenge is the stimulation which the leader derives from the group. It would appear that both presidents, Long and Oakley, were stimulated by the Alpha Club. They were challenged. One may guess, however, that Mrs. Long was a bit overwhelmed by the challenge of her new situation and new leadership responsibility. Mrs. Oakley was more ready to accept the challenge and respond comfortably and appropriately. Her "group confidence" was a result of past associations and her attitude that all of the club's affairs were group affairs, not her personal responsibility.

7. Emulation

The principle of emulation works only when there is unity or agreement on objectives. In the early days (perhaps the first year) of the Alpha Club, unity existed. Everybody was agreed on a desire to get educational help from Miss Ryan's office and other sources. So the group emulated or followed enthusiastically the pattern established by Miss Ryan and Mrs. Long for reaching that objective. The club moved along successfully the first year.

But during the second year a cleavage was beginning to form. Segments of the group began to have ideas of their own. Their organizational and process objectives were different from Mrs. Long's. The new group continued to emulate only those qualities and services of their leader which they could wholeheartedly endorse and accept for themselves. These were principally in the educational and subject matter field.

8. Training

It is not clear from the record available just what assistance in leadership was given to club officers and members in Beta County. Probably they received no more than a handbook containing organizational suggestions on order of business, suggested constitution, and what is expected by way of participation in county programs and activities. There is no evidence that any of the Alpha officers enjoyed opportunity for special help for anything except subject matter fields.

It would appear that the Extension Service may have overlooked an important need, exemplified by Mrs. Long. She was dedicated, respected, and willing. But she obviously lacked those skills and principles of leadership which can be most easily acquired if organized pre-service training is provided.

Mrs. Oakley apparently brought with her to the Alpha Club a basic leadership competence and experience. Where she acquired this is not clear. Perhaps her experience on the County Council may have given her some of this. But observations of other clubs and other Extension activities in Beta County lead the writer to conclude that leadership training for group work was almost entirely lacking.

9. Experience

Experience is probably the best teacher. One immediately recognizes that members of the Alpha Club grew rapidly in leadership capacities as soon as they enjoyed leadership opportunities. After only one year of Mrs. Oakley's term as president the chair might have been ably filled by any one of several women. After two years there were a dozen who could have performed more effectively and democratically than Mrs. Long did the first year.

Prior to 1953, the members had no observations and experience with democratic leadership in their club. But when Mrs. Oakley and the 1953 officers provided them with opportunities for participation the response was electrifying.

Experience is the best teacher. What a tragic waste of human resources results when rich, developmental experiences of leadership are lacking! What a thrill it is when they are present and operating in harmony!

10. Flexibility

Two elements of flexibility need pointing up in this case example. One is the flexibility of adjustment to our rapidly changing communities. Alpha, which was a farm community less than 20 years ago, is urban or suburban today. If the home demonstration program of the Extension Service was restricted to farm or strictly rural families, Alpha women would be ignored completely.

If Miss Ryan followed the same procedures and objectives today that she probably used 30 years ago it wouldn't work. The fact that she permits the groups to plan their own programs and have a council for the development of county programs is a tribute to her leadership and the flexibility of Extension. It also explains why Extension work is even more popular today than it was 30 years ago. Flexibility should not be confused with indirection, however.

The other element of leadership flexibility is more personal. It relates to the desire and ability of the leader to adjust herself to the group situation, interests and needs. Mrs. Long started the club in keeping with a need and interest of the Alpha homemakers in 1950. They wanted information and help in home economics. They needed a homemakers' club to get it. Mrs. Long served ideally their purposes and needs at that time because she had contacts with Miss Ryan, status in Alpha, and she was interested in starting a club, —a perfect combination at that time.

Then the club's needs and situation changed. The problem of starting a club was solved. The problem of making the club serve as an effective learning and doing tool was a new situation. Some of the members possessed more skill at this than their president. Members became restive. They tried to help Mrs. Long change her methods—to be more flexible. She was unable or unwilling to do this. So the group changed leaders and achieved flexibility in this manner. This is the course of democracy.

Frequently people get hurt in the flexing, adjustment process. Emotion and hurt feelings sometimes result from changes of a group's course. Providently, this did not happen in Alpha. The reason it didn't is the next principle.

11. **Empathy** (Imaginative projection of one's own consciousness into another being)

The concept of empathy was not presented as a principle in Chapter V because it is more of a personal quality than a principle of leadership. Considering the critical period of 1953, however, it is easy to reconstruct that Mrs. Oakley possessed this quality of empathy to a remarkable degree. And it was important that she did. She *sensed* that Mrs. Long might feel a little hurt and resentful as the club moved forward into new activities and used new methods.

First, it was arranged that the club should present Mrs. Long with a gold pin and to recognize her significant and everlasting contribution to the club in its first two years. This recognition was given by the new officers with sincerity and dignity.

Second, Mrs. Long was elevated to a position of "senior citizen." Her views were invited and used when appropriate. The club did not ignore her but moved on so rapidly that she had no time or reason to protest.

Third, the new regime immediately set about to involve *all* members in useful and acceptable work assignments, *including the old officers.*

Here was the use of empathy at its best! An understanding of personal feelings and needs. A recognition of the good. An overlooking of personal limitations or mistakes. Moving forward as a body on things that everyone could agree upon. Taking time to discuss more fully those issues where agreement comes slowly. All of these tools of effective leadership depend primarily on one quality—empathy. It's the ability of a leader to *sense how his members feel.* It is not only sympathy or tolerance but *understanding.* It is imaginative projection of one's own consciousness into another person. This was clearly demonstrated by the Alpha Club in their handling of Mrs. Long and the "old guard" in the early months of 1953.

12. Service, and Leadership Satisfactions

It would appear that the ideal of service to others was genuinely demonstrated by the leaders and members of the Alpha Club. They engaged in numerous social service projects, like the new fire department; they sponsored a new 4-H Club, a second homemakers group; and they were very supportive of health, education and welfare projects of many kinds. From the club's minutes one might conclude that they spent more time and money helping others than they did in their own educational programs. Probably this is an illusion, however, caused by sheer numbers of items in the secretary's minutes. Obviously it takes a lot more time and effort to put on a demonstration of child care at a meeting than it does to send a $5 check to help the well-baby-clinic. But each item occupies about the same space in a minutes book.

It would not be possible to draw comparisons between individual leaders in the Alpha Club with respect to their service dedications and ideals. There usually is no ulterior motive such as political prestige, monetary pay, or job promotion to be furthered by home demonstration work. For this reason it seems safe to say that all or most of the members were non-exploitative in their reasons for belonging and sharing.

It is probable that each leader or member of the Alpha Club best remembers the meeting or meetings where she helped. Little did she realize at the time that through helping others she helped herself even more! Service and satisfaction are almost synonymous in group work. Service and leadership bear a cause and effect relationship.

An interesting and deeply significant clue to the reasons why Mrs. Oakley succeeded as a leader is contained in this direct quotation from a statement that she wrote some months after she was president of the Alpha Homemakers' Club. She discussed the job of a good president thus:

> "The word president means presiding officer. As such the duties involved are sometimes confused. A good president does not solve all problems, dictate the actions, direct the activities, or in other ways assume the role of a single authority. To me,

a president's role is one in which she attempts, with the help of the other officers, to provide a situation in which there is a freedom of exchange of ideas, a confidence in expressing one's thoughts, even when they may not agree with others, a mutual respect for each member's differences in reactions to problems, and finally an atmosphere in which *all members feel responsible for the final solution and resulting action.*"

CHAPTER XIII

The Solution to an Economic Problem in Southern West Virginia

PART I[1]

INTRODUCTION

An economic transition is taking place in southern West Virginia where an entire area is lifting itself out of the dangerous situation of depending upon a single industry for its economy. The people of the area are using their own leadership and the professional leadership of others to make this change. For years, certain rural areas have been specialized farming sections. This is particularly true in the South where cotton has been king. More recently, diversification has been recommended and a more stable economy has been the result. The transition that is taking place in West Virginia is being accomplished by injecting sound agricultural projects into the economy of an area which had been primarily dependent upon coal production for many years.

The program has been labeled the Beckley Area Rural Development Council. R.D.C. is an urban-rural partnership sponsored by business interests in Beckley, West Virginia, to add another arm to the area's economy. Its supporters realize that much of the success and accomplishment is yet to come. However, they have promoted many worthwhile accomplishments of which they are justly proud.

The program was started in 1949 and within its first six years it sponsored the development of 18 million dollars worth of new business. R.D.C. is no longer considered a fancy dream around Beckley and its supporters are growing in number.

Historical Background. Beckley is roughly the geographical center of the Smokeless Coal Region of West Virginia. It grew

[1]The basic data for Part I of this chapter were contributed by Mr. C. T. Shackelford, Manager, Beckley Area Rural Development Council.

from a village of 542 people in 1900, to a city with a population in 1950 of almost 20,000, with the economy based on coal. Beckley is the county seat of Raleigh County which has a population of 96,000. Figure 13 shows Beckley's retail trade area which comprises all of two counties and parts of six others with a total population of 250,000 and an area of 3200 square miles.

The area has an average elevation of around 1500 feet, varying from 800 feet at Jarrold's Valley to 3600 feet on Huff's Knob. This region is hilly as can be seen by a few statistics on the slope of the land: Land with 0 to 12 per cent slopes makes up 17 per cent of the total area, 12 to 25 per cent slope accounts for 23 per cent of the acreage, 25 to 40 per cent slope accounts for 34 per cent of the acreage, and 26 per cent of the total area is composed of land with over 40 per cent slope. Most of the

Figure 13. Counties Comprising the Retail Trade Area of Beckley, West Virginia

soil is residual and shale in origin with some residual limestone
in three of the eastern counties.

Raleigh County came into being in 1850 with a population
of 1,765, and it experienced a normal growth with a purely agricultural economy until the completion of the Chesapeake and
Ohio Railroad in 1872. The railroad provided an outlet for the
vast stores of timber and coal which Raleigh and surrounding
counties had in abundance. By the turn of the century, agriculture was rapidly giving way to coal and timber in economic importance. This was particularly true in Raleigh and the other
western counties of the area. Farmers flocked to the coal mines
and the sawmills where wages were better and working hours
were shorter. In 1944, less than 30 per cent of the population
were classified as farm people and over half of these had full-
time jobs off the farm. Only about 2 per cent of the farms had
yearly production valued at over $2500.

At the peak of coal production in 1947, the Smokeless Coal
Region yielded 66,000,000 tons of coal at a payroll cost of $194,-
000,000. This money was distributed over an area of 2500 square
miles—four counties and part of a fifth. Much of the money
was spent in stores operated by the mining companies. A great
deal also went to independent merchants and to professional men
in other towns in the area. About $40,000,000 of it was spent in
Beckley through retail trade channels.

The Problem. In 1947, there were a few forward-looking individuals, whom we would like to call leaders, who began to feel
that it was not wise for the community to continue to depend
on a single industry—coal, for its economy. Foremost and most
vocal of these individuals was Charles Hodel, publisher of Beckley's morning and evening newspapers. Hodel, who is of Swiss
descent, says that both of his parents were steerage immigrants
of the 1880's. He came to Beckley in 1910 at the age of 21 with
a background of experience as a printer and newspaper reporter
—as he puts it, "just in time to grow up with the town."

He points out that from 1947 to 1954 there was a mine payroll shrinkage of about 40 per cent. That did not occur because
coal sales had dropped so low, but because production per man-
day had been greatly increased through mechanization of mines.
Fewer and fewer men at work were meeting the demand for coal.
That, in turn, reduced the production cost per ton and made it
possible to retain some markets that might otherwise have

joined the switch to the more convenient fuels. So, the amount of community income from the coal industry had shrunk very low. Something needed to be done.

When it became plain that industrial diversification offered no relief from the diminishing payrolls, Hodel's attention turned to the soil. He reasoned that if the arable land of the area could be brought into production eventually to supply the major food requirements of the half million people still living off mine payrolls, an advanced state of prosperity could be permanently maintained.

The situation was one in which agriculture had been abandoned by farmers for work in the mines. When these farmers became miners, they continued to live on their farms. The workers preferred to receive their pay twice a month rather than to wait from one harvest to the next, especially in the absence of a properly organized system of marketing and distribution of home-grown products.

Hodel harped on the fact that since there was little local food production and since the largest part of the average family's income goes for subsistence, the mine payroll money poured into the area twice a month was swept right out again for food that had to be secured from other parts of the country. This, he insisted, made for an unstable economy.

ATTACK ON THE PROBLEM

In the spring of 1948, Mr. Hodel visited Tupelo, Mississippi, where a decline in the estate of King Cotton had proved as devastating to the economy as that with which the decline of King Coal was threatening Beckley. In Tupelo, a diversification of land-use had been accomplished. Beckley, on the other hand, simply needed more use of the land. Mr. Hodel felt that perhaps they could adapt the Tupelo idea to the Beckley situation.

The most important thing Hodel learned at Tupelo came from a fellow publisher, George McLean of the *Tupelo Journal*. He learned that the Tupelo development council had employed the Doane Agricultural Service, Inc., of St. Louis to survey its area's resources, and that Doane had made recommendations as to how to bolster the sagging Tupelo economy.

Returning from his trip, Hodel held a luncheon meeting with about 30 of the key men of Beckley. He outlined to them what he had observed at Tupelo and how he thought a similar effort might be successfully applied to Beckley. Out of that meeting came endorsement of the plan and a recommendation, solidly backed, that the Beckley Chamber of Commerce consider employment of the Doane Service to avoid costly mistakes in developing a workable program.

Correspondence with True D. Morse,[2] then president of the Doane Agricultural Service, Inc., soon brought him to Beckley for a preliminary study. An agreement was made by which the Chamber of Commerce of Beckley agreed to pay for a complete survey of agricultural possibilities. The survey was made in the fall of 1948. The findings of the survey along with recommendations were submitted at a public meeting near the end of the year by Mr. Morse and Morris L. McGough, the latter a member of Morse's staff who did much of the field work of the survey.

Later came the "Report of Factual Data, Plan and Program," dated January 20, 1949. This report was the result of considerable study by leaders in the Beckley area and the principles laid down in the plan were based on Doane's long years of experience in farm management and agricultural development.

Objectives. It was decided that before a program be inaugurated to meet the problems, there should be agreement on the objectives and the long-time agricultural pattern best adapted to the area. It was also decided that the institutions, agencies and individuals who would be primarily responsible for carrying forward the work be designated. They felt that the plan should be relatively stable and change very little from year to year. However, it should undergo refinement as further study from year to year showed clearly what was needed to be included as part of the agricultural plan for the area. It was decided that it would be advisable to pick out only a few of the more important features of the plan for special emphasis and development, in the beginning at least. As these become well developed, other parts of the plan could be given special attention until the whole had been covered.

The trade area of Beckley was to be served irrespective of county lines. It was recognized that the limits of the area might shift from time to time, depending upon road improvements and other developments. It was recommended that in the beginning, work be carried on largely in the primary trade area with the

---

[2]Mr. True D. Morse is at the time of publication Under Secretary of Agriculture, United States Department of Agriculture, Washington, D.C.

rural people who regularly visit Beckley. As any one phase of the work became well established, its extension into the area less intensively served by Beckley was to be considered.

Basic to the long-time plan for the area was the realization that it was to combine the work and influence of both town and rural people and institutions. It was felt that there must be a teaming up of business and industry with the farmers and agricultural agencies. Otherwise, best results would not be obtained in the development of the area. Beckley and the smaller towns and villages were to provide the markets and the kinds of goods, implements and services needed for satisfactory progress of the project. All agricultural agencies, state and federal, were to work toward the same objectives. Backed by businessmen, farm leaders and farm organizations, with a clear understanding of the types of production and methods best adapted to the area, they were more effectively to point the way to greater farm prosperity.

It was decided that all activities must lead to development of conditions that would result in a high level of health, education and character of the people. Their homes were to be improved to give the population stability which must be realized if steady long-time progress was to be achieved.

To coordinate the efforts of the many organizations and agencies of Beckley and the surrounding rural areas, it was decided that a *Rural Development Council for the Beckley Area* be organized. The Council was to have two broad functions: (1) To bring together all the organizations and agencies that were or should have been working with the agriculture of the area. The Council was not to do the work. Its purpose was to plan and coordinate, and put the influence of all the area back of the approved projects and programs. (2) To focus the work of all agencies upon the various parts of the Plan that had been agreed upon for the area.

It was felt that special commissions should be set up to guide and supervise the development of the most important long-time features of the program. For example, there should be a Dairy Commission and a Forestry Commission. Committees to supplement the major commissions and not duplicate or conflict with their functions were to be used from time to time as needed to guide particular projects or short-time programs. Every commission and committee was to contain both businessmen and farmers along with representatives of the public agencies primarily interested in the work involved.

After agreement of the leaders on what was to be developed as the primary source of agricultural income for the area, major commissions were to be set up to guide their development from year to year. Major emphasis of the development program was to be built around the activities that bring in the dollars. The thinking was that major sources of income in the immediate Beckley area would be poultry, dairy, beef and other livestock, fruits and vegetables, and forest products. Other sources of income were not precluded, but major emphasis was to be placed on the above as the most productive items.

Some of the people felt that the community development should be concerned with the enterprises that affect the majority of farmers and especially the low-income groups that may limit the growth and prosperity of the community. In the immediate Beckley area, the majority of farm operators had small acreages. They should follow intensive enterprises.

The long range objectives developed by local and professional leaders for the Beckley Rural Community Development Program were as follows:

(1) Business, agriculture and labor to work together to build a stabilized area surrounding Beckley and the rich coal mines of the region.

(2) Payrolls of the mines to be used to establish comfortable and attractive homes on the land. Thus wholesome living in desirable communities would make the area more than just a place to earn wages.

(3) Small farms, intensively operated, to be developed. The homes on these farms can be attractive and comfortable places to live. The income from the coal mines could thus be balanced with complete use of the agricultural resources, giving the economy of the Beckley area a major secondary foundation even more dependable than the mines.

(4) Home units to be interspersed with the farms on sites in rural areas where the land is not adapted to farm units. This is where the mine laborers and other workers of the area should live. A combination of a country home and good wages would give a high standard of living.

(5) Farms to produce the health foods needed within the

area including milk, meat, eggs, poultry, meat, and vegetables. This would provide more healthful diets for labor and higher priced markets for the farm products.

(6) Forests to be so developed as to become a productive crop that would produce a sustained yield and thus a continuous source of income. Woodworking plants could then be established within the area with assurance of a steady supply of timber. The mines would continue to offer a market for small timber.

(7) Country areas to have continuing development until every rural community had good schools, recreational buildings, parks, ball fields, playgrounds, and strong churches.

(8) Labor to be made the means of acquiring a desirable home, environment and old age security.

The people reasoned that if these objectives were attained in the Beckley area, people would continue to congregate there because of the good facilities.

Formation of the Beckley Area Rural Development Council.
Organization. The overall Council was formed in March of 1949 and five commissions were established; namely, Dairy, Poultry, Forestry, Health and Recreation, and Savings and Investments. Selection of membership for the commissions followed closely the suggestions in the plan as interpreted by True Morse who believed in harnessing personal interests and in selecting men to serve on commissions who stand to profit most from the success of their activities.

The next step was the employment of a full-time manager. Doane had said that this was almost a must. After careful checking and screening for a competent individual, the Executive Board of the Council employed Charles T. Shackelford as manager. Mr. Shackelford was reared in Fayette County which adjoins Raleigh. He had graduated from college in 1932, taught school for five years, served as a county agent for six years, and had spent three years in the Army during World War II. In June of 1949, he received a second college degree at Virginia Polytechnic Institute with a major in Engineering. Mr. Shackelford assumed the duties of manager for the Beckley Area Development Council in July, 1949.

After the first two years Oscar C. Hutchinson was employed as an assistant to the manager. Later his duties were changed to managing the Beckley Farmers Market, Inc.

The original council had 92 members representing all segments and interests embodied in the program. The plan looked
good on paper, but it didn't work so well. It was impossible to
get any major part of the membership out for regular monthly
meetings. Since that time, the council has narrowed down to
around 25 faithfuls who attend the regular monthly meetings.
The council as such does very little of the actual work. Each
month it hears progress reports from each of the commission
chairmen and discusses and approves their proposed new projects and activities. In a few instances projects have been initiated by the council and turned over to one of the commissions
or to a special committee for execution. The council holds an
annual dinner meeting in June of each year. The program includes progress reports and achievements of each of the commissions, the presentation of goals for the new year, the president's annual report, and an out-of-state speaker. A four-page
brochure on activities and accomplishments is printed annually
and distributed at that time. All matters pertaining to finances
are handled by an Executive Committee of the council which is
made up of the five officers and the four directors.

Finance. In the beginning, the council decided to raise
money to finance the program for an initial period of three
years. The Doane report said that it would take three years to
show sufficient tangible results to prove to the doubters that the
program would work. So, a finance committee of five was appointed. Their goal was to get 24 subscriptions of $1500 each,
payable at $500 per year for three years. They compiled a list
of 25 of Beckley's leading business and service organizations,
and each member of the finance committee selected five prospective contributors to contact. The list included the three banks,
the larger wholesale and retail hardware stores, feed dealers,
lumber dealers, bakeries, a department store, a furniture dealer,
Murphy's, Grant's, J. C. Penny, Montgomery Ward, the dairy
plant, the Newspaper Company, the water, gas, telephone, and
electric companies, the Elks, Moose, and District 29 of the United
Mine Workers of America. Of these 25, they succeeded in getting
14 subscribers, nine for three years and five for only one year.
A number of the others on this list subscribed for amounts less
than $500, after the committee relaxed its policy of $500 or
nothing. Others were added to the list and after three weeks of
intensive campaigning they had secured signed pledges totaling

$34,400, with promises from a few of the one-year pledgers to continue on a year-to-year basis. This was to be enough money to operate the program for four years instead of three.

The program was refinanced at the beginning of the fifth year, again with both three year and one-year pledges. In 1956, the council operated on a budget of $15,000 with 75 subscribers.

OPERATION OF THE BECKLEY AREA RURAL DEVELOPMENT PROGRAM

As indicated earlier, all of the work required to carry out the program is done by the commissions. Each of the commissions is treated separately in this chapter. To show how they function, the work of the poultry and dairy commissions will be described in considerable detail.

Poultry Commission. The chairman of the poultry commission is a power company executive and the membership includes feed dealers, a banker, poultry farmers, hatcherymen, the county agent, and a small broiler processor. The commission sensed in the beginning that southern West Virginia with an annual consumption of 10 million broilers afforded an excellent market potential close at hand. They had been told that the high altitude with low humidity and cool summers provided an excellent climate for poultry.

Delegations from the commission visited the large poultry areas in northeastern West Virginia and in Virginia to study their plans of financing, types of housing, and production practices. They also observed the mistakes these already-established areas had made. They learned that before production could get very big, they would have to have at least one processing plant in the area. They decided to start with the existing outlet, a processor in Charleston, 75 miles away. Production financing in the beginning was handled by two feed dealers who adopted the 90-10 contract system used in some of the broiler areas. The local banks were very slow to take hold of the financing of buildings. The commission appealed to the Farmer's Home Administration which cooperated to the limit of its facilities on new broiler houses. Other producers converted old barns and outbuildings.

A series of community meetings were scheduled to allow farmers to hear the broiler story. A team of three or more commission members attended each meeting, explained the program and listed prospective producers. From then on, it was a matter of working with the individual farmers, drawing building plans, assisting in laying out the buildings on the ground, designing heating systems, and visiting after the flocks were placed. A lot of work went into getting the first few producers into operation. As the number of producers increased, they learned from each other and the job became a little easier.

When this program began in 1949, there was almost no broiler production in the area. In 1950, 200,000 broilers were produced and even with that small number marketing became a problem. The output was not evenly distributed from week to week and at times there were more than the Charleston processor could handle. Some of them were trucked 125 miles to Huntington and a few all the way to Cincinnati. The commission started a search for someone who would come in and build a processing plant. They found a plant operator in Harrisonburg, Virginia, who agreed to build a plant in Beckley when they had 200,000 birds on feed. That was four times the existing capacity. By late 1951, that goal was reached, and the processor built a $150,000.00 plant in Ronceverte which is 50 miles from Beckley on the fringe of the trade area. Shortly after this plant was built the Charleston plant doubled its facilities and more recently has made an additional enlargement. Production rose to 620,000 in 1951; 1,240,000 in 1952; 1,500,000 in 1953; went slightly over 2 million in 1955, and has continued to increase.

During their early planning, the commission decided that a poultry show would help to arouse interest in this enterprise. It would give the newspapers and radios a chance to encourage further development of the project and get more people to thinking poultry. The first show was a two-day affair held in the city recreation building early in January of 1950. It was financed by 25 commercial exhibitors renting booths at $25.00 each. The show also included 57 live poultry exhibitors, 15 egg exhibits, 6 educational exhibits, 75 4-H, N.F.A. and F.F.A. boys in judging contests, 8 4-H team demonstrations, and 4 educational meetings including speakers, movies, and discussions. One hundred and seven dollars in cash premiums and many ribbons were awarded. Attendance was only fair. Three other shows were held in succeeding years, but somehow interest and attendance never quite measured up to the commission's expectations. The show was discontinued after the fourth year.

The commission felt from the beginning that egg production had even greater potentialities in the area than broilers but realized that layers require more "know-how" and heavier financing. It was not until 1955 that an all-out promotion of commercial eggs was started. Since then, there has been considerable interest in cages, and 10 new producers with cages ranging in capacity from 700 to 3,000 were started in the summer of 1956. Five new floor flocks of similar capacity also started production that summer, and this activity has also continued to expand.

Dairy Commission. The Dairy Commission began under the chairmanship of the manager of the local dairy plant. The other 10 members of the commission were all men who had a personal and financial interest in the dairy industry. The first project undertaken was that of establishing an artificial breeding unit of the West Virginia Artificial Breeding Cooperative Association because this was the fastest and best way to upgrade the commercial dairy herds of the area. The dairy herds were small and it would have been impractical to use the quality of bulls in a natural breeding program that would bring the improvement that could be accomplished by artificial breeding. The A.B.C. manager agreed to establish a unit when 1300 cows within a 25 mile radius of Beckley were registered with the program. The county agent accepted the assignment to make a survey to learn who was interested and the number of cows owned. Survey cards were printed and the job of determining which families owned cows was begun by using the same neighborhood leaders who had been used in the wartime food program to contact their neighbors. Members of the commission agreed to contact the commercial dairies. The neighborhood leaders were slow to act and some of the local dairymen hesitated. This method of breeding was relatively new in the state. Farm magazines were carrying pro and con articles and doubts prevailed. After one full year of plugging, the owners of only 400 cows said they were interested. The commission went back to the A.B.C. manager and he lowered the requirement to 1,000 cows. A series of 12 community meetings were scheduled throughout the area to explain the program, but few attended. Finally the state A.B.C. Association agreed to sell semen to independent associations, and such a group was organized as a local cooperative and started operations in July, 1951. It started with only 80 members who owned a total of 435 cows. The first inseminator was a young married man who was attending night school at Beckley College under the G. I. Bill and accepted this part-time job to supplement his income. He was trained by the State Association and bred the first cow on July 21, 1951.

The breeding fee was $5.00 per first service, $2.00 of which went for semen, the other $3.00 to the inseminator. He got an additional $.50 as a subsidy from the State Department of Agriculture. He did an excellent job of promoting, maintained a high conception rate, and bred 500 cows the first year. In October of the same year, the cooperative had him trained for Dairy Herd Improvement Association testing. The program was launched with 6 herds containing 184 cows.

The Artificial Breeding Program has maintained a small but steady growth, although never achieving the desired total participation. The D.H.I.A. Program has been less successful. It was increased to 8 herds with 235 cows, but later during the milk price squeeze in the area, 4 of the herds dropped out at the time when they needed the service most. Both programs were operated under one Association. The Rural Development Council gave some financial help to the Association in the beginning with a grant of $150.00 for artificial breeding equipment and $300 for D.H.I.A. equipment. Since that time, the association has been able to pay its own way and has a little money in the bank.

Other projects sponsored by the Dairy Commission include a Dairy Day each year and dairy school one night per month during the winter. They have promoted the establishment of new dairy herds and increases in the size of existing herds. Six new dairy herds have been established since 1951, and the new number of cows in commercial herds has more than doubled. All dairies are Grade A. Later, the commission organized a campaign to promote greater consumption of locally produced milk. This is being done through the use of the "Land O' Hills" seal of approval and through the school milk program.

A more recent project is the establishment of an Honor Dairy Farm system. This program attempts to incorporate the desirable dairy practices into a score card which can be used to recognize good dairy farm operators. It is not a contest in the usual sense. All dairymen who meet the standards set up by the score card will receive recognition and awards. Any dairy farm scoring 90 or more points on the score card will be recognized by the presentation of a metal Honor Dairy Farm Sign at an appropriate public ceremony.

The purpose is threefold: (1) To provide recognition for good dairymen. (2) To create more public interest in local dairy production. (3) To provide more local income from the dairy industry.

In discussing the work of the Poultry and Dairy Commissions, considerable detail has been presented in order to show how they function. The other six commissions function much in the same manner. The projects and accomplishments of these commissions will be discussed briefly.

Forestry Commission. The Forestry Commission continually promotes better woodland management through tours, demonstrations, the sponsorship of three annual state-wide woodland equipment shows, and a one-day forestry conference. They have promoted the production of Christmas trees, an enterprise especially well adapted to the area, planting and pruning demonstrations, and the establishment of an organized outlet through the Beckley Farmers Market. In one year more than 300,000 trees were planted under this project.

Health and Recreation Commission. The Health and Recreation Commission has been primarily interested in better public health programs with particular emphasis on trash dumping and garbage disposal. Pressure water systems in rural homes have been a major promotion. Annually, one-week training schools for rural community recreation leaders have been held in crafts, social recreation and square dancing.

Savings and Investments Commission. The Savings and Investments Commission set out to induce large landholding companies to make available for sale their large holdings of desirable agricultural land. They pointed to the many advantages which would result from getting coal-mining families to establish homes on small acreages for subsistence living. This project never got quite off the ground. The commission set up a committee to receive requests from farmers seeking loans and channel them to the proper lending institutions. The committee did some good work in the beginning but this job was soon taken over by the other commissions. After two years, the commission died a natural death due to inactivity.

Country Life Commission. The Country Life Commission was organized during the second year of the program to sponsor the New River Country Life Program, a rural community improvement contest. A staff member of the State Agricultural Extension Service had come to the Rural Development Council with a proposal that the Council furnish the prize money, pay the printing costs, and assist the county extension staff with organization and promotion. The proposal was accepted. At last report, the contest was operating in 31 communities in 5 counties. This program has had far-reaching effects in changing the lives of rural people. The job of promoting greater agricultural production has been made easier through these organized communities.

The program is flexible and encourages balanced community improvement in agriculture, education, health, home improvement, and religion. The program is producing good results: (1) It is enabling the people in these communities to increase their income. (2) It is enabling the people to live better with the money they have. (3) It is developing a spirit of cooperation within the community, resulting in better homes, better churches, and better schools. (4) It is building better relations between the rural residents and urban dwellers. (5) It is stimulating growth and development in the people themselves.

This program could be the meat of the whole Rural Development Plan. If enough communities in the area were organized and working like a few of them, the jobs of the other commissions would be vastly simplified.

Fruits and Vegetables Commission. From the very beginning of the Rural Development Program, the establishment of organized marketing outlets was a major problem. The council requested the United States Department of Agriculture and the State University to make a survey to determine the feasibility of a producers market for fruits and vegetables in Beckley. The survey was made in 1950 and a negative report was returned. The report concluded that such a market was sorely needed for independent retail grocers and farmers of the area, but that such a market could not expect a sufficient volume of business to justify its operation by private enterprise. The idea was dropped for a couple of years, then came an opportunity to secure funds from the County Court and the State Department of Agriculture for building the facility. A Fruits and Vegetables Commission was organized to serve as sponsor and to promote production. The facility was built at a cost of $40,000 and opened for business in July of 1954. It consists of a permanent masonry building 60 x 100 feet to be leased to wholesalers for year-round operation; a quonset hut for grading and packing; and a farmers' shed with 30 stalls.

The market operates as a non-profit corporation with a Board of Directors as the governing body. The Board realized from the beginning that it was desirable to secure one or more full-time wholesale operators in order to make the market function properly. A number of prospective full-time wholesale operators were contacted but none were secured.

The market has been operating as a traders' market serving as a place for farmers and retailers to get together. It has provided a good service to the 100 or more farmers who have used it, but the volume has not increased as rapidly as was expected. The wholesale operator is still needed. The Poultry Coordinator was transferred to Market Manager and the Department of Agriculture provided an Assistant Manager. A project in green wrap tomato production for Southern markets proved quite successful with the 30 farmers in the project averaging $250 per acre labor income. The market is also handling black walnuts and has a contract for the sale of one-half million pounds. Christmas trees are also being sold through the market. It is felt that the Farmers' Market has a vast potential and that the difficulties encountered in the beginning will be overcome.

Livestock Commission. The Livestock Commission was established in the spring of 1956 with two specific objectives: (1) to promote the building and operation of a public livestock auction market facility, and (2) to promote sizeable increase in area sheep production. A site has been secured for the livestock market, building plans have been drawn, and enough money has been allotted by the County Court and the State Department of Agriculture practically to complete the facility.

The promotion of sheep has been carried on through community meetings, through attempts to solve the dog problem through the legislature, and through pooling orders for importation of western ewes.

In addition to the activities of the 8 commissions, the council has also sponsored a few special projects.

Special Projects. In 1954, the council decided to find a trade name that could be used in the promotion of various phases of the program. A contest was conducted through the newspapers. Two hundred names were submitted and the name "Land O' Hills" was chosen. A commercial artist created the insignia shown in Figure 14.

The Land O' Hills insignia is copyrighted by the Rural Development Council and is used to promote all phases of agriculture and rural living in the counties of Fayette, Greenbrier, Mercer, Monroe, Nicholas, Raleigh, Summers, and Wyoming. On agricultural products, it indicates local production and high quality. It is being used on dairy products and eggs and is intended to be used on vegetables, fruits, broilers, and other products. To encourage local consumption, a promotional campaign was carried on to inform people in the area of the significance of the insignia.

Figure 14. The "Land O' Hills" Insignia

A regional watershed conference was sponsored in 1954 by the Council as a follow-up to a state-wide conference which had been held earlier by the West Virginia Chamber of Commerce. The general idea of the conference was to have it serve as a fore-runner for a local water-shed development program. The conference was well attended, made many worthwhile recommendations, but nothing has happened since.

A number of small services are provided by the council. Furnishing prize money and ribbons for a soil conservation contest; F.F.A., N.F.A., and 4-H shows and exhibits; ribbons for purebred cattle shows and for county and community fairs.

SUMMARY

The Beckley Area Rural Development Council, operating in eight counties of southern West Virginia, has realized a large measure of success. It was organized to improve an economy that had been dependent on a single industry, coal. This improvement came about by diversifying the economy, supplementing income from coal mines with a stable income from agricultural products raised and sold very largely in the area. The result has been a more prosperous area with happier people with good rural and urban relationships.

The Beckley area's rural development project was first envisioned by Charles Hodel, publisher of the two Beckley newspapers. The Doane Agricultural Service, Inc., of St. Louis, Missouri, surveyed the area and made recommendations designed to improve the dwindling economy, which the people of the area accepted. A plan was developed which provided for year-to-year as well as long-time goals. In the beginning, only a few activities were started. As these were understood and developed, additional ones were added, until a total of seven different commissions were operating in the area.

The achievements and successes of the Beckley area Rural Development Council assures continuation of the program. The program affords the area a balanced economy for future stability. Coal, which will remain important in the area for many years to come, is being supplemented by a strong agriculture. Each dollar invested in this program is returned many times. Each dollar of increased income that the farmers realize is turned over *Five Times* before it leaves the community.

Finally, all persons in the area stand to benefit from this program. The businessman will benefit through the increased business received as a result of the increase in the purchasing power of farmers. As farmers prosper, so do Beckley and surrounding towns. Industry will benefit because 72 per cent of the farm operators in the county work on jobs off the farm, causing the income and the standard of living of these families to be improved. The farmer benefits through increase in his farm income. As new income is developed, living opportunities of rural families and rural communities are greatly expanded. Each citizen benefits through healthful foods that are available fresher and at lower cost.

PART II

ANALYSIS OF THE BECKLEY AREA
RURAL DEVELOPMENT PROGRAM

Democratic Principles Used. There was an early and continuous display of the use of democratic principles of *leadership* in the organization and operation of the program to solve the Beckley area problem. It took keen mental power to detect early stages of the problem. Therefore, *knowledge* of the problem was not widespread very early. The few who had *knowledge* of the problem were immediately *challenged* to give individual and small-group thought to a possible solution of it. As soon as a good idea for the solution of the problem was arrived at, key men in the community were called to a meeting to discuss the idea. At the meeting, these men were able to get an interchange of *knowledge* about the problem and how it might be solved. This *participation* resulted in a *challenge* that led to action. The action had *purpose* that was clearly understood.

Knowledge, participation, sharing, and *challenge* were continually expanded to larger and larger segments of the population. By starting out in this way rather than having an all-out activity in the beginning, *group mind* was better achieved and *process* was better understood. Finally, reports on *purpose* and *process* were given at a public meeting where all could get *knowledge* of both and *participate* in the discussion and clarification of both. In addition, several media were used to publicize what was being considered and what was being done. All this increased general *knowledge* of *purpose* and *process* as well as *challenge* and *group mind.* Many persons *participated* directly by helping to make the initial survey, by soliciting and giving financial assistance, by being members of commissions and committees, and by taking other active roles in various parts of the comprehensive program.

Direction was spread over a large segment of the persons *participating* in this program. Responsibility for success or failure of the program was *shared* with all these persons. Members and officers of the council itself gave much of the *direction*. Also, *direction* was *shared* in the commissions and in the committees that worked closely with the commissions.

The principle of *experience* was observed when an outside agency, The Doane Agricultural Service, Inc., was employed to help determine *process* and to help give *direction* to the program. As local people worked with, for, and under the *direction* of this organization, they received valuable *experience* which was helpful to them and to the program. Out of this *experience* with the Doane Agricultural Service grew *emulation* and *training* for the local people.

The Beckley Area Rural Development Program covers a large area, several economic enterprises and many activities which require much *integration*. Only through the *integration* of activities have committees, commissions and the council been able to realize their successes. The council receives, coordinates and disseminates commission reports and all activities of the program. Through such *integration*, *knowledge* of *purpose* and *process* of all phases of the program is always *shared* with participants in the program and with the public at large. *Integration* of this kind also facilitates *flexibility* which was amply demonstrated in this program.

Evidently the *habit* of democratic group activity was already established before the beginning of this program. At no point was autocratic behavior evidenced. By having the *habit* of democratic group behavior, no time was lost in having to convert the group to this method of making decisions and taking action.

The democratic principle of *service* above self permeated the leadership activity from top to bottom. At every level there was an eagerness to promote the program rather than to promote self. The persons who were most responsible for bringing about the success of the program have been most vocal in praising others for the progress made. This was true even though people with special interests were most often selected for commission membership.

Leadership satisfactions are evidenced even in objective reports of the operation of the program to participants. This is not surprising for when great success is achieved through the adequate use of the principles of democratic leadership in a program of great magnitude and potential, *leadership satisfactions* might well be expected.

Principles Omitted.

> Whoever thinks a faultless piece
>   to see,
> Thinks what ne'er was, nor is,
>   nor e'er shall be.
>   Pope . . . Essay on Criticism

All of the principles of democratic leadership were used to some extent. For the most part, each one was very well used. However, in a few instances there is evidence of weakness in the use of certain principles. The failure of the finance committee of five to secure the $1500 subscriptions from a list of 25 of Beckley's leading businesses and service organizations in 1949 may have been due to one of several things. First, the potential subscribers may not have had a sufficient *knowledge* of the *purpose* for which the money would be used or the way in which it would be used. Second, the potential subscribers may not have felt themselves to be real *participators* or *sharers* in the total program. Third, rigid adherence to the $500 down or nothing prevented many from subscribing. When *flexibility* of payment was put into operation, the number of subscribers rose from 14 to 55 cooperators. Also, *flexibility* in permitting year-to-year pledges rather than three-year pledges probably caused an increase in subscriptions.

Disinterest and poor attendance at four poultry shows that were started in 1950 and continued for three succeeding years may have been due partly at least to the insufficient use of certain democratic principles. It is evident that *knowledge* of the events was widespread due to the large amount of publicity that was given to them. However, the principles of *habit* and of *experience* may not have been given enough attention in the planning. People who do not have the *habit* of *participating* in certain kinds of activities have to develop a liking and appreciation for them. They had no previous experience with poultry shows. Farming itself had become of little importance and concern to the people in the Beckley area prior to the activities of the Rural

Area Development Council. With this history and background, it might have been better to delay the poultry shows until later when the people had learned to appreciate farming and recognized its importance to the area.

Difficulty in getting membership in the State Artificial Breeding Cooperative Association was also probably due to the lack of *habit* and *experience,* plus the lack of *knowledge* and *training.* Traditionally, rural people have been hesitant to accept new ideas about which they have little *knowledge* and *experience.* With *knowledge* of this characteristic of rural people, leaders of a program must exhibit extreme patience in trying to initiate new projects. This type of weakness may have caused less than expected success and progress in some of their other projects such as was experienced by the Savings and Investments Commission, the Fruits and Vegetables Commission, and the watershed development program.

Alternative Actions. There are several instances in the development and operation of the Beckley Area Rural Development Council where alternative actions could have been taken. Most may not have added to the success of the venture, particularly in the organizational stages.

To finance the program in the beginning, an effort could have been made to solicit smaller pledges from a larger number of subscribers. This would have resulted in getting more people directly involved in the program, which may have made them better cooperators and boosters. If small pledges from individual farmers could have been secured, some of the later programs that depended on the cooperation of farmers might have been more successful.

The council showed good judgment in selecting a qualified and able manager. This had a great deal to do with the success of the program since much of the responsibility for coordination and the use of democratic principles rested on his shoulders. The selection of a less able person might well have meant the failure of the program. Too often, organizations of this kind seek the cheapest rather than the best qualified personnel.

The primary responsibility for the development and conduct of the various projects could have been vested in the council rather than in commissions and committees. To have done this would have restricted the spread of the leadership, directly involved fewer people in the program, and overburdened members of the council. Such an organization would have been inadequate for a program of this magnitude. It would have resulted in either failure of the program or in restricting it to a smaller size that could be managed by the council.

Although other action might have been taken, the type of leadership exhibited in the Beckley community provided opportunities for a large number of people to work together through special commissions and committees to improve their economic welfare. It is significant that the experiences shared during this undertaking not only met an economic need, but gave much personal satisfaction and enjoyment as well. Such a dual accomplishment is typical of real democratic leadership.

CHAPTER XIV

A Civic Club Sponsors a Rural Improvement Program in an Arkansas Community

PART I[1]

A person visiting Carthage, Arkansas, in 1940, would have been no more impressed with it than he would have been with any other small rural community. He could have entered Carthage from Fordyce which is 30 miles to the south, or from Malvern which is 30 miles to the north. He would probably have arrived in Carthage by car or train since the bus did not pass through the community. The visitor to this south central Arkansas community would probably have observed general farming and timber-growing as the principal agricultural activities. Large acreage held by lumber and paper mill companies dominated the economic scene.

If this visitor had returned to Carthage, Arkansas, in 1950, he would have seen essentially the same situation that he saw in 1940 except for two things. First, the school had been enlarged and its activities expanded due to a consolidation of several small districts. The school had become the center of community interest and had prevented the complete disintegration of the spirit of the community. Second, the population of the community had declined from 687 to 533, a loss of 154 or 22.4%.

Naturally, a loss of almost 1/4 of the population in a period of ten years had resulted in a depressing effect both on the people who remained and on the economy. It was in response to this felt need to improve community spirit and economy that the Ruritan Club was organized.

ORGANIZATION OF THE CARTHAGE RURITAN CLUB

Ruritan National is an American rural service organization that was started in 1930. It is a civic organization whose objec-

---

[1]The basic data for Part I of this chapter were contributed by Mr. Samuel Key, who was, at the time, Vocational Agriculture Instructor, Carthage, Arkansas.

tive is to make rural communities better places in which to live. The Ruritan Club is composed of farmers, businessmen and professional men who are desirous of helping rural people to meet their needs and the needs of their communities.

Early in March, 1954, Mr. Jack Snider, who was then assistant executive secretary of the Ruritan National, contacted Mr. Samuel Key, Vocational Agriculture teacher at Carthage High School, concerning the possibilities of organizing a civic club in Carthage. Mr. Snider had been introduced to Mr. Key by Mr. O. J. Seymour, a District Supervisor of Vocational Agriculture in the State of Arkansas. Mr. Key was born and reared in the community and had taught Vocational Agriculture there for eight years. During this time he had demonstrated his leadership ability among rural people. He had a love for the community and for the rural way of life. Much of his time and effort were devoted to church and civic activities with a view toward elevating the welfare of the people he loved. In working with youth and adult groups he had demonstrated patience, kindness, friendliness and vision. It wasn't long before he earned the affection and the respect of the people in and around Carthage.

Immediately on hearing about the objectives and the work of the Ruritan Club, Mr. Key saw in it an organization which might offer an opportunity to improve the Carthage community, and make it a more attractive and better place in which to live. This, he thought, might be accomplished through a program of cooperative action instigated, inspired, and centered around a civic club.

Immediately Mr. Key discussed with other local and professional leaders the possibilities of improving the community by working through a civic club. They thought well of the idea and letters were sent to each farmer, businessman and professional man in the community inviting them to attend a meeting to consider and discuss the organization of a local Ruritan Club. The meeting was to be held at Carthage High School on March 18, 1954. At the meeting, which 32 men attended, Mr. Snider explained fully the organization, operation, and objectives of a Ruritan Club. He informed the persons present that if a club at Carthage were organized, it would be the first such club west of the Mississippi. After a full discussion which included many questions and answers about the needs and possibilities of such a club in Carthage, the men present voted unanimously to organize a local Ruritan Club. Officers for the club were elected and at the following meeting, Mr. Marvin L. Grey, Executive Secretary of the Ruritan National, presented the charter to the Ruritan Club of Carthage.

Since its inception, the club has held its regular meetings the first Friday evening of each month in the high school cafeteria. These are dinner meetings, and the local P.T.A. prepares and serves the meals monthly for a charge of $1.00 per plate. This arrangement has proved to be very satisfactory. Each club member pays quarterly dues of $3.75. Three dollars of his dues money per quarter pays for meals received at meetings. The remaining 75 cents is used for local expenses and national dues.

GOALS AND ACCOMPLISHMENTS

The Carthage Ruritan Club, being composed of civic-minded rural people, has been active and successful in bringing about community improvements. Members of the club have worked hard, but they have enjoyed both the work and the results of their labors. The members felt that their first action should be to make a penetrating study of the community needs, which they did over a period of three months. It was decided that the study should be made in an informal way. They felt that an informal approach would be just as productive and more pleasant than a formal approach. Club members would talk with other people in the community and get ideas of the greatest community needs. These ideas would then be discussed in club meetings where decisions were made on the problems to attack and ways of attacking them. As a result of their study, it was decided that needs of the community could best be attacked through committee work. Twelve committees were organized in the areas of welfare, youth, agriculture, recreation, fellowship, finance, public highways, education, the home, forestry, rural church, and industry. Club members were assigned to work on one or more of these committees depending on their individual interest, time, and ability. The committees met from one to four times a month depending on the nature of their assignments. Plans, problems, and progress of the committees were discussed at monthly club meetings.

Early Achievements. The type of activities engaged in by the Carthage Ruritan Club provided a new type of experience for many of the club members. For this reason much time was spent by the various committees in planning and organizing group activities. Mr. Key and several other members of the club who were more experienced in group work gave assistance to all of the committees as needed.

Through the efforts and stimulation of the local Ruritan Club, several community projects were completed by April, 1956. These projects are discussed briefly below. In order to get a better appreciation of the leadership activities involved in the accomplishment of these projects, the state highway improvement project will be discussed in more detail than the others.

State Highway Improvements. The highway committeee was composed of three club members who volunteered to serve on this committee. Because these men often used state highways leading into Carthage, they were well acquainted with the poor conditions of these roads. These highways were very inadequate for modern day traffic. They were too narrow and rough in many spots. It was felt that because of the inadequacy of the roads, many motorists took alternative routes which were often out of the way and less convenient. This limitation of traffic of course affected the economy of Carthage. Since earlier, but poorly organized efforts to get State Highways 48 and 9 improved had failed, the highway committee realized that its attack on the problem must be well planned. Aspects of the problem such as how much of the highways needed improvement, type of improvement needed, estimates on the cost of improvements, and estimates on loss in out-of-town traffic to the economy of Carthage due to poor highways, were studied by different committee members. These topics were then discussed and refined in the committee meetings, which were frequently held. After all related facts were outlined by the highway committee, they were presented at a Ruritan Club meeting for further discussion and suggestions by the entire club membership.

After the plan was approved by the membership of the club, the highway committee met with the State Highway Commission and on the basis of evidence of need, requested that State Highways 48 and 9 be improved. After several additional meetings with the State Highway Commission, the commission finally agreed to improve State Highways 48 and 9 in the vicinity of Carthage, providing the right of way was given to the state by property owners affected. With this commitment from the Commission, the highway committee members sighed in relief, for it had required tenacity, persistence and great energy to secure this milestone. And yet the work of the highway committee was not completed. Members of the Committee had to contact all the property owners who were affected in order to secure the right of way for the state. Highway committee members were challenged by this task and were able to get the cooperation of the affected land owners, and these highways were improved.

To make their leadership job with the highway improvement project complete, members of the committee arranged for donations of labor to help land owners who needed it remove and replace fences. Also, farmers who were unable to purchase wire or posts for replacing fences were aided by donated funds solicited by committee members from local citizens.

County Road Improvements. The highway committee met with the County Judge and town council several times to discuss improvement of county roads which was badly needed. As a result, three blocks inside the town of Carthage were black-topped, and several miles of county roads between Fordyce, the county seat, and Carthage were completely reconstructed. Also, several miles of country roads from outlying neighborhoods to Carthage were black-topped during this time.

Dumping Grounds. The town of Carthage received its first suitable garbage disposal site through the efforts of its local Ruritan Club. Realizing that a dumping ground was a need of long standing in Carthage, the club located a suitable acre of land, and influenced the town council to buy it. Total cost for the dumping ground was $250.

Clean-up Campaign. Before the organization of the local Ruritan Club, there was no organized program to keep the town of Carthage clean. With the local Ruritan Club taking the initiative, plans were formulated for two clean-up campaigns a year, one in the spring and one in the fall. This plan, which was agreed upon by the town officials, has worked out very satisfactorily. During the period of the campaign, the town truck picks up rubbish that has been sacked and placed at the side of the street by citizens.

New Fire Truck. The Ruritan Club Committee concerned with welfare met with the town council to make plans for the purchase of a fire truck. The need for one was emphasized when several buildings burned, including a saw mill which was the town's only industry. It was decided that a used fire truck might meet their needs, but when none was found after repeated ads in state papers, the council purchased a new fire truck at a cost of $5,500.

Rodeo Arena. The recreational committee of the Ruritan Club met with a local riding club to discuss possibilities for the construction of a rodeo arena. The end-result of the efforts of this committee was the construction of a rodeo arena at a cost of $1,125. This reasonable cost was possible because a saw mill operating in the community donated the lumber and the labor was donated by citizens of the town and adjacent area.

Church Improvements. The rural church committee of the Carthage Ruritan Club contacted various churches and their auxiliaries to encourage the improvement of church property. After several contacts in which plans were made, the local Presbyterian church raised $100 to be used for the purchase of kitchen articles, and roofing material was purchased and laid by the free services of members of the church.

The local Methodist church was painted and re-roofed by its members. Both labor and materials to do these jobs were donated, thereby saving the church an estimated $750.

Cemetery Road Markers. The Carthage Ruritan Club, in co-operation with the local Home Demonstration Club, placed road markers leading to the Hampton Springs Cemetery. Although this activity might be considered one of the smaller accomplishments so far as capital outlay is concerned, it satisfied a felt need in the community. It required the cooperation of several groups, including the F.F.A. boys who made and painted the signs and a local merchant who did the lettering.

School Lunchroom. The committee on education met with the county superintendent of schools to discuss the possibilities of remodeling the school lunchroom which was in obvious need of repair and enlargement. The superintendent took the matter up with the local school board and soon the recommended re-modeling was under way. It included the enlargement and re-decoration of the lunchroom. New lights, new counters, and new cabinets were installed. Purchase was made of additional dishes and silverware, and the exterior of the building was painted. This was accomplished at a cost to the local school board of $2,000.

Town Street Improvement. As a result of the cooperative efforts of the Ruritan Club and town council members as well as other interested citizens, 20 blocks of town streets have been black-topped, 16 blocks graveled, and three new streets graded. Citizens of Carthage paid $100 per block for black-topping the streets, the county judge furnished the necessary equipment and labor, and all gravel was hauled by the town's newly purchased truck.

Dump Truck. At a cost of $1,200, a used truck in good condition was purchased by the town to be used in the clean-up campaigns, for hauling gravel, and for other hauling jobs.

As is true with most endeavors, even in the face of resounding success, the Carthage Ruritan Club has not been entirely without failures. Two proposed projects that the club initially failed to achieve were:

(1) The possession and development of an F.F.A. Forest. Members of the Ruritan Club who volunteered to work on this project approached their jobs with the same vigor, vision and enthusiasm as did the members of the highway committee. It is felt by club members that failure to achieve this project at an early date was not due to neglect on the part of the committee members but rather to lack of cooperation of a lumber company in a nearby city. Continued efforts did result in the achievement of the F.F.A. Forest project at a later date. (2) The possession of a clubhouse for the youth of the community. The only available and suitable building in Carthage for a youth clubhouse was constructed with funds donated by several people. In order to acquire this building all of the donors had to agree to release their share in the building. This some of them refused to do, which caused the failure of the project. However, the desire to have a clubhouse for the youth of the community has not diminished, and it is felt this project is now in sight of achievement.

Later Goals and Achievements. At the regular monthly meeting in April, 1956, members of the Carthage Ruritan Club discussed areas of continued prevailing needs for community development and improvement. At the May meeting, the club members decided to sponsor the election and organization of a committee to be called the "Community Development Council" through which, it was believed, a large part of the future community improvement activities could be allocated, coordinated, sponsored, and conducted. While enabling each organization to have more appreciation and respect for the other, the council could also serve as a "clearing house" for many community projects. The idea was presented to all the organizations in the community, where it received enthusiastic endorsement. Immediately, each organization in the town and its patronage area elected someone from its group to represent it on the council. The council elected Mr. Key Crouse, secretary-treasurer of the local Ruritan Club, as its general chairman. It decided to hold its regular meetings on the third Monday night of each month in the high school auditorium.

This council has worked diligently toward improving the community economically, socially, physically, and spiritually. Its efforts have not gone unrewarded. From a long list of community needs, representatives of the various organizations selected projects on which their groups would work. The goals and achievements of organizations represented on the Community Development Council along with the name of each organization and its representative to the council are listed below. The activities of the Parent-Teacher Association are described in some detail to enable the reader to follow more closely the leadership involved.

Parent-Teacher Association.—Representative, Mrs. Obie Higgs. The P.T.A. has functioned at Carthage High School for many years. It is a wide-awake and active organization that has contributed much to the excellent school program and the very favorable community-school relationships that exist at Carthage. Mrs. Higgs, who represents the P.T.A. on the Community Development Council, is a long-established resident in the community. She is a housewife with a determination to do her best in whatever organization she belongs. Actually, she often ends up doing more than what would be her share, because she works in terms of getting a job done and not in terms of having done her part. Mrs. Higgs possesses an abundance of zeal and enthusiasm for her civic, church and social work. She has what is often referred to as "lots of get up and go." This trait along with her ability to understand and work well with others makes her very well liked and respected in the community.

From the list of community needs developed by the Community Developement Council, Mrs. Higgs tentatively selected the development of a town park and recreational area as the project for the P.T.A. to undertake. At the next P.T.A. meeting she made a report of the activities of the Council. After some discussion of the project that Mrs. Higgs had tentatively selected, it was agreed that the P.T.A. would undertake a long-range plan to provide a town park and recreational area. A committee was selected immediately and work on the project was begun.

The P.T.A. committee with Mrs. Higgs as chairman selected a site for the park in an excellent location that was accessible and large enough to provide the needed space. Next a committee member contacted Mr. and Mrs. Roy Rogers and explained to them their need for some tables. Mr. Rogers is a contractor and a very civic-minded individual. He and his wife agreed to build the tables free of charge, which they did without delay.

The committee decided that a Bar-B-Q pit would be needed, and discussed how it might be secured. Knowing that Mr. Key often had the F.F.A. boys perform community services, it was decided to request his assistance on this project. Mr. Key and the school principal agreed that construction of the Bar-B-Q pit was a worthy community activity and at the same time it would provide some vocational training and experience for the F.F.A. boys. The idea was presented to the F.F.A. boys, and they were eager to do the work under the supervision of the Vocational Agriculture teacher. The end-result of this coordination and cooperation was the actual construction of a very good Bar-B-Q pit by the F.F.A. boys.

Through similar planning, coordination, and cooperation, the committee now has underway the construction, by local citizens, of an outdoor kitchen. Also, a miniature golf course, croquet area and clubhouse are in the plans for construction as soon as possible.

Mrs. Higgs reports the decisions and activities of her committee to the P.T.A., where they are discussed and suggestions are made. With P.T.A. approval of activities of the committee,

Mrs. Higgs reports on the project to the Community Development Council. At the council the report is discussed and again suggestions to facilitate the work are made. The same type of coordination and cooperation exist between the Community Development Council and the other organizations that have representatives on it.

Ruritan Club.—Representative, Key Crouse. As a member organization of the Community Development Council, the Ruritan Club has sponsored the following projects:

The black-topping of 15 miles of country road on Highway 48.

The black-topping of approximately 20 miles of country road on Highway 9.

The submitting of bids for a new town clinic.

The purchasing of grounds for a new clinic.

The purchasing of grounds for a city hall.

The purchasing of grounds for a new fire house.

The purchasing of materials for a new fire house.

The securing of a medical doctor to be located in the community.

Education.—Representative, J. W. Tolleson. Forty acres of farm forest were donated on a long-term lease to the school board by the International Paper Company of Camden, Arkansas. Mr. Samuel Key, local Vocational Agriculture teacher, in cooperation with School Superintendent J. W. Tolleson and the local school board, is responsible for the forest management. The forest, which is used to train F.F.A. boys and other youth and adult groups interested in forestry, has a good growth of Pine Timber and is set up on a four-year rotation basis.

American Legion.—Representative, Mack Treadwell. The local members of this organization erected a flag pole on the school grounds and presented the school with an American Flag. They also initiated a basketball tournament to be played annually with the proceeds to go to the local polio drive.

American Legion Auxiliary.—Representative, Mrs. Edna Mae Lea. This organization collected and shipped several boxes of clothes to the Hungarian Refugees, among other worthy projects.

Home Demonstration Club.—Representative, Mrs. S. W. Treadwell. The local Home Demonstration Club sponsored the organization of a Ground Observer Corps. Thirty-three of the members have qualified for the basic training certificates, and thirteen of them have qualified for Ground Observer Corps Wings which requires 21 hours of service. In addition, this organization sponsored the beautification of the Hampton Springs Cemetery and has elected to make this project a part of its year-round program.

Women's Society of Christian Service.—Representative, Mrs. R. L. Scudder. This organization selected the difficult task of meeting with certain families and groups in an effort to get adequate housing through remodeling of old and construction of new homes.

Presbyterian Church.—Representative, Mrs. Harris Wylie. The local Presbyterian church has given leadership to the development of plans for the construction of a Youth Center to serve all the young people of the town and its outlying areas.

Baptist Auxiliary.—Representative, Mrs. James Pierce. This organization has been able to get an adequate parking area near the church grounds through soliciting donations of money, tile for ditches, and labor for construction of the project. The organization sponsored the landscaping of church grounds and the erection of a sign in front of the church. Plans have been made for the construction of a cross by the church members who will furnish the labor plus two bricks each.

Town Council.—Representative, Earl Kelly. The Town Council agreed to erect street stop signs where needed, and to keep grass clipped in vacant lots and ditches.

Riding Club.—Representative, Harris Wylie. The Riding Club has elected to sponsor a rodeo annually on the 4th of July and to compile the history of the town from its beginning.

SUMMARY

The Ruritan Club of Carthage, Arkansas, has furnished the stimulus, guidance, and initiative necessary to give life, spirit, improvement and progress to a community that for more than ten years had been going in exactly the opposite direction. The people of Carthage proved that there is strength in cooperative effort. They found that civic ends can be attained through the cooperative struggle of civic-minded people and that joint efforts for the common good can be not only mutually beneficial, but personally gratifying and rewarding as well.

If the person who visited Carthage, Arkansas, in 1940 and again in 1950 were to return now, he would see a very different community. Not only would he see many physical improvements, but probably more important, he would see a much happier and prouder people whose community spirit is wonderful to behold. If this visitor were to inquire about the many improvements in the community, practically anyone there would sing the praises of the Civic Club.

If the visitor were to inquire about how such improvements might be realized in his own community, a Carthage citizen would probably relate to him the history of his Civic Club. He might then give the visitor the Biblical admonition: "Go ye and do likewise."

PART II

ANALYSIS OF THE CARTHAGE, ARKANSAS IMPROVEMENT PROGRAM

Democratic Principles Used. Rural leadership and community improvement often result from a felt need. In the case of Carthage, Arkansas, decline in population causing a depressed community spirit and economy was the problem. All the people in the community had some *knowledge* of the problem. However, little progress was made before Mr. Jack Snider and Mr. Samuel Key introduced the idea of a Civic Club through which a solution of the problem was realized.

The principle of *participation* was observed when consideration was given to organization of the Civic Club. Through action and interaction brought about by *participation,* a *group mind* which is basic to successful democratic group activity was developed.

There was no question as to *purpose.* All members of the Civic Club had *knowledge* of the *purpose* which enabled the group to move along more rapidly and with fewer misunderstandings, misgivings, and blunders. The *purpose* was decided at the organizational meeting and was kept before the group thereafter.

A thorough *knowledge* of the *purpose* aided *direction.* Members of the group understood the problem and were *chal-*

lenged to reverse the recent trends in their community. Leadership was *shared* first within the club through committees and later extended to other organizations represented in the "Community Development Council." The leaders were *challenged* to use well their skills of leadership to insure healthy group decisions and action (see Chapter VII). The principle of *direction* was observed by leaders both in decision-making and in taking action.

Wise use of the principle of *process* kept means and ends in balance. To have overemphasized *process* at the expense of product might not have resulted in improvements. To have overemphasized product at the expense of *process* might have further depressed community spirit causing dissatisfactions that might have further increased decline in population.

The *habit* of democratic group activity helped to make rapid achievement possible. Early *experiences* of successful activities gave encouragement and stimulus for additional successes. It was not long before a pattern was established, and success itself became a *habit*.

Service was the motive behind all leadership acts. By keeping *purpose* in the forefront, self-edification was left in the background. That leadership was not for personal gains can be seen from the extent that it was *shared*. *Sharing* of leadership resulted in the development of leadership qualities in younger members of the community. Development of leadership in others is one measure of successful leadership and it ensures continuation of desirable community development. The fact that Carthage, Arkansas, continues to be improved through self-help measures even though several who gave leadership to the early activities of the group have moved to new locations, died, or retired from active leadership, is added indication of the *service* and *sharing* of leadership roles. Widespread *sharing* of the leadership role and of responsibilities for many different projects required unusual *integration*. The need for *integration* was so clearly seen that a community development council was organized through which objectives and procedures could be channeled.

As successes began to be realized, *leadership satisfactions* began to unfold. Just as nothing satisfies a thirsty person like a drink of water, nothing pleases a leader more than seeing fruition of the efforts of his group. Physical improvements in

Carthage are gratifying, but the greatest satisfaction was due to the improved morale of the people.

Principles Omitted. Although there is no tangible evidence that the principles of *emulation* and *training* were used, due to the size and success of the program, it is very likely that they were. Unlike some of the other principles, *emulation* and *training* are not always readily noticeable. It may have facilitated the work if a short *training* course had been planned for the chairmen of the various committees as the success of the activity depended in large measure upon them. A course designed to acquaint these leaders with techniques and approaches to help them perform their tasks efficiently might have developed their abilities and strengthened their confidence in themselves.

Although the principles of *knowledge, purpose* and *challenge* were adequately used, the danger is ever present in a project of this kind, that they may be neglected due to a relaxing of effort which sometimes follows success. This would cause the community spirit to sink back to the low level which existed before 1954. A community needs change. If there is no *knowledge* of changing needs, or if the Civic Club or some other group is not *challenged* to meet them, a community spirit will eventually fall to a low ebb again. Also, *purpose* must continually be in harmony with needs if continued success is to be expected.

Alternative Actions. There are several alternative actions that could have been taken in an effort to prevent slow death of the community, which the decline in population and its accompanying ills actually amounted to. Mr. Key showed vision and imagination in seeing in the Ruritan Club the possibility of an organization through which the community needs could be met. The farmers, business and professional men who participated in the organization of the club were similarly endowed. It is unlikely that the goal could have been met more effectively in any other way, though civic clubs with other names may have done as well. However, to accomplish similar ends, it is possible that one of three alternatives could have been used, each of which has some limitations. (1) An outside agency could have been employed to study the situation and make recommendations for solution. To have done this might have left the people without a real feeling of personal accomplishment. Also, many wholesome personal experiences might have been lost, and the cost of the service might have been a burden on a community of this type and size. (2) An existing organization might have been used to accomplish the same goals. This would have called for a change or at least an addition to the objectives of such an organization. Non-members of the organization in the community might not have given full cooperation because of prejudices toward the members and knowledge of the previous activities of the group. (3) A community development council, such as the one that sponsored the later achievements, could have been formulated at the suggestion of one of the already-existing organizations. Here again, response to such an attempt might not have been as complete as it was to the call of the Ruritan Club. The Ruritan Club probably received good response partly because it recognized needs that all community citizens recognized, it demonstrated success in helping the community, and it made its purpose known by all.

CHAPTER XV

Leadership for Living—4-H Clubs in Middletown

The countryside around Middletown is richly endowed. It has good soil, temperate climate and thrifty, agrarian-minded people. The area was first settled by German immigrants about 1733. Later others joined them from Pennsylvania Dutch settlements farther north.

The Middletown valley, of Fredrick County, Maryland, is known for its highly productive dairy and general livestock farming. A few industries came in during World War II but most of the people continue to look to the land as their basic resource. How the people of Middletown first began to develop their skills and attitudes toward good farming and satisfying family living is a fascinating story. But there are only time and space here for a sentence about that. By some grace or miracle people learned early to work together, to team up with agricultural research, the cooperative Extension Service, the schools, the churches and with business and cooperatives for community development. Probably a very provident succession of superior educational leadership had much to do with expanding the talents and horizons of a fundamentally thrifty and industrious but conservative people.

Since 1917, Fredrick County has employed county extension agents to work with farm families. Boys' and girls' clubs were started and a succession of popular agricultural and home demonstration agents were employed. Henry R. Shoemaker, the present highly respected county agricultural agent, has been a modest but potent leader in all rural affairs since 1926. Much of the following chronology about the Middletown 4-H Clubs was first related by the county extension agents and all of it was later checked and verified with the local leaders.

The Middletown Boys' 4-H Club first selected Maurice Ahalt as volunteer leader about 1935. He has been helping the boys and girls ever since. He is mild mannered, about 45 and a modestly successful dairy farmer. Perhaps you would not immediately select him from a crowd as being outstanding. His leadership ability springs from a sincere personal interest in youth and people. You are likely to observe him sitting in the back row at a meeting. Or maybe he will be chatting amiably with neighbors about crops, cows or Mickey Keller who has just left for his stretch of military service. But to more than 100 young men and women of the community, Maurice Ahalt is a counselor, confidant and a teacher *par excellence*. "He's our Club Leader." That title symbolizes a whole bookful of principles, a galaxy of richly educational meetings, and more than two decades of events, marriages, and family incidents.

To most of the 125 present and former members of the Middletown clubs Maurice is not thought of as the man who did 4-H Club work. His service is more valuable and significant than that. He is the one who was available for help while they ran the club themselves. Many former 4-H members may even need to stop and reflect a moment before they can describe just how Maurice Ahalt helped them keep the club moving. But even if they cannot verbalize his contribution, members know he was important in their lives.

By 1945, ten years after Maurice Ahalt was chosen leader of the Middletown Boys' Agricultural Club, there was a concern about a suitable meeting place. Members preferred to meet in homes but with 40 to 45 active youth this was a problem —especially in the confining winter months. So they tried the community schoolhouse. This worked all right until the school board adopted a policy of charging a fee for use of the school buildings outside school hours. Besides this, the school desks, fastened to the floor in soldierly rows, permitted no games or active demonstrations.

For many years now the 4-H Club meeting was an established part of the community's social and cultural life. Parents were no longer able to take part in the meetings—there just wasn't room. But they drove to the meeting place, chatted with neighbors outside for a while and usually returned to pick up the young folks again about 11 p.m., after the meeting was over.

The problem of too many members or too little room dragged along. Several solutions were suggested. One obvious idea was to divide the membership into two clubs by geographic location. The homes covered an area about six miles in diameter. Travel distance to meetings would be reduced. But this would mean separating life-long friendships and pals. No go! How about breaking up into smaller project groups for alternate meetings? The dairy, livestock or crops boys could work together in smaller study groups every alternate month, meeting in members' homes as before. Then regular meetings of the entire club could be held in the schoolhouse every two months. This plan had a few supporters but no one really wanted to divide the club this way.

Maurice Ahalt didn't say much about the dividing business. Not that he was unaware of the problems. During his first years as a leader, the club frequently met in his home. And even considerate, well-behaved boys can leave their marks on the floors, walls and curtains of a farm home when 40 or 50 pairs of wiggly feet are sardined into a living and dining room built for a family of five. Besides, Maurice is a leader who recognizes boy-nature. He knows that there should be demonstrations, illustrated talks and a chance to do and show things at any good 4-H Club meeting. Learning by doing is a reality in the Middletown 4-H plan. This kind of learning takes space and elbow room. A club of 40 to 45 is just too large to work with efficiently.

But even so, Maurice hesitated about dividing the club. Most of the available youngsters in Middletown belonged to this club, came to meetings and believed in it as "the thing to do." One doesn't consider dividing up such a group without some hesitation.

About 1945, the club arranged for the help of an assistant leader. There were so many 4-H activities going on all the time that even a live wire like Maurice Ahalt couldn't keep up with the needs and interests of 40 or 45 young dynamos.

It came about gradually. Charles Remsberg, a jovial, strapping six footer, of about 40, returned to Middletown to farm. He and his wife had been 4-H Club members. Charlie had started out as an assistant county agent after going through the University of Maryland Agricultural College. But agents' salaries were low. He had a young growing family of four children, and besides, he always wanted to farm anyway. So Charlie moved to a large grain farm in the Middletown valley with his family.

Members of the club were quick to discover that the former extension worker was a good resource. He knew a lot of things about dairy and livestock. He liked young people. He responded to their needs and interests. Soon he was coming to regular meetings of the club with his own children. From then on nature took its course. Charlie Remsberg was assistant to Maurice Ahalt as a second volunteer leader for over two years.

The club continued to thrive. As soon as young people reached the age of 10 they made their choice of agricultural projects and worked out a little business deal with Pa and Ma in preparation for 4-H membership. A youth considered 4-H one of his citizenship rights, like going to school at six or voting at 21.

But what to do with all these kids? The older boys and girls were not dropping out of 4-H at 13 or 14 years, like they do in so many communities. Why should they? It was fun. They were learning about science and life and the world around them. They earned money and accumulated stock, equipment or cash from 4-H projects, sales and prizes. And they enjoyed the feeling of achievement from serving on programs and tours committees, giving demonstrations out of their own experiences, and holding twilight judging practice. Every member of the club had at least one important job in it. The more experienced helped the new ones so there were few failures. Membership continued to grow and something had to be done about bulging meetings.

Another problem was the wide span of need and interest between 10-year-olds and high school graduates. If the club planned a meeting to figure out whether it was more profitable to sell butterfat to the cream station or to sell whole milk to the co-op milk producers association, the young kids couldn't work the arithmetic. They fidgeted and made noises. They didn't want to be left out but they didn't really understand the issue. They were not ready for a 4-H marketing project.

On the other hand, if a meeting was planned for the young new members, the older ones lost interest in the "kid stuff" they had learned five years before. The older boys tended to hang around outside and talk about cars and tractors, the draft or maybe girls. They didn't dislike the younger kids of 4-H either. But there were more important things to do at 17 or 18 than to hear a 10-year-old tell how to mix a simple feed ration for his first-year fat pig project.

Psychologists and educators recognize immediately the need for *planning programs around the developmental needs and interests of the child.* Volumes have been written on the subject.[1]

Charlie Remsberg and Maurice Ahalt as 4-H leaders recognized this need also. But what could they do about it? The 4-H record books, project outlines, bulletins and leaders' guides were all printed in the State Extension office at the University, 60 miles away. There was a general suggestion in the guide for leaders, pointing out that something of interest for every member should be included as a part of each club meeting. Also, it was suggested that older members serve as junior leaders to help the newcomers. But nothing was said in these materials about how to divide a club nor specifically what would appeal to the needs of the first year and tenth year 4-H members at the same time. And to further confuse their problem, it was generally understood that Extension leaders preferred something vaguely called the "family approach to extension work."

When Charlie Remsberg first suggested that the club might be divided into junior and senior groups it was recognized that this might create some problems. For some families it would mean two or even more 4-H meetings a month. Who would drive the junior members to their meetings? At first a few of the younger boys and girls protested. There is an important prestige factor for an 11-year-old to be in the same meeting with the "big guys."

The older members thought dividing was a good idea. They recognized that they could have better meetings. They could more easily meet in the homes. They could have a square dance, organize a softball team or make an overnight tour without having to worry about how to take care of the small fry.

Gradually there was recognition that younger members in the club were not getting as much out of the big club as they should. Club procedures were democratic, but younger members were at a disadvantage in holding office, giving demonstrations or planning programs. On this basis it was agreed that

---

[1]For a highly useful pamphlet on this subject applying to all ages, see "Developmental Tasks and Education," by Robert J. Havighurst, Longman's, Green & Company, New York, 1954, 100 pp.

Charlie would begin to work more intensively with the younger members.

At first the juniors met separately for extra project instruction meetings only. They gained new interest and started advancing in their work and their confidence.

Soon they were getting as much fun out of their own meeting as they did from the larger group and they weren't so restricted in their behavior patterns. Charlie has always been a firm disciplinarian but he has a ready wit and enjoyed a hearty laugh, even at his own expense. There was always something new going on in the junior club. It "clicked" right from the start. Charlie's own children are or have been active 4-H'ers. Angela works hard in the junior club. Bob is a member of the seniors. Betty, the oldest, is now a nurse and has moved away. Bill is beyond 4-H age now also. Careful and understanding observations of the needs and interests of his own children helped Charlie Remsberg become a top-notch leader for the junior club.

There was always the best of cooperation between the two clubs and the two leaders. It was agreed and expected that the junior club would feed members into the senior group. At about 14 years a member "graduated" from the juniors. He has a new 4-H leader who understands that he is growing up and that he is ready for adult-like experiences. He may serve as a junior leader to "help out" Charlie and the "younger kids" with their beginning projects. But for his own personal 4-H experience, he is ready to move on to bigger and broader horizons in the senior club.

By 1957 there were about 25 4-H members in the junior club and 18 in the senior. Both clubs meet in homes all or part of the year. At least twice a year there is a joint meeting with parents and the entire neighborhood turning out. One is an annual Christmas party. Few young people of club age in the Middletown community fail to be attracted by 4-H programs. Leaders also work with both clubs on special project activities. This is shown in Figure 15.

A yearly plan of work and the monthly meeting topics are developed by the members in both clubs. This procedure was started by Maurice in the original club and it is still standard operating procedure for both groups. Early in the 4-H year the county extension office sends to each local leader a list of na-

Figure 15. Local 4-H Club Leaders in Middletown Work on Special Projects with Members of Two Clubs. Charlie Remsberg demonstrates to officers and junior leaders of both clubs some new features of dairy equipment for his milking parlor. Maurice Ahalt is looking on with some 4-H dairy members.

tional, state and county events and program suggestions. These are general. Local clubs use only the ideas that appeal or apply directly to their interests. About the same time the clubs make up and send out a localized questionnaire. It asks for evaluation of last year's programs and ideas and interests for the next 12 months. Included are such questions as: What would you like to have included this year that was not done last year? What activities, games or educational topics will you be willing and prepared to lead? On which committees would you prefer to serve?

After homework on the questionnaire is completed a committee of the officers, leaders and a few members hold a "blackboard" planning session. Major features are decided, a month-to-month schedule of topics is worked out. Committees are named for each meeting and other events or activities of the club. The date and place for each meeting are planned in advance by this group. The entire 4-H program of work for the year is submitted to the club for discussion, refinement and adoption at the next meeting.

This process takes time, patience and perseverance. The leaders are "on tap" but not "on top" during the program development. They jokingly agree that after all these years they "could do it quicker and a lot easier by themselves." And they are probably right, in the short run. But for the long run both Maurice and Charlie are dedicated to the concept that 4-H is a citizenship training program. It is not enough to learn practices and skills. They know that our democracy depends on people learning to work democratically together. They know that young people learn fastest and best by doing. So it follows that youth must be involved and participate directly in the planning of programs for their own betterment.

The members verbalize it more simply and effectively: "Gee, we did it ourselves. It's in the groove. I mean really, solid."

It's not only within the club membership that Maurice and Charlie arrange for a sharing of responsibilities and the attendant credit. Throughout the entire community "everybody gets into the act." Nearly every modern practice and convenience known to dairy farming could be shown to the Middletown juniors right on Charlie's own 50-cow establishment. From milking parlor and loafing shed to vitalized dairy rations and improved pastures, the Remsbergs are good farmers. They have completely changed the old grain farm of 1945. But more often than not, the 4-H members get their new ideas from the facilities and lips of other farmers in the community. They take tours, ask in guest speakers or gain judging experience all over the area. There isn't a farm or home in the whole Middletown valley that escapes 4-H. In one way or another every family is involved. Even the very few needy or indigent are remembered and aided with food, fuel or services. And the countryside is more beautiful because of 4-H scrap drives, cleanup campaigns and roadside improvements. Godliness, neighborliness, thriftiness and friendliness are their working tools for carrying out the Golden Rule.

Over the years, what are the results of such leadership and 4-H efforts? First of all must be recognized that no single individual, group or influence is responsible for communities like Middletown. Many forces are at work. Probably most of the

good things in Middletown are a result of interaction of numerous factors. Churches, schools, farm organizations, business and
civic leaders, cooperatives, the press and many others have
played important roles in this community improvement symphony.

An agricultural historian recently studied the genesis of
every purebred or high grade livestock herd in the Middletown
area. Without exception each was traced back to a 4-H Club
project or family. Many of the farms in the Middletown valley
are currently operated by men who got started by way of vocational agriculture enterprises or 4-H family partnerships. Many
were thus enabled to "grow into farming" and saved some of the
excruciation of "going into farming" with sudden commitments
to present-day high capital costs. Many members of the Senior
Club are working in partnership with a parent or actually owning
and running a farm themselves.

Agricultural leadership is an important by-product of 4-H.
Five years ago Charlie Remsberg decided it was time to move
over and make room for new adult leadership in the juniors.
The members and parents were encouraged to talk about a replacement. This took some time. Finally three or four candidates
were presented and the members voted their preference. Paul
Coblentz was first selected. He had a long and successful experience in 4-H Club work as a member. Later he was succeeded by
John Burrier. John married a former member of the Middletown
club and Paul himself was an alumnus. Both were elected 4-H
All-Stars from Fredrick County at State 4-H meetings. All
leaders of these two clubs are active in church, civic and community affairs besides 4-H.

ANALYZING THE LEADERSHIP OF
MIDDLETOWN'S 4-H CLUBS

Think back now to Maurice Ahalt and Charlie Remsberg.
Why and how did their 4-H Clubs succeed so well? Consider that
an average 4-H Club in the United States is active only three
years and a typical 4-H volunteer leader about the same. Why
is Middletown so delightfully different?

Browse through Chapter IV again on Dedications of Leaders. Is there anything familiar about Maurice as a living personi-
fication of the highest and best in value dedications? Is he trying

to help others to help themselves? Does he answer your description of a democratic leader—a friend of man by the side of the road of life? Is he motivated by a sincere interest in boys and girls and in helping them to develop sound bodies, skilled hands, happy personalities and good citizenship attitudes?

Probably you have answered yes to each of the rhetorical questions in the preceding paragraph. Most assuredly Maurice Ahalt's dedications and values are in keeping with the highest of ethical standards in Middletown and in our American culture. The same may be said of Charles Remsberg. Would you conclude from this that there must always be a positive relationship between the lofty dedications of a leader and success of his organization? Yes, but we would caution that other things are needed too. There are many qualities or factors of leadership in addition to dedications. A wide range of qualities including leadership skills and use of sound principles are important and may bear directly on the leader's successful relationship to the club.

Let's now flip back through the pages of Chapter V and see how effectively the Middletown 4-H leaders are applying Principles of Democratic Leadership. For the Middletown 4-H leaders we have selected or combined 13 principles from Chapter V as the basis of the following analysis.

APPLICATION OF PRINCIPLES OF DEMOCRATIC LEADERSHIP
TO THE MIDDLETOWN 4-H CLUBS

1. **Knowledge**

   About subject matter. Both Maurice and Charlie are successful farmers and give evidence of knowing subject matter about agricultural practices.

   About people. There is evidence also that they understand developmental needs of their 4-H members. Parents and community leaders are supportive.

   About group techniques. Mr. Remsberg displayed keen insight into peer group processes by his persistence in getting two separate groups established on the basis of age and developmental needs of the 4-H members.

2. **Participation**

   In decision-making. The Middletown Club members and leaders make their own decisions. The leaders advise but do not decide.

In planning. Every member has a part. A committee actually develops the plan and submits it to the Club.

In conduct of meetings. Officers, committees, and members all have regular and important parts.

In project instruction. Members give demonstrations and share their experiences.

Outside the club. The entire community is involved.

3. Service and Sharing

For the benefit of present members. If the welfare of members vs. the leader's personal interest must be reconciled, the needs of the club become the dominant concern. The leaders subjugate their own interest to that of the group.

For future development. Provision is made for strong and continuous leadership by using junior leaders and by arranging for fresh younger adult leadership.

4. Habit

In democratic action. These clubs are consistently democratic in their planning, activities and human relationships. Through the years it has come to be expected that each club will enjoy complete control of its own destiny.

In constructive work. Middletown considers 4-H Club work to be an important and integral part of its educational, social and economic pattern. Any leader that failed to observe or promote this pattern probably would be resisted by members, parents and others.

5. The Group Mind

In planning. Many people in these clubs share in the development of ideas and decisions. More and better ideas come in geometric ratio to the number of people involved.

In operation. Group participation reduces the amount of resistance to changes planned.

6. Purpose

In planning. Objectives are established in advance. Programs are agreed upon as a group process and their fulfillment thereby becomes an individual and a group concern.

In action. Total action is thus greater because of united and concerted action.

7. Process

As the citizenship objectives of 4-H become more clearly and generally understood the methods and process followed assume greater importance. Middletown is an example of learning how to be useful, happy and successful citizens by practice. Practice develops into habit. Both individuals and the community have gained from the knowledge, skills and attitudes internalized through this process in Middletown.

8. Direction

In stimulation. The Middletown 4-H leaders share their ideas and experiences. They perform more than a laissez-faire role. They ask thought-provoking questions. They set up situations that will stimulate group thinking, decision and action.

In administration. Available when needed. Alert when there is danger. Enthusiastic when there is apathy. Stable when there is emotion. Understanding when there is disappointment or sorrow. These are working tools of the Middletown leaders.

9. Challenge

Significantly, Charles Remsberg recognized that size and character of the 4-H job must be adjusted to the developmental needs and interest levels of the members. It was not realistic to maintain uniform challenges for 10-to-20-year-old members in the same club. Accordingly, a separate club was formed for juniors. Everyone moved faster and farther as a result.

10. Emulation

These leaders know that precept is power. Deceit means defeat. Imitation and emulation are universal stimulators. Middletown 4-H leaders are good farmers, good fathers and husbands, good citizens.

11. Training and Experience

New leadership capacities are growing and developing every day within the club. Competence grows out of situations and experience. Middletown is "growing" a new crop of leaders for all walks of life. Their leaders are not born, they are developed and trained.

12. Flexibility

Adjustment of the leaders to new and developing needs of young people was exemplified when Charles Remsberg began to concentrate on needs of the junior members. Many 4-H Clubs throughout the United States are failing to recognize the new situations and needs of suburbanites and youth who will leave farming for college, the city or other opportunities in an atomic age.

Individual differences among youth and communities compel an attitude of objectivity and alertness. Members of the Middletown clubs are encouraged to work and progress on their own problems and at their own rate, for greatest and best total results.

13. Leadership Satisfactions

People are the most important component of the Middletown 4-H Clubs. The projects, awards, events and community services are secondary to the development of members, parents and families. The leaders measure results of 4-H in terms of its effect on Johnny, Tina and Tim. Some will recall the words of the wise Chinese peasant. When asked what satisfactions had come into his menial existence, he replied, "The greatest is the joy of watching a little girl go skipping down the road after I have helped her find her way."

CHAPTER XVI

An Adult Class of Farmers Solves
a Long-time Water Problem

*"The wise man of Miletus (Thales) thus
declared the first of things is water."*
—*J. S. Blackie*

PART I

INTRODUCTION

Approximately twenty-five miles southwest of Montgomery, Alabama, is Haynesville, Alabama, a rural village with a population of about 1500. This village, located in Lowndes County, which is in the Cotton Belt, is a typical southern rural settlement. Eight and one-half miles southwest of Haynesville is Central Community,[1] where for years cotton has been the main farm cash crop. Recently, the trend in this community has been toward more diversified farming with livestock taking a more dominant role. As one approaches the community, he sees moderately rolling land of grayish brown to reddish brown acid clay soil which is closely associated with the true "Black Belt" soils.[2] This classification (land type) grades into relatively level land with black clay soils on flood bottoms of the "Black Belt" area, in which Central Community is located. Typically, areas of this type overflow with water during the rainy seasons, yet the streams go dry during the summer. The homes, though modest, appear comfortable and compare favorably with rural houses in this section of the state.

The community is about two and one-half miles long and is composed of 40 families. In addition, there are three families on the western periphery. Thirty-seven of these families are land-

---

[1]Sociologically, Central Community is a *rural neighborhood*. However, since this chapter is based on an actual situation, the writers will refer to this locality as a Community to be in harmony with the description given to it by the people living there.
[2]Alabama Department of Agriculture and Industries, Soil Map, State of Alabama, Montgomery, Alabama, 1953.

owners with an average of 60 acres per farm. The people in the community seem happy and content with the expectation of living to the fullness of their days in their present locations.

On the northeast edge of the community is located the Lowndes County Training School, which conducts public education from grades one through twelve. The school was organized some 46 years ago by consolidating three grammar schools that were located in the county. At present, the school has 47 acres of land. Of this, 10 acres are devoted to the campus site and 37 acres to general farm land for the school. There are five buildings on the campus. One is a brick administration building with seven classrooms and a combination library and auditorium with a seating capacity of 450. Another is a classroom and shop building used for teaching of Vocational Agriculture. A third is a frame building used for teaching the elementary grades, and the fourth is a concrete block building used as a vocational home economics classroom. The building program for the near future calls for an extension of the administration building to house 27 classrooms and a new Vocational Agriculture Building.

Vocational Agriculture has been taught at the Lowndes County Training School since 1918, only one year after the passage of the Smith-Hughes Act.[3] The influence of the Vocational Agriculture department with its two teachers extends to 17 neighborhoods which the school serves, over an area of more than 20 miles.

THE WATER PROBLEM

Of all the necessities of life that have an economic value, water is the cheapest and most plentiful. It is also indestructible. Water costs less than dirt and is abundant. Three-fourths of the earth's surface is water and it is continually being formed. Most water is in the atmosphere. Some is on the earth's surface, and some is under the surface of the earth. Even with the earth's abundance of relatively cheap and indestructible water, it becomes a scarce commodity at certain times and in certain places.

---

[3]The Smith-Hughes Act, passed by the Sixty-fourth Congress of the United States, was enacted for the purpose of developing and promoting vocational education in agriculture, trades and industry, and home economics, and for the training of teachers for those fields through a plan of cooperation between the Federal Government and the States.

Such was the case in Central Community, Lowndes County, Alabama, during the 1940's and the early 1950's.

Water is an important item that has many uses. The primary uses for water in agricultural communities are for human, animal, and plant consumption. When discussing the weather, the farmer is engaged in "shop talk" for the success or failure of his business enterprise depends largely on it. In recent years, the farmer has more and more been able to do more than just talk about water. He has been able to do something about it so far as meeting his own needs are concerned.

Alabama is located in the humid section of the United States where the average annual rainfall from 1886 through 1938 was 53 inches.[4]

In recent years greater uses of water in rural areas, decreased annual rainfall and increased livestock production have caused a need for increased efforts to secure and preserve water for domestic and farm use in some areas of Alabama.

The farmers freely described the water problems that existed in Central Community before cooperative efforts of the people achieved a solution. Said one farmer who owns a country store and sells gasoline from two gas pumps in front of it: "We had no water fit to drink even when it rained often. Surface water is no good for a family to drink. Then the drought came and we had no water for our livestock." Another farmer in the community commented: "People were drinking water that smelled. It was where cows drank water." As the discussion went on, he reiterated, "I actually saw people drinking water from places where cows drank." Another farmer who was a blind preacher and evidently well-thought-of in the community observed: "Son, we couldn't even offer a visiting friend and neighbor a drink of clean water during the hottest days of summer."

Such descriptions of the water situation in Central Community were plentiful. The water supply for home use had been secured largely by dug wells which ranged from a few feet to 25 or 30 feet in depth. Some farmers in the community traveled as far as eight miles to secure water for domestic use. To get this water some farmers paid nominal fees, some did chores, and some secured water free of charge from gracious owners.

---

[4]Climate and Man: *Yearbook of Agriculture*, 1941, United States Department of Agriculture, Washington, D.C., United States Government Printing Office, page 753.

There were only a few farm ponds in the community, and fewer still with adequate depth and breadth to supply water for livestock during the summer. Live streams, common in some communities, are practically nonexistent in this section. Farmers within the community who owned farm ponds shared them with others. Naturally this required herding farm animals from one farm to another which caused inconveniences and loss of time, with the possibility of spreading contagious diseases over the community.

For the farmers in Central Community, Lowndes County, Alabama, a paradox prevailed. Water, which is in plentiful supply over the earth, was not conveniently available to them in sufficient quantity. And they knew, as expressed by one of the farmers, that "Wishful thinking has never accomplished any task. It requires wishful thinking and work."

First Attack on the Problem

In July, 1940, J. T. Haynes accepted a position as teacher of Vocational Agriculture at the Lowndes County Training School. After two years in that position, he was inducted into the army. However, from 1940 until 1942, he was able to make his presence in the community felt and was well accepted by the time that he went into the army. The school superintendent assured him of re-employment when his tour of army service terminated.

Mr. Haynes returned to his job in September, 1945, after having served three years in the army. Immediately he conducted a farm survey, the results of which gave him indications of the acute need for more adequate water in addition to other such needs as sanitary toilets, screen windows and doors, painting of homes, and general farmstead and farm improvement.

In November of the same year, Mr. Haynes organized two adult classes, one in McDuffie Community, the other in Central Community. A unit of work was started in each class on the farm water supply. Due to interest in other subjects, this unit was later dropped in the McDuffie Community but continued for 15 meetings in Central Community. While various lessons in the unit were concerned with subjects such as the water needs for plants and animals, construction of farm ponds, purification of water for domestic use, and testing of water for sanitation, the instruction consistently referred to more adequate sources of water for human consumption.

Increased numbers of livestock that were being recommended and brought into the community during this time gave greater emphasis to the need for providing adequate farm ponds. Also, Mr. Haynes was instrumental in getting a farm pond established on the school farm which was used as an example of what was needed to be done. Largely because of these classes, many of the farm ponds were improved and made more adequate. Also, the total number of farms having farm ponds increased from about 30 percent in 1945 to 100 percent in 1948. At this point, the Vocational Agriculture teacher continually made the comment to farmers in the community that water provision for animals was more adequate than it was for humans.

A period of restlessness and agitation existed from 1948 to 1952. During this period, Mr. Haynes said, "I was still preaching the same sermon—an adequate water supply for humans."

Since it was known that most farmers in the community were not able to finance water systems on their individual farms, in March, 1952, the Adult Farmer Class of Central Community appointed a committee for the purpose of investigating and planning a community water system. That committee appointed the Vocational Agriculture teacher as the "contact man." It was his duty to make contacts over the state wherever and with whomever he could find to get enlightenment, suggestions, procedures, etc., on the subject. Mr. Haynes was to report his finding to the committee where they were to be discussed and presented with recommendations to the adult class. The contact man made an effort to get in touch with all persons and agencies suggested to him by members of the class.

The contact that seemed most promising to the adult class was one made by Mr. Haynes with a representative of a lending agency located in Montgomery, Alabama. Robert R. Pierce, who is principal of Lowndes County Training School and who occasionally attended adult class meetings, felt that this project was a very worthy endeavor and he actively gave his support to it in every desirable way. He suggested that Mr. Haynes see a Capital City Gas Company representative from Montgomery who was a friend of a representative of the lending agency. During this time the Capital City Gas Company representative was in the community installing gas at Lowndes County School.

He was able to get Mr. Haynes in contact with the representative of the lending agency who agreed to meet with the adult farmer class and discuss how his agency might be used to finance the proposed community water system.

In October, 1952, representatives of the lending agency and the Capital City Gas Company met with the Central Community Adult Class at the county training school. The Vocational Agriculture teacher, who presided over the meeting at the request of the president, gave the background of the water problem and the type of solution that the class was seeking.

The representative of the lending agency explained the agency for which he worked and how it might be used to finance the proposed community water system. At the conclusion of his discussion, the representative made some recommendations to the group and opened the meeting for questions and comments from the floor. A lively question and answer period ensued, and the farmers appeared to accept the recommendations that had been made. Most of the discussion was in terms of success of the venture. Finally the question of possible failure arose. The representative of the lending agency then explained that this was a very unusual type of project for his agency to finance, and that in case of failure, his agency was not going to lose money. If some farmers, for one reason or another, became unable to pay their share of the debt, other members of the group who were able would be compelled to pay the entire loan. Personal property could be confiscated in case the debt was not paid. The discussion indicated that this liability feature "threw cold water on the project" though it was not expressed that night.

The representative of the lending agency was thanked for his time and patience and he was informed that the group would subsequently let him know its decision. Actually, the matter died right there. During the ensuing days and weeks, farmers discussed the plan informally and an attitude developed which was hostile to the plan. The farmers disliked the liability feature of the plan.

THE WATER PROBLEM SOLVED

After the failure of the attempt to get water for domestic use in 1952, no direct effort was made again until 1954. According to the Vocational Agriculture teacher: "This delay was necessary in order to let the scar of the first attempt heal over. Also, the domestic water problem constantly got worse as a result of severe droughts in 1953 and 1954. Persons who had water became increasingly reluctant to give or sell it to others." The Vocational Agriculture teacher felt that this was an appropriate time again to attempt a cooperative solution to the domestic water problem.

In September, 1954, the Agriculture Department at Lowndes County Training School was made a two-teacher department by employing Lee Ernest Jackson. As principal of a Junior High School in northwest Lowndes County for four years, Mr. Jackson had previously demonstrated his ability as a professional worker and a leader among rural people. The two agriculture teachers, Mr. Haynes and Mr. Jackson, immediately began to think and work on a solution to the water problem. On November 16, 1954, they mailed a letter to each member of the Central Community Adult Class calling for a special meeting on Tuesday, November 23, at 7:30 p.m. at the Lowndes County Training School to reconsider the community water problem.

Twenty men and one lady attended this first meeting. Mr. Haynes, acting as chairman of the meeting, asked Rev. J. C. Lawson to conduct the spiritual devotion, after which he thoroughly explained the purpose of the meeting and the need for pure water for healthy bodies. Following the remarks of Mr. Haynes, a discussion period gave indications of a serious determination to solve the problem at hand. Such questions as these were asked and discussed: 1. Where should the well be located? 2. What would be the cost of construction? 3. Who should be employed to drill the well? 4. What terms for financing the project could they expect?

Mr. Haynes then introduced J. W. Mathews and Scott Billingsley, County Agents in Lowndes County, who gave informative and inspirational talks on the possibilities of a community water system.

By this time the group showed eagerness to get organized for an attack on the problem. Officers for the group were elected as follows: R. C. Maye, President; Coley Whiting, Vice President; L. E. Jackson, Secretary; Carnelius Williamson, Treasurer; Rev. J. C. Lawson, Chaplain; J. T. Haynes, Reporter; Ed Crosby, Counselor.

The newly elected president appointed a board of directors consisting of Messrs. Whiting, Williamson, Stallworth, Maye, Logan, Crosby, Haynes, Jackson and Lawson. The first assignments of the board of directors were (1) to suggest a site for the well some place near the half-way distance between the Ross home and "Rudolph's Hill," which were the extreme ends of the community, (2) to get estimates of cost for a deep well from well-drillers, and report their finding to the group at the next meeting. It was suggested that the driller with the best bid be invited to the next meeting. The group agreed to hold weekly meetings on Tuesdays at 7:30 p.m. at the County Training School.

At the second meeting held on November 29, 1954, the board of directors reported that the distance from the Ross home to Rudolph's Hill was two miles. The halfway mark, which would be one mile from either place, would fall on property belonging to Ed Crosby. It was reported that Mr. Crosby, a member of the board, had agreed to sell one-half acre of land on the highway and at the desired spot for $50 which was considered a very reasonable price. The board recommended that the land be purchased for the stated price and that $1.75 be collected for that purpose from each member that night and put in the treasury until the deed could be drawn up and the transaction made. The group accepted the recommendation and readily began paying the fee at the meeting.

After $38.50 was collected from 22 of the 30 members present, a member of the board introduced W. J. Bozeman and his son as the prospective contractors for drilling the well. Mr. Bozeman explained that for $2800 his company would drill a well of about 1200 feet depth with not less than 200 feet of 4-inch black steel casing at top and 3-inch black steel casing with not less than 10 feet of brass screen at bottom. He said the well would furnish not less than 30 gallons of potable water per minute.

Mr. Bozeman also stated that for $650 his company would install a pump in the well with all switches and a 120-gallon pressure tank that would pump 22 gallons of water per minute at 20 pounds of pressure and 17 gallons per minute at 40 pounds of pressure.

After a period of questioning Mr. Bozeman for purposes of clarification on his proposal, the president thanked him and stated that the group would study his plan and notify him of its decision.

At the next regular meeting, December 3, 1954, the group decided to accept the bid of W. J. Bozeman and Son, Contractors, and the board of directors was ordered to enter into a contract with the company on behalf of the group. Members of the group decided that the project would be financed by equitable assessments on individual family participants. After the total cost, to include cost of land, deeds, well and pump, was calculated, the group voted to sell shares in the project for $114.75 per family member. A total of $1,371.75 was collected from 15 of the persons present at this meeting.

The president asked Mr. Haynes to have a surveyor survey the land to be purchased for the site and he requested that all participants pay their share at the next meeting. The real work on the project then got underway.

With the exceptions of those weeks when people were too busy, weekly meetings on this project were held until the middle of May, 1955. (By that time, the project had been completed and it was decided in the May 28th meeting that subsequent meetings would be on a quarterly basis primarily for the purpose of making reports and checking on the progress of the use of the well.)

At the December 13, 1954, meeting, the treasurer reported a total of $2092.75 in the treasury. The money was always deposited in the Fort Deposit Bank, Fort Deposit, Alabama, and could be withdrawn only on the basis of a written statement by the president countersigned by the secretary. At the same meeting, Mrs. Martha Lawson suggested that the well be named the "Ed Crosby Community Well," in honor of a lifetime member of the community, counselor for the project, and member of the board of directors. Mr. Crosby, a man of high moral and spiritual values, had long ago earned the respect and esteem of the people in the community. His pleasing personality enabled him to get along well with others and to be liked by others. The suggestion of Mrs. Lawson met the approval of the group.

At the February 7, 1955, meeting, the contract between the board of directors of the Ed Crosby Community Water Project and W. J. Bozeman and Son, Contractors was read and approved by the group and signed by the directors. The president asked the secretary to write the manager of the Pioneer Electric Cooperative at Greenville, Alabama, requesting him to have installed a 220-volt electric line to the pump with a switch box and meter. At the next meeting a committee of five was appointed to formulate a Constitution and By-Laws for the project. At a subsequent meeting, this committee submitted the Constitution and By-Laws which were read and accepted with minor changes.

At the regular meeting held February 17, 1955, a committee of seven was appointed to develop a program for the dedication. The eight women who were at this meeting volunteered to raise the money needed for the construction of a pump house. At the next meeting, on February 28, 1955, these women turned in $61.60 which they raised at a Box Supper. Mr. Haynes was instructed to have a local builder build the house at a cost of $62 which had already been agreed upon.

The report made by the program committee on the dedication ceremony was read and adopted at this meeting. The main speaker was to be James Pierce, a young man who was born and reared in the community and was now teaching at Alabama State Teacher's College. The dedication held on April 7 was an inspiration to the community.

In the meeting on May 28, 1955, it was decided that persons who were not members of the project be permitted to use all the water needed for a fee of $2.00 per month. Provision was also made at this meeting for a person not already a member to join the project by paying the full share of $114.75 at any time, or he could pay one-third down, $38.50, and pay the remaining two-thirds within the same year. Dues for full members were set at 25 cents per month.

At the present time there are 38 shareholders in the project, and 6 monthly renters, some living outside the community proper, who pay for water privileges by the month. All debts are paid and the financial balance sheet looks encouraging.

As one talks with farmers in the community who are members of the project, he senses the pride that these individuals have in their accomplishment. He realizes that this achievement took courage, vision, determination, faith in God, faith in self and fellowman, good leadership, and good followship. Many problems were faced and conquered, which is largely the reason for pride in the project. This pride is evidenced in the eagerness of farmers to talk about the project and in such statements as: "and we did this all by ourselves."

In talking with these farmers, one finds that they encountered skepticism on the part of some, adverse circumstances and sometimes hostile attitudes as they worked toward a solution to the water problem. Certainly raising almost $4,000.00 among farmers who had been victims of droughts for four consecutive years was not easy.

Although major credit for the success of the project goes to the Vocational Agriculture teachers and the nine members of the Board of Directors, one is impressed by the constant use of the term "we" when talking to any of the adult class members. You get to feel that these farmers really have the feeling of oneness with each other. That they know the meaning of fellowship, brotherhood, and love for God and man.

Of all the farmers interviewed, there was unanimous agreement that the Ed Crosby Community Water Project was operating very satisfactorily. They also agreed that they could think of no better way to proceed if called upon to do the same project again. When asked what would be their advice to persons starting a cooperative activity such as this, the farmers replied: "Be sure there is a need for it. Get the people interested in the activity by helping them to understand the need. Bring the women in on every phase of the activity. Make it voluntary. Select leaders who have integrity. Be honest with the funds. Organize and have a well-balanced plan and work according to it."

FUTURE OUTLOOK

> "Now understand me well: It is provided in the essence of things that from any fruition of success, no matter what, shall come forth something to make a greater struggle necessary."
> —Walt Whitman

Success breeds success and a longing for it. Having subdued the domestic water problem, the farmers in Central Community, Lowndes County, Alabama, now look for new problems to attack and solve through cooperative action. The pleasant experiences gained through this cooperative activity have sparked members of the project to a desire to help others with similar needs, and to surge further in cooperative activity in their community.

As to the future of the water project, two things are planned: (1) Other communities in the county are now anxious to start such projects, and the Board of Directors of the Ed Crosby Community Water Project plan to give aid and assistance to them. (2) Plans are underway to install an overhead reservoir and to run a water main from the well site that will eventually pass the house of each member of the project. These persons will be entitled to tap into the water main where it passes their houses.

Although the farmers plan to attack only one problem at a time, they are already looking beyond the water main into the possibility of cooperative buying and servicing of expensive farm machinery such as cotton pickers. Also, the cooperative purchase of purebred livestock has been thought of as having possibilities for future cooperative action by farmers in Central Community, Lowndes County, Alabama. One thing is sure, a need has been met through cooperative enterprise in this community. The farmers have come to recognize strength, joy, and success through cooperative activity. They now plan to use this instrument for solving new and bigger problems in the future.

PART II

ANALYSIS OF CENTRAL COMMUNITY PROJECT

The success of the water project in Central Community, Lowndes County, Alabama, can be attributed to the wise use of several principles of democratic leadership. Principles used to achieve this milestone are common and yet important for successful democratic group activity.

Democratic Principles Used. There had been *knowledge* of the water problem for some time. However, farmers in the community had formed the *habit* of depending on others to meet their water needs. It was not until the water problem became serious due to severe droughts and increased livestock in the early 1950's that farmers felt *challenged* to attack the problem seriously. This *challenge* was intensified by the Vocational Agriculture teachers who continually explained the dangers of inadequate water supply and helped to give *direction* to the attack on the problem.

The principle of *participation* is clearly evidenced. Farmers attending the first meeting to consider the water project were encouraged to *participate* fully in discussing the what, who, why, where, and when of the project. This type of activity continued throughout the planning, development and operational stages of the project. Also, the women actively *participated* in the venture. This widespread *participation* increased *knowledge* of need and possibilities for solution. It also helped develop the *group mind* which is so vital to a feeling of oneness or singleness of *purpose.*

Sharing of the leadership role was widespread and probably increased the "we" feeling among the farmers. A corps of officers of the parent body was functional. Also, several subcommittees with their officers played important roles in the development of the project. Wise use of the principles of *knowledge, participation, sharing, group mind, purpose* and *challenge* facilitated the effective use of the principle of *direction.* That leadership is a group phenomenon is evidenced from the way that *sharing* and *direction* operated. All *direction* and other activities were *integrated* through the parent body and with full *knowledge* of it.

Flexibility of two sorts was demonstrated. The first attempt to solve the water problem failed in 1952 due in part to undesirable features of making a loan. The second and successful attempt used direct subscriptions as the means for raising the money. The change in approach was the result of the first *experience* the group had. Secondly, leadership was selected for particular phases of the work depending largely on the interest and ability of members of the group.

Finally, the principle of *service* ran throughout the development of this project. All phases of the leadership evidenced unselfish efforts toward group goals. Members of this group amply demonstrated a belief in *service* above self, that a life of *service* is a life that counts. Actually, they contributed most to themselves when they tried hardest to help their neighbors. And so, through the use of the principles of *leadership,* the people of Central Community, Lowndes County, Alabama, have developed a facility that will contribute to the health and well-being of their families and yield them personal satisfaction that can come only through achievement.

Principles Omitted. All *principles of democratic leadership* were used at one time or another in the establishment of the Ed Crosby Community Water System. When the first attempt to solve the water problem was made, there was insufficient *knowledge* concerning various methods of financing the project.

If a variety of possible methods had been presented and studied in 1952, it is likely that the acceptable one used in 1954 would have been discovered two years earlier. This would have prevented the delay in the progress that was made toward the solution of the problem. When the only method considered in 1952 was not acceptable, the group considered no alternatives and disbanded. If the method considered in 1954 had not been acceptable, disintegration and failure would have been the result a second time for still no alternative method had been presented. To prevent such faltering, *knowledge* of several possible methods to attain group *purpose* should be decided upon. The group might decide the order in which possible methods will be explored. *Flexibility* of this kind is usually desirable.

Alternative Actions. Possibly other methods might have been used which would have enabled the citizens of Central Community to develop their water system. However, the one finally agreed upon by the group was the most feasible as it eliminated the borrowing of money and long-drawn-out legal transactions. This was a saving of time and money.

There is hardly anything that is done that could not be improved upon. Experience is still probably the best teacher. Future group activity in Central Community will probably make even better use of the principles of democratic leadership.

CHAPTER XVII

A County Library Is Developed in Missouri

This story is one of defeat and success. It contains evidences of failure to use democratic principles of leadership and examples of their effective use in determining techniques. X County remains anonymous in this example because many of those who were involved in the errors in planning for a county library might be embarrassed were it identified. The authors believe that this should not be so since in leadership for community betterment, mistakes are often made and provide the basis for later and correct actions. It appears that this was the case in obtaining the county library to be described.

In this story particular attention should be focused on the initial need for cooperative efforts which leaders overlooked; on the effect of disruptive forces at the state level; on the changes in the use of principles, methods, and techniques during the ten-year period; and on the reasons behind the present success of the county library. The analysis following the story will be made in terms of the principles used, principles overlooked, and alternative courses of action which might well have been taken.

A LIBRARY FOR X COUNTY[1]

In 1945 it did not appear that a county library with book-mobile service was wanted in X County. The need for better library service may have been recognized by only a few people in the county. In fact, most citizens probably had not realized such a service existed unless they had heard from friends or read about such a project in other areas. Nevertheless, it was at this time, immediately following World War II, that the Missouri State Library was introducing a promotional campaign to develop county and regional libraries supported by local tax levies. They believed that it was their professional responsibility to get citizens to see the need for library service. The State Library

---

[1] The basic data for this story were contributed by Miss Doris Beebe, Home Demonstration Agent, Jefferson City, Missouri.

was short of funds but attempted to sell the library idea in the state by the use of a state bookmobile. One gift bookmobile was available for demonstration to 114 counties. It was the hope of the State Library that through publicity and talks to organized groups (and a general promotion program) interest might be aroused among local people to the point where they would make one of two decisions. The first would be complete acceptance of the need for better library service, followed by the holding of elections and voting of a tax levy to support such a project in the county. The second, considered less important but still very desirable, would be for citizens to contribute funds toward the purchase of additional demonstration bookmobiles. These bookmobiles would be controlled by the State Library and used for demonstrations in all parts of the state.

A women's state organization with headquarters in X County heard about the library idea and voted to have a year-long fund raising campaign to aid in the purchase of a bookmobile for the State Library.

Subsequently, other state organizations were contacted. The Home and Community Department of the Farm Bureau and the Missouri Federation of Women's Clubs gave bookmobiles to the State Library. Because the headquarters of the women's organization was in X County it was recognized by having the bookmobile brought to their courthouse square for a two-day stay. Visitors were welcome to examine the bookmobile and ask questions. Favorable publicity was given through press and radio.

Later, a representative of the State Library came to X County. One of his first contacts was with the personnel in the Cooperative Extension Office. "Would the agents assist in the promotion of the project by introducing the representative to the Women's Extension Council and the 4-H Council?" The extension agents were new to the county and hesitant to begin work on such a project without more information. They had no knowledge of how their cooperating local leaders felt about library service, but though hesitant, they agreed to have the library representative appear for 10 to 15 minutes on the program of the next Women's and 4-H Council meetings to explain the State Library's proposal. At this time there were three city tax-supported libraries located in the county. Librarians and library boards were contacted by representatives from the State

Library. They also contacted the county superintendent of schools, P.T.A. officers, local editors and civic organizations. When the city librarians and library boards were consulted, they were not ready to help. They felt that suggestions for greater service were a personal insult to their efficiency in serving the people; "County as well as town people could obtain library cards." The county superintendent of schools and county P.T.A. officers thought it was a good idea but made no concrete offers to aid the project. State Library representatives appeared before a number of groups, sometimes through the half-hearted efforts of extension personnel and at other times through their own persistence.

The Women's and 4-H Councils had no objections but did nothing to improve the county library service. No one made any efforts to coordinate the thinking of the various groups. The first step was mainly to present the desirability and the procedure for obtaining service to anyone or any group that would listen. Attempts to get several groups to look at the need jointly were never made. It appeared that county library service was not a community concern of high priority.

Several years after the first bookmobile demonstration, extension club leaders inquired as to how they might start proceedings to get the matter of better library facilities before the public. This was quite different from the initial contact, at which time the extension agents "allowed" them to hear the library story. This time they were asking for it themselves.

By this time, the State Library had secured a very good colored sound film which very aptly displayed the operation of the library and bookmobile in another state where this library service had been established. They were most willing to bring this film to extension groups in the county. Promotional leaflets were distributed. In most instances, a short, effectively-led discussion followed the film showing. This seemed to help considerably in arousing enthusiasm.

About 1950 there was a change in the administration of the State Library. The next contacts between the County and the State were by a librarian who was unfamiliar to the local people and with what had gone on before. The newness to the job and the inexperience and insecurity of a person under such conditions made it most difficult. The response of the local people lacked enthusiasm. This led to the entire project being dropped in 1953.

In the meantime the effective promotional efforts of the State Library and strong local leadership had resulted in the establishment of county libraries in several neighboring counties. These counties were considered less wealthy and progressive by people in X County. Once again a favorable attitude toward county library service began to appear in X County. One cannot be sure just how the idea spread, but the nearness of service in other counties was definitely related to acceptance. Perhaps relatives and friends were a factor. Interest in the possibility of a county library service increased and it was discussed by a number of organized groups. In late 1954, the County Farm Bureau took the lead in sponsoring a meeting of representatives from the following organizations: women's extension clubs, 4-H clubs, P.T.A., newspaper, radio, TV, school administrators, library boards from the three cities, chambers of commerce, and civic organizations. The purpose of the meeting was to explore possibilities of a county library system. A representative of the Farm Bureau presided. A member of the State Library was invited to attend as a resource person to explain the potentials of such a service.

This time the State Library had added incentive to get a library started in a county like X County. The librarian explained that free demonstration bookmobile service could be made available to the county for one year beginning with a summer vacation reading program for children as well as adults. If, after one year of free demonstration, a number of people felt that the service was worthwhile, they could cause an election to be held on the question of establishing a permanent service. If the election was favorable, this service would be financed by a one-mill tax.

At the meeting of representatives of the various organizations, a chairman and secretary were elected. The group voted to sponsor the demonstration for one year. A number of committees were established to provide the necessary action to map bookmobile stops, plan publicity, develop plans for long-time financing, and to appraise results.

The bookmobile service provided by the state became available a few months later. A very able librarian was in charge.

A local family in each community was named by the planning committee to assist the librarian with the stops for the bookmobile. The schedule was remapped when schools opened in the Fall. An early appraisal showed that parents and children used the service a great deal. When schools opened, the rural teachers welcomed the library as a service which would be very helpful in expanding the resources available to the rural schools.

To promote additional interest, the librarian encouraged the formation of reading clubs. Certificates were given to boys and girls who read a certain number of books. Displays concerned with books for both children and adults were established in store windows and at local fairs. The librarian and the local committees made every possible effort to bring the library service to the attention of the county public.

Members of the local committees and the State Library staff were very desirous of obtaining the cooperation of one of the city libraries for headquarters, storage, and interchange of books. After considerable study, the library board in the largest of the three cities saw the advantage in greater exchange and circulation of books and cooperated by offering space in its building. No additional funds were needed for rent.

The local executive groups started early in the winter to promote the idea that this was a free service for one year only. They made it clear that it was for demonstration only. If the people thought the service was worthwhile, they would have the opportunity of voting a one-mill levy at a special Spring election. Only after a favorable vote would library service in X County be of a more permanent nature.

Papers and radio stations cooperated as much as possible by using stories and pictures showing local people enjoying the service, printing testimonials from teachers, and describing the opportunities that could be available on a permanent basis. When the election was held the vote carried by a good majority. The permanent project is now in operation. From all appearances and reports, it is a successful community service.

ANALYSIS OF THE LIBRARY PROJECT

Democratic Principles Used. The Missouri State Library attempted to use techniques in keeping with the principle of *challenge* as they began their promotional campaign in X County.

The challenge was to lead to two positive decisions or the alternative of no action whatever. From the story, one sees that for the most part the groups were not *challenged*. One consideration which should always be made in the practice of this principle is the necessity for knowledge and understanding of a problem or a proposal before *challenge* is possible. In this instance it appears that the foundation of knowledge concerning good library service was very weak, thus the citizens had no basis upon which to be *challenged*.

There is considerable evidence in this story that as the library project progressed the principle of *participation* was used more and more. The two-day exhibit made possible by the earlier contributions of the women's civic organization was the first example. It appears to have been used effectively by the State Library. The Farm Bureau must have had the type of leadership that recognized the importance of others *participating* when it took the lead in getting representatives of other groups together to study the possibility of a county library system. The results of this effort show the first big step toward the ultimate goal, even though the efforts which had been made before showed some progress.

The best examples of use of the principle of *participation* came at the stage where committees were formed to aid in the one-year demonstration. The committee system with the attendant responsibility given to the committeees is one of the very best ways of getting people involved. In this instance it was most effective because it was associated with a demonstration designed to reach a large number of citizens. The library demonstration technique is one which is directly related to participation. The potential of success after getting people to use the service is far greater than are attempts to obtain a library system without the citizen's first *participating* and experiencing its contributions to them as individuals. Also very effective was the use of one local family in each community to assist the librarian during bookmobile stops in their community. One could be confident of real support for the long-time project from the families who participated in the demonstration.

Related to participation in this example was the principle of *sharing*. The opportunity to *share* in the purchase of book-mobiles for demonstration purposes and then to see their contributions come back to the county in the form of a two-day demonstration must have been a thrilling experience for the women's civic group. The evidence shows that they were completely sold on the project through the opportunity to *share* that which was given to them. Later the Farm Bureau recognized that the project was too big and important for just their own group and willingly *shared* both the problem and the solution with their fellow organizations in the county.

Throughout the ten-year period groups recognized that *knowledge* was important to a successful outcome of the project. Often the lack of understanding and *knowledge* stood in the way of acceptance of the plan for a county library. Yet, from the beginning it was emphasized. The use of the bookmobile as a means of acquainting citizens with service was an attempt to inform. The request to talk to any and all groups was made in order to give them the *knowledge* necessary to make an intelligent decision. The development of leaflets and films by the State Library was both to challenge and to provide knowledge. The extension club leaders looked for ways to bring the matter to the public for the second time. They wanted the "know-how." The executive committee and the librarian made many efforts to bring *knowledge* of how the library worked and how it could become permanent to the attention of the public. Though some people will act without knowledge of results, most citizens are seekers of facts, reasons, and outcomes. They want to *know* why and how.

It is interesting to note how the total plan of the county committees and the State Library depended upon *habit*. The one-year demonstration idea is designed to get people in the *habit* of using the library service. Both groups seemed to have the confidence that once people became accustomed to what the library had to offer, they would want to continue such an experience. Every effort was made during the year-long demonstration to get people to use the service. The more use that could be made during the demonstration year, the more likely would it become *habit* for those who used the service. This would be the core group to aid in the campaign to make the county library a permanent service.

The principle of the *group mind* seemed to be recognized more by the Farm Bureau leaders than by any other group. Their meeting with representatives of other organizations, not to sell their own plan but to study potentials and develop a joint plan for action, was an excellent approach. Even though the alternatives were limited, representatives of many groups could use their cumulative wisdom to make the final decision.

Though the *purpose* of good library service was not well understood during the early stages of the campaign for a county library, every group involved made an effort to bring the *purpose* of the plan to the attention of others. The early attempts seemed ineffective more from lack of communication than from lack of desire. Effective communication of the *purpose* of good library service and clarity of *purpose* on the part of all concerned didn't come until after the Farm Bureau sponsored its group meeting for representatives of other agencies and the demonstration year was begun. During that year the variety of methods used made more citizens aware of the *purpose* and more willing to pursue it as their own goal.

One criticism which could well be made of the early stages of the plan for a county library is the lack of attention to the *processes* (methods) by which it could be accomplished. More will be said of this later, but an examination of the first years of the story shows little attention given to the *process* by which the goal was to be reached. However, when the demonstration year began, excellent methods were used to bring good library service and an understanding of it to the public. It may well be that one person, the librarian, was the first really to take the principle of *process* into account.

There are few instances in the first nine years of efforts to gain a county library that show real *direction* to the project. No one person or group had or was willing to take the responsibility of keeping the efforts for a library on a straight and forward path. The representatives of the State Library may have believed that as an outside resource they could not direct; the extension agents believed that they knew too little about libraries; the city librarians were afraid that it would reflect on their own libraries; and civic groups were more interested in learning than in *directing*. It was only after the formal selection of officers and committees prior to the demonstration year that responsibility to give *direction* was given to and taken by anyone. From then on, by means of committees and assistance by the librarian during the demonstration year, there was able and ample *direction* given to those ideas and plans which were suggested.

One good example of the use of the principle of *emulation* is the use of community families to aid the librarian with the bookmobile stops. Whether this was considered by those leaders planning this system is not known, but the setting to *emulate* is ideal.

Two examples of recognition of the principle of *training* are clear in the story. The extension agents and the representatives of the State Library, in their first discussion in 1945, considered the Women's Extension Council and the 4-H Council as the groups to hear about the potential of the library demonstration. These councils are often the best *trained* leadership core in the rural areas of the county. The second example is one of *training* rather than recognition of *training*. It involves the selection of one family in each community to help with bookmobile stops. The *training* possible under such a system did have a considerable effect on the final results.

The demonstration method in its operation can be related to a number of principles. Another important one is the principle of *experience*. The key to the State Library program appears to have been that of getting people in a county to *experience* what a good library would do for them. The State Library seemed confident that the demonstration would result in the establishment of permanent service, but realized that active support and participation of all county-wide agencies were essential. Undoubtedly it is an effective method, but it is entirely possible that putting too much emphasis on one method may lengthen the time needed to gain acceptance of a service as comprehensive as good library facilities.

Neighboring counties had established county libraries before the State Library Demonstration was available. The State Library, however, stressed the demonstration method as the most advantageous. This emphasis on demonstration may have led to their overlooking other methods. The greatest *flexibility* was that demonstrated by the Farm Bureau when they became interested in the project. It is here also that the initial efforts to *integrate* ideas and work together can be noted. From this point on, the results were rapid. All groups and individuals became aware of the plan for and accomplishment of the demonstration.

The *integration* among agencies which is needed to accomplish a project of this type is often a stumbling block to success. For several years it was that in X County.

From the representatives of the State Library to the community helpers, one principle was emphasized more than any other. It was the principle of *service*. There are even hints that, as in many other such projects, the early leaders so wanted to help the citizen that they moved faster than he was able to follow. The Women's Civic Club wanted to be of *service* to their county and the state; the extension agents felt a *service* responsibility to their council; and the community helpers would never have accepted the work responsibility they did unless they wanted to be of *service* to their neighbors. It is through the principle of *service* that one gains *leadership satisfaction*. This principle provides that extra dividend which comes with knowing that what they attempted to do for others was accomplished. The ten years of effort to improve library service in X County and its achievement must certainly have given *leadership satisfaction* to all of those involved who believed in the democratic approach to their efforts for community improvement.

Principles Overlooked. From the analysis of the principles of democratic leadership which were used, it is noted that all can be identified to some extent in the campaign for library service for X County. A number of the principles may have been followed more by accident than by design. These will be given consideration here because they do not appear to be followed consistently in the example.

The ineffectiveness of *challenge* in the early years of efforts for library service can be traced to the lack of *knowledge* of what good library service really entailed. The State Library made several efforts to impart *knowledge* during these years, yet made little progress. The *purpose* may have been clear to library representatives, but it is likely that others didn't have it clearly in mind. Extension personnel very likely aided the library without being clearly aware of the *purposes* of their effort. Analysis of the ten-year period shows considerable limitation in the recognition of the principle of *process*. From the story one gets the impression that two or three methods were all that were tried during the period from 1945 until 1953. The two main ones were talking to groups of people and encouraging the use of the demonstration bookmobile to create interest and desire for library service. After this point, films, brochures, group discussions, community helpers, and many other means were considered. During the early years the State Library may have been responsible for this limited outlook on the *process*, but they apparently got no guidance in that direction from the county leadership.

Related to lack of consideration of the various methods by which goals might be accomplished was the lack of *flexibility* in the entire *process*. The alternatives were limited, the choices to be made were always presented in terms of yes or no, and the opportunity to strike out in new directions was blocked by the alternatives presented. This *inflexibility* also appeared in the action of the city librarians who objected initially to the entire concept of a county library, and possibly on the part of the State Library and their contacts in the county.

By the lack of positive considerations for the principles of *process* and *flexibility*, certain other principles could not be adequately followed. The principle of *sharing*, though recognized in certain stages of the story, could not be used as a guide when almost all of the initial leadership rested with one person, the representative of the State Library. The principle of the *group mind* was left by the wayside during the first few years, either being overlooked or considered unimportant. Early efforts of the State Library, Cooperative Extension, and others, were all on an individual basis with only a limited chance to *integrate* the efforts of individuals and groups. On the first contact with the State Library representative *participation* was limited to listening or giving money for another demonstration bookmobile. It was possible to write a successful conclusion to the experience in spite of the fact that several principles were neglected, and others used only casually.

Alternative Actions. In this story the alternative ways of accomplishing the objective of good library service in X County are focused on ways in which the entire process could have been accelerated. Four suggestions will be made, all relating to the early promotional aspects of the county library system. The suggestions are: initial coordination among agencies; initial patience; emphasis on information before promotion; and a more positive "help seeking" attitude on the part of State Library staff.

Initial coordination among agencies. The early efforts for library service were largely "State Library Centered." Although help was sought from local groups it appears that it was to help the general cause of bookmobile service to areas of the State without it, and to purchase bookmobiles and to demonstrate the need for the service. The examples of cooperation described were typical of that shown when a group or agency is helping someone else. "We think it is a good idea," but after that no offers of help. It may have been much better to have sought suggestions and ideas on library service from the groups contacted than to have sought help. An attempt to coordinate efforts with existing libraries in the county is essential even if the anticipated outcome is negative. In attempts to sell a project rather than to find a project, the State Library had a tendency to put other groups "out on a limb." No local group feels comfortable if they're not sure that what they are doing is their own project.

Initial patience. Seeking coordination of ideas on a local problem which is only partially recognized takes time. The leader or leaders trying to get others to see the problem as their own have to combat within themselves the "I'll take over" attitude. In the example described this "taking over" delayed coordination until the time when the Farm Bureau recognized the need to follow the principle of *integration* in dealing with county library service. Direct action occasionally brings positive results. Joint action, with common purpose, brings greater accomplishment. Patience is an essential ingredient to joint action.

Emphasis on information before promotion. One and even two years of education on what good library service is and what it provides for the county would have given a more substantial basis upon which local groups could have made intelligent decisions on the problem. As it turned out, one of the important factors leading to acceptance of a county library was getting acquainted with it by association with people in the neighboring counties that had such service.

It was possible to see in the example some evidence of "railroading" through a project that isn't understood by the local citizen. If we expect to promote democratic community life, then leadership actions in line with democratic principles are a necessity. Democratic action on the part of the county citizens depends upon the basic information and understanding which undergirds their decisions.

A more positive "help seeking" attitude. Related to the first three alternative actions is a fourth which is specific to the leader or leaders of a state agency making contact with county or rural community. This is a suggestion to individual leaders who are categorized by Essert as "outside inventors."[2] Their role in initial community contact should be that of a willing listener, a seeker of local ideas, a stimulator without "needling," and an unselfish coordinator of local ideas. It is only after acceptance and direction by local leaders that an "outside inventor" is able to work for the group. The most necessary time in the story for this role to have been taken was when a new representative of the State Library visited the county. True, it should have been the attitude and action of the first representative also, but after local leaders have once looked at a problem, regardless of the elementary level, they do have sound ideas to offer. "Outside inventors" must always keep in mind that they begin their county or community leadership roles on the "outside."

The project described took ten years from the initial exploration to its acceptance by election. This is not an unusual amount of time to take to accomplish something as big and important as the development of a county library. More attention to sound democratic principles would certainly have aided the project at several stages. In spite of the identified weaknesses in developing this service, X County, its local leaders and citizens, and the Missouri State Library are to be congratulated on their accomplishment.

---

[2]Paul Essert, *Creative Leadership in Adult Education.* New York, Prentice-Hall Book Company, 1955, pp. 140-141.

CHAPTER XVIII

A Farm Organization's Part in Total Community Development

Cox's Chapel is a distinctive community. Its isolated geographic location contributes to this uniqueness. In this respect it reminds one of a mythical "Brigadoon."[1] Its people have a century-long, almost pure Anglo-Saxon, agricultural heritage in this same community. There is a unity of spirit and purpose which is believable only when one sees it through his own eyes.

Several preceding case examples dealt primarily with the subject of individual leadership for a special group. For the sake of interest and variety this chapter will illustrate and discuss *group* or community leadership as a whole. Here the principles of integration and the group mind are notably important. Cox's Chapel is a real community, admirably suited as an example for this discussion. The persons named actually lived the experiences described.

Four factors were considered essential in the selection of this case example:

1. The community should be rural and should be one which provides a comfortable living for the residents.
2. The work program of the groups should be of a noncontroversial nature in order not to bias a consideration of the principles involved.
3. The community should be located in such a way that its actions could be distinguished from those of other communities.
4. An adequate documentation and record of community activity, through time, was needed.

This record is developed from successive Community Service Reports of Cox's Chapel Grange, No. 954. The Grange Community Service Contest, conducted for ten years in cooperation with The Sears Roebuck Foundation, provides a remarkable

---

[1]The lost village in Scotland that kept itself pure from temporal earthly influence by going to sleep and awakening only one day every hundred years.

fund of authentic cases of community development. Cox's Chapel was one of the ten highest-scoring local Grange units in this national contest in 1953, 1955 and again in 1957. This analysis was checked for accuracy by several members of the community.

Cox's Chapel Community is located in Grayson County, Virginia, on the south or Carolina side of the New River. As noted in Figure 17 on page 304, it is divided by the Virginia-North Carolina state line. In 1953 when this record begins, twenty-two families were living in a horseshoe-shaped area bounded on three sides by streams. Farming was the only means of livelihood for the residents, except for five school-teaching sons and daughters and a very few others who commuted to work in villages some distance away.

There was one church (Methodist) in the community. The school was consolidated into another district many years ago so all the children must now travel out of the area for school. Likewise the nearest railroad and market place were about 20 miles away over circuitous mountain roads. To reach Independence, the county seat of Grayson County, Cox's Chapel families travel south, east and then north through Carolina territory to use Doughton interstate bridge.

Some of the children must ride a school bus 23 miles (46 miles round trip) to reach their school which is just across the river and less than two (crow-fly) miles away. One boy, after riding 18 miles, is just across the river from his home. He can use a small boat to cross the river part of the year but this is too dangerous because of high water or ice much of the time.

Agriculturally, Cox's Chapel is a dairy and livestock area. The average of the 19 farms has 113 acres of cleared land. Better than average husbandry and management practices bring to most of the families a fair income and level of living. The ground is hilly and the topsoil is shallow. Recurrent drouth seems to be an increasing problem. Nearly all of the farms are owner-operated. Farmsteads are neatly maintained. A few modest brick homes are replacing the older frame structures which in turn replaced the log houses of the first settlers. All of the roads are of secondary grade and standard. In order to keep them passable, neighbors pool their time, labor and equipment.

In 1955 there were just six organizations in Cox's Chapel. The Methodist church was the most important institution. Most of the families belonged to it. Next, and perhaps most active, is Cox's Chapel Grange. In 1955 it had 39 members and the chronology of this chapter will prove its vitality and influence in the community. A very good 4-H Club was the major youth activity at that time. A Methodist Youth Fellowship group was subsequently started. An active home demonstration club is organized in Cox's Chapel as a part of the Allegheny County, North Carolina, Cooperative Extension Service. This is by special agreement, because of the isolation from Virginia's services. There is a Community Club that embraces about the same group of families as the Grange. Mouth of Wilson, Virginia, provides postal service for the community.

The most significant feature of Cox's Chapel community life is the manner in which the people have recently integrated and coordinated their organizational efforts toward improvement. In Chapter V we defined integration as concern of each group or organization for every other and a willingness of every group to learn from the others. It fits perfectly and more! In Cox's Chapel there is not only integration; the situation approaches unity! It is difficult to tell one organization from another because the membership of each is drawn from the same homes.

If one could trace the individual and family participation in the institutions of this community he would become involved in a maze of threads leading from nearly every family into every group. The membership and leadership in church, Grange, 4-H Club and others appear to have fully sorted themselves into organizational bins according to eligibility. All the youth of 10 to 21 belong to 4-H. Most of the families belong to the Grange. Most of the women belong to the homemakers' club. Practically everyone belongs to the Methodist church. It's a sociologist's dream, so far as community integration is concerned.

The 1953 Grange Community Service report, prepared by several of the citizens, states it simply and accurately this way:

> "When you speak of the Grange, Community Club, Church, etc., you are really talking about the same people, because the Community is so small and the same people, for the most part, comprise all of its organizations.
>
> "The Grange sponsors the Community Club as its community service organ because here the Grange members work shoulder to shoulder with non-Grangers for the general good of all and the community as a whole."

One gains an impression that the people of Cox's Chapel may have discriminated carefully as to just which institutions or organizations they invited. One thing is certain. Nothing was started without the full knowledge of everyone. Communication, though informal, is practically 100% perfect. If a crow with one white wing entered the community from the west, it is likely that someone would have its photograph before it reached the east side, six miles away. And they might have phoned the museum in the meantime. The people are just that alert and communicative.

If you want to find out who are the chosen leaders in Cox's Chapel, it's important to specify the date and year of your interest. For leadership is rotated and seems to be interchangeable, to a remarkable degree. Women share leadership about equally with the men. The 1955 Grange officers included a woman master and secretary, and a man lecturer, all from different families but probably all related. There have been many intrafamily marriages in Cox's Chapel since its settlement over a century ago. But there is no evidence of congenital deterioration sometimes associated with such communities.

In order to study and analyze the leadership of Cox's Chapel let us first examine the results of leadership. Then we will trace backward from result to the causes. This is done for the reason that it is impractical to isolate one or a few persons and recognize them as the key group leaders of this community. In one way or another nearly every person has a part in motivation, execution or policy making. It is indeed an integrated community with a group mind. So let's take a look at *how* the community works and *what* is accomplished. The *who* in this formula will be developed later.

Here are some excerpts quoted from the 1955 Grange Community Service Report:

"Our number one project for the year was to get a bridge across New River near the mouth of Bridle Creek. This is something that our grandfathers and fathers worked to get and something we have worked on for years but to no avail. It is true that our section, cut off from the rest of the State as it is, is small but we feel that as citizens and taxpayers we are due some consideration.

"Hundreds of letters have been written to the State Highway Department by concerned parents and interested citizens. Years ago the Board of Supervisors appropriated money to build a ferry to help the situation. It was used until one day it sank with the school bus loaded with our children. Only a kind Providence caused it to happen on the shallow side of the crossing. They were marooned for hours as it was, but had it happened on the other side of the crossing where the river is deep the entire group would have been drowned.

"High water washed the ferry away and mothers breathed a prayer of relief. So the long way around has been the way used.

"Once the Highway Commission wrote and suggested to our people that the area was too small to justify a bridge and suggested that the area be given back to the Indians.

"This was hard and only the strong of will could keep on working.

"However, a new Commissioner was finally appointed.

"Delegation after delegation pleaded our cause in Richmond (a three-hundred-mile trip each way).

"One by one the excuses and the 'run arounds' were overcome and we forever kept our cause before them and each year we worked harder and harder. Finally, a delegation to see our Senator in Washington, D.C., started the ball rolling. This year we got our 'rollers' lined up in the best manner possible and here is what happened. A revolving bridge fund, which had been abolished for many years, was activated. It came to our district this, the first year.

"Over half of it came to our county and a two hundred and eighty foot bridge was approved for our location!

"Bids have been received, the right of way secured and we have been assured that construction will start as soon as possible.

"We look forward to the day when we can change the slogan on our community welcome sign from 'The Most Isolated Community in Virginia' to 'the Most Progressive Community in Virginia.'

"Our number two project for the year has been our Community Grange Center.

"The Situation: For the past three years we have had our Grange Hall in the basement of the church and we have there carried on a somewhat limited Grange program in certain phases of Grange work. We have a few people in the community who are not Grangers and question in their minds if we should use any part of the church as a means of making money. (Example: feeding some group for pay.) Then some of our Grangers question square dancing in the basement of the church even though it is the Grange Hall.

"Instead of a limited program, our Grange group envisions a greater and wider program of service to itself and to others. With this in mind we bought 2.18 acres of land for $400. The price was high but we bought the most desirable piece of ground in the community and from a man who didn't live in this section.

"Our Community Grange Center is to be more than just a Grange Hall. However, it does contain the nicest, most complete Grange Hall in Southwest Virginia. The hall is 70 feet by 30 feet and is of granite block, (ground granite and cement). It contains a stage the full width of one end of the hall with curtains and dressing rooms. There are also provisions to add rest rooms in the future when we get running water.

"The hall will be used for all Grange work, a meeting place for all organizations in the Community, a Community meeting place, a recreational place for young and old, a meeting place for 'Family Night,' and any other for which we have a need. It will be second only to our church itself. When we move out of its basement we will be able to carry on there a fuller church program.

"In addition to the Grange Hall with all of its uses, there are other features: a memorial park where 'Old Glory' waves in the breeze, an outdoor theatre where we present special programs, a playground for young and old, a picnic area with tables and fireplace, an area for agricultural purposes and a grove. Since our land was a wooded area, we have had the help of nature's work for many years.

"All of these features will be improved and others added as we use them and see the need of other things we can do.

"Our people—men, women and children—have donated more than 2100 hours of work, given all the logs for all of the floor joists and subflooring, (4,484 board feet of oak lumber conservatively valued at $500), and have done all of the other jobs that they could do. We have hired masons and electricians. Grangers and non-Grangers have labored to make this a reality."

The new bridge and the new Grange Community Center are but two of more than 31 projects reported by the group in 1955. They gave food and shelter relief to a new young tenant family whose home burned. They supported four aged "Farmer Girls" who had very little other income. They made improvements on the roads, the Community recreation area and their church parsonage. They maintained a cemetery and a lunchroom, and gave aid to a hospital, TB drive, health clinic, Polio Fund and a 4-H Club.

They bought a movie projector, exhibited at both the Virginia and North Carolina State fairs, and they installed highway direction signs and farmstead location signs. They supplemented the meager church budget with $150.00 in order "to get a better type minister and not an old man or a college student."

Since incomes of these farms were modest, funds to pay for all of this community work posed a problem. It is not practical to put on a bake sale in Cox's Chapel. There are not enough customers to purchase from the producers. However, women of the community packed their dishes, food and salable articles many miles, dozens of times during the year, to Sparta, Independence, or Galax where they could find a settlement large enough to provide a market or a hungry crowd.

Another money-raising device is "Grange Acres." The report reads:

"As (another) means of raising funds we have Grange
Acre projects. They provide an opportunity for the group to
work as a unit and at the same time to make money to be used
in some of our many projects.

"We raised snap beans, tobacco (one of the members 'donated'
his precious tobacco acreage base earlier, according to the
1953 report), and cane in our acres. They netted us a little
over $300. This amount would have been more except for the
fact the dry weather almost ruined all the crops in this area.

"The cane we are raising now should give us better figures
for next year."

For a more complete insight into the dedications and value
systems of the Cox's Chapel community, we refer now to sections from their 1953 Grange report:

"The Methodist church is a single but all-important spiritual
symbol of the community; a chronology of the known history,
through four building programs, includes the heartaches and
the evolution of community life since 1832. The first church,
near the present site, was a log building with an open fireplace
and chimney at one end.

"The second was one of the first frame structures to be
built in the area. It still employed an open fireplace as the sole
means of heat and was constructed about 1871.

"The third church was a single-story frame structure built
about 1905, from materials and labor largely donated. By
1952 it was sagging, bulging, and inadequate for the full program of youth, Grange, and community activities that the
people wanted."

The Grange report modestly imparts the inspiring story of
how the fourth church was developed in a cooperative manner.
All families of the community worked and shared. But it was
agreed in advance that the Grange should be the spearhead
group. It had been organized originally in the church and still
held part of its meetings there. Other meetings were held in two
discarded rooms of an old home.

Figure 16 shows the new church. Its development is described in the report which reads in part:

"The community was in need of a new church and we proposed that when the new church was built that we have a
basement to be used as a Grange Hall and other desirable
Community activities. The entire building committee selected
for the church were Grange members and suitable plans for
a Grange Hall were made into the plans.

"So, we now have a new Grange Hall that is ample for all
Grange work—the total cost of building and furnishing so
far is $14,997.36 and represents 3,877 hours of (donated)
labor.

"This is a beautiful brick country church, with paneling
in the pulpit area, plastered walls, modern pews, oak floors,

carpet and memorial stained glass windows. It has an automatic oil furnace which is an air conditioner in summer. In addition to the sanctuary, there are two Sunday School rooms and a vestibule on the main floor. The basement is full sized, has a cement floor and is the Grange Hall. There are provisions for a kitchen and inside toilets, stairway and also the furnace room. The Grange Hall can be made into a dining room when any of the organizations want to serve a meal.

"A period of eight months to the Sunday was used from the last service in the old church to the first in the new church.

"Our second biggest dollar project (1953 Grange report) was our parsonage. Last year the five churches (in our charge) raised the money to buy our present parsonage. It represents a total investment of more than $8,000. Our unit now carries 49% of the total budget because two of the other churches have dropped out."

Figure 16. The New Church in Cox's Chapel, Virginia

It is obvious from this report that the Cox's Chapel Methodist Church was the most important institution in the community. In second place was the Grange, but actually all six of the community organizations and groups are integrated and coordinated by the people that belong to them and manage them.

Also we can tell that the community leadership was largely indigenous to the area. Even the minister had four other churches in his charge and was himself moved every three to five years, in keeping with Methodist practice. There was no school and therefore no formal educational leadership except on an itinerant basis.

The Dynamics of Leadership in Cox's Chapel

The people of Cox's Chapel know what they want to get and do. The principle of the group mind is working among them to stimulate new ideas, to expand community services and to keep the area "on its toes." One might speculate too that good, fast and complete communication of ideas and opinions takes place. The spirit of "love thy neighbor" and "service above self" spreads like osmosis into every facet of community life and apparently into nearly every home. These factors taken together provide a degree of community integration and group mindedness seldom achieved in the adult world.

If one were seeking to do so, he might identify and glorify the leadership contributions of several persons in Cox's Chapel. But in so doing he had best be careful. He might only photograph the contributions and situation going on at a particular time. If he arrived earlier or came back later he would see a different picture.

If one were seeking to do so, he might identify and glorify nities we have ever seen. Relatively few new families come in. There is no room for more. A normal number move away. One might expect from this that other elements of community life would be stable, too. And they are! Why doesn't the leadership remain stable then? Well, in a way it does. Let's take a broader look.

Because there is good communication among the families and because there is unity on dedications and ideals the people know what services they want. There is one church, one farm organization, one youth group, one community club and one women's club. Probably they selected these on the basis of need, rather than because an outside promoter saw an opportunity to exploit his organizational goals and gain memberships. Perhaps, too, the people feel they cannot afford the luxury of too many services that would compete for the time, money and facilities which are so limited in this community.

The people brought in these organizations and institutions as tools, not masters. Each serves a purpose—the community's purpose. Each group exists only for the people. People own them as a home or a suit of clothes. The groups help to facilitate community life because there are some things that people can do better in groups than they can alone or as families.

Coming back to the leadership—we might again observe some uniquenesses. In Cox's Chapel, leaders, like organizations, are representatives or servants of the people, not masters. They are spokesmen, not prodders. They are pushed forward by the groups and out of the groups. One gets the feeling that the community has a Grange Master only because it needs one to carry on its business. Flora B. Dutton served for a while. J. R. Walls was master for another period. Now it's someone else's turn. Joe B. Cox seemed to have an inquiring mind and a broad knowledge about many subjects, so they made him the Grange lecturer.

The Community sorts and sifts its leadership talents, then matches square pegs into square holes and round pegs into round holes. There is little thought of whether Flora has a *vested right* to inherit the master's job. It seems to be much more pragmatic than that. It's a case of the Grange needing Flora to preside at Grange meetings, moving the business forward while everyone else pushes or pulls or helps at some other job, this time. Next time Flora may be lecturer or may be chairman of the home demonstration club. And Joe Cox may become just a committee worker. Or they may push him along up the ladder to a State Grange job. There is quite a bit of talk about that.

Students of community and group organization have long recognized the relationship between action and group morale, spirit and esprit de corps. No one has successfully established which comes first, the high group spirit or the activity. But certainly they are associated together. A group that is *doing* probably is *growing*, too. People want to be associated with successful things. They will be loyal to a dying cause for a while but eventually will find other, more productive outlets for their energies.

Certainly the organizations of Cox's Chapel have morale and spirit. A subordinate Grange with 31 completed projects in a single year! There must be cooperation to run that kind of a show! Did the projects start first and the group morale follow along as a result? No, we doubt that. There must have been good team spirit and optimism present or they never would have undertaken that many. Maybe it's like having an orchard—if you want good fruit today you had to plant good trees a long time ago. And then you needed to husband them with good nutrition and cultural care after that.

Perhaps we can get a look at the basic drive or force in a different way. One of the subtle but fundamental truths in man's makeup is an urge to drive or push toward the frontiers of knowledge, and the outer edges of the earth's resources in an effort to find or secure more satisfaction, or better living for self and family. This is the motivation for most of our earthly progress. If you trace this concept carefully and far enough it's the reason why the people of Cox's Chapel do things and have things together. The 21 families of the community feel needs . . . They want satisfactions or things they don't have now.

Take the bridge across New River as an example. They gathered facts and they knew there was a better way than driving all the way around through North Carolina to cross that river. They discussed it together long enough and fully enough to know that everybody felt the same way about it. They tried a ferry. It nearly drowned their loved ones. No more of that!

Individuals and families couldn't break the inertia. So they called in stronger and more potent tools to help. Their organizations and groups carefully built up a case. They used reason, emotion, friendships, indeed every ingenious device available. They considered the timing. They delegated responsibility. They acted as one person but with the multiplying benefit of group power and influence. As a well-organized group they were successful. The bridge was finished and dedicated in 1957.

Such a group in such a community will not stop with a bridge or a church or a new Grange Hall. They will do many more things together, so long as they are united with a group mind and an integrated approach to their life and problems. If they should become careless and forget to keep everybody informed and involved—watch for trouble. If they should forget to stop and discuss each idea or issue fully, before planning ahead, watch out again. They may lose their group mindedness. Or if some one or two individuals should start to grandstand, looking for fame and acclaim, there might develop some cleavages. If the community becomes complacent—satisfied with its lot and willing to sit at home and enjoy life—watch for a plateau of activity and a firming up of current leadership roles. This in turn may be followed by a gradual decline of community activity, spirit and progress. The younger potential leaders will move out. Neighborhood rigor mortis will set in.

But as long as Cox's Chapel permits the free play, open-end existence of group mindedness to continue, they will move along cooperatively. So long as there is an opportunity for the basic drive and force of the inquiring mind to exist and explore new horizons, progress will continue. But when complacency or ultra-conservatism sits at the wheel the machine will stay mighty close to the ground and at its present location.

SUMMARY

In this chapter we have explored a few principles relating to how groups work, using a community farm organization as a case example. Now let's summarize briefly.

1. There is a basic drive or force which pushes the minds of men toward the frontiers of knowledge or experience in an effort to satisfy his needs and wants.

2. Men will use their individual talents and resources first. If they are unable to attain their goals they will join with others to multiply their own power and to stimulate additional ideas (the group mind).

3. Successful working conditions (togetherness) within the group depend upon thorough discussions of issues, good communication of ideas and complete involvement of all the members.

4. Leadership for a group is most effective if it is pushed outward rather than inflicted inward. Leaders should be spokesmen, not bosses. They should be servants rather than masters.

5. Success makes more success. A group that is dynamic attracts members and inspires more work from them. No one wants to die—either inside or outside of an organization.

6. An integrated community is more productive than a disintegrated or a competitive one. Many groups and organizations are needed to fulfill the specialized needs and interests of people in our modern society. But these should complement one another rather than fragment and splinter the talents and efforts of the population.

But is this six-point formula practical in today's world? Does it work? Is it reasonable to expect a community to know what it wants—to work together—to achieve organizational integration and a group mind? Is togetherness good for America and Americans, or must we stress individualism, diversity and competitiveness? Take another look at Cox's Chapel before you decide. Their way is good enough to give 22 families a satisfying level of living, even though basic resources are very limited. As to its appropriateness for America—more than 7000 Granges in 1957 acclaimed this tiny community as one of the most progressive in all our land. It received the national grand prize award for community improvement.

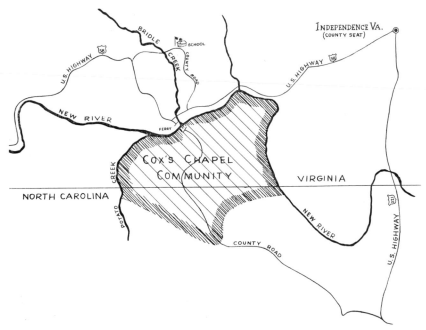

Figure 17. Cox's Chapel Community, Grayson County, Virginia

CHAPTER XIX

Rural Churches Working Together

PART I[1]

THE PRAYER OF JESUS

Neither do I pray for these alone, but for them also which shall believe on me through their word;

That they all may be one; as thou, Father, art in me, and I in thee, that they also may be one in us: that the world may believe that thou has sent me.

John 17:20-21

For years rural churches have done their work independent of each other. This has been an independence of operation of one church in the community from another of the same denomination. However, the most noticeable independence of operation of churches has been between churches of different denominations. Traditionally rural people have experienced contacts with fewer different individuals than have urban people. Rural people have traditionally seen, worked with and cared for others who are like themselves economically, socially, and psychologically, as well as spiritually. Out of this background, rural churches have developed denominational independence of each other. This was true in the Cumberland Mountains of Tennessee where this story takes place.

According to Beata Mueller, "Back in 1800 the Great Revival swept across the frontier country of Tennessee with the crackling intensity of a brush fire. Camp meetings sprung up everywhere. Men, women and children gathered by the hundreds, spent days and weeks at a time listening to ministers of various communions take turns preaching fervent evangelistic sermons.

---

[1]The basic data for Part I of this chapter were contributed by Dr. Henry Randolph, Department of Town and Country Church—Indian Work, Board of National Missions, Presbyterian Church, U.S.A.

"When the emotional fervor passed, however, disputes arose among the various denominations. The bitterness of these disputes can be measured by one preacher's characterization of his rivals as hirelings, caterpillars, hypocrites, seed of the Serpent, dead dogs that cannot bark, men possessed of the Devil, rebels and enemies of God!

"The factionalism of that time died slowly—slowest of all, perhaps in the isolated rural communities."[2]

THE ALPINE RURAL LIFE CENTER

In Alpine, Tennessee, as in many other rural communities, the rural churches with their denominational separateness have furnished leadership that has greatly improved human welfare economically, recreationally, educationally, and spiritually. However, in 1945, local leaders with the help of national church leaders of the Presbyterian Church, U.S.A., the Methodist Church, and the Disciples of Christ Church, organized the Dale Hollow Larger Parish to meet better the needs of that area through cooperative denominational endeavors.

The area has a very interesting history centered around Alpine, Tennessee. This volume will not permit an extensive discussion of the area and the personalities involved in its development, but a brief background might prove informative and interesting.

Location. Alpine is in Overton County, Tennessee, about twenty-five miles south of the Kentucky border. The Alpine Parish is the southern part of the Inter-denominational Dale Hollow Larger Parish. The village was named by John Dillard who in 1818 left his home in North Carolina for a journey through the mountains of Tennessee. John Dillard settled in this Cumberland Mountain area and for nearly 40 years served as scholar, teacher and theologian. There is no railroad through these hills. The nearest station is at Algood, 25 miles south.

Population. In this country, inhabited until 1778 only by Indians, now live Scotch-Irish folk of the Southern Highlands. The population is surprisingly dense, considering the small proportion of the land which is tillable. Until the 1930's, many people in this area were without formal public school provisions.

---

[2]Beata Mueller, "Revival in Alpine, Tennessee," *The Country Christian,* November, 1949, pp. 11-13.

And yet, Alpine is one of the superior populations in the Cumberland Mountain range. The mountain people are poor, proud, and mannerly. Their poverty and hardships have been borne cheerfully. They do not apologize for their poverty nor shrink from it. There is a certain tone of culture in their lives which springs from the continuous emphasis on religion and education.

Mountain people help to replenish the white population of many southern states. Some of the outstanding individuals native to this part of Tennessee are Tennessee Governor A. H. Roberts of Alpine; the father of Mark Twain; a World War I hero, Sergeant Alvin York of Jamestown; and a Secretary of State of the United States, Cordell Hull of Pickett County. All were born within 30 miles of Alpine.

Industry. The major portion of income has been from farming and lumbering. Poor practices in these industries have had tragic effects upon the economy and life of the people. Largely through leadership activities sponsored by the Presbyterian Church and the Dale Hollow Larger Parish, which will be discussed in more detail later, slowly and persistently the fertility of fields is being improved and the forest is being protected from fire and slash cutting.

Schools. The original settlers of this part of Tennessee were Presbyterians. They brought with them from Scotland and northern Ireland a belief in the importance of a well-trained mind. The early schools in this area were church supported and operated and they emphasized religious training.

The first school at Alpine was started in a log building on the top of Alpine Mountain in 1821 by Rev. John L. Dillard, a Presbyterian minister, and Mr. Christopher Organ. This school flourished and favorably affected the life of the area and contributed leaders of importance to a wide section of the South until it was destroyed by fire during the Civil War. In 1880, the school was re-established as Alpine Academy by leading citizens of the Alpine Community under the principalship of a Mr. Davis. The school took the name of Alpine Institute in 1889 when Albert H. Roberts and his father-in-law, B. O. Bowder, a graduate of Hiwassee College, assumed the operational leadership of the school as teachers. Under the able leadership of these teachers, the school again played an important role in training people of this area. Near the close of the century, Mr. Roberts gave up teaching to study law, the profession which led him to the governorship of Tennessee. After the Roberts family moved away, the school situation again became grave. Local leaders worked heroically to keep standards high, but inadequate tax resources, coupled with isolation and unimproved roads, made the task too great.

There was an apparent need for help which came following the union of the Cumberland Presbyterian Church and the Presbyterian Church, U.S.A., in 1906. At that time it was decided to re-establish Alpine Institute under the auspices of the Presbyterian Church. This was accomplished in 1918 under the leadership of Dr. J. H. Miller, then supervisor of the Cumberland Mountain Presbytery, and Dr. Warren H. Wilson of the Board of National Missions, in cooperation with the local citizens of Alpine community.

Miss M. K. Schoenhals was the first principal of the re-opened school. The minister of the local Presbyterian, U.S.A., Church usually taught classes and helped raise money from all possible sources to pay other instructors. The institution continued to grow until in 1936, grades 1 through 12 were represented, and State Department of Education accreditation was gained. Alpine Institute had courses in Bible, home economics, agriculture, and industrial arts, in addition to the regular courses. In view of the location of Alpine Institute, the curriculum continually emphasized subjects designed to help students live a better Christian life in the country.

In 1936, the county was able to provide the education for students in the first eight grades. At that time the county relocated these students in a new building. With the coming of better roads and busses, the need for this type of semi-boarding school declined. As attendance decreased, each year the county assumed more and more responsibility for the education of its citizens until 1945, when the Alpine High School was consolidated with Hilham High School and Livingston Academy and moved to Livingston, the county seat.

Transition. While the Presbyterian Board of National Missions was withdrawing gradually from formal schools, the leaders were exploring possibilities of rendering service in other areas of great human need. Already several key families had moved away and with the loss of the school as the nucleus of community organization, there was a danger that Alpine might almost completely fall apart. Through many conferences held by church leaders and lay people in the community, it was decided that an organized attack on community ills could best be accomplished through an organization set up for that purpose. In 1940 the Alpine Rural Life Center was organized to re-think the potentials of Alpine and to help organize the attack on community problems.

During this period of transition, the area was fortunate to have Rev. Bernard M. Taylor serving as minister of the Presbyterian mission at Alpine. Mr. Taylor, who had arrived at Alpine with his family in November, 1936, was born in Georgia. He had a love for the way of rural life. He was a naturalist who knew and loved birds, trees, flowers and wild life in general. While at Alpine, he was considered a walking encyclopedia on such matters. In addition, Mr. Taylor was aware of the problems of poverty and ill health that often beset rural people. He had come to Alpine from Pennsylvania where he had served as pastor to a group of rural churches. In Alpine, he found farms where the vitality of soil had been leached away through the porous limestone underneath. He found homes where the only light came from smoky kerosene lamps, the only heat from an open fireplace or an old barrel made into a stove, the only water supply fifty feet or more from the house.

The situation at Alpine during these days has been described by Beata Mueller.[3] "Tuberculosis was a scourge. Pellagra added its dragging fatigue to overwork. The average family income ranged from $86 to $200 a year. As the children grew up, many of them left home for work in the factories of the North because there was no adequate living to be made at home.

"Both people and land had inherent resources that could be developed. And Taylor, a 'born pioneer,' as one of his family described him, loved both the people and the land." This man, affectionately called "Bernie," had a personal magnetism that grew out of his warm desire to help people. He believed that Christian religion should affect favorably all aspects of life, health, education, politics, land, crops, and the vocations of the people. He believed that the Church should be central to the life of the community, and that the most effective help could be found only in church cooperation.

---

[3] Ibid.

The Alpine Rural Life Center, sparked by the leadership of Rev. Bernard Taylor, realized outstanding success with several projects for the Christian development of the people and their community. These projects were usually preceded with conferences or workshops for the purpose of planning steps to be taken. These conferences were often started after two or more members of the community had discussed the idea. It was not unusual for Mr. Taylor to ride horseback or go on foot to visit little churches and the homes of the area, in the gullies and up on the crest of the hills, to discuss with different people some project that might bring improved living and happiness to the people.

In order to get a better understanding of the activities carried on during this transition period, one notable project will be discussed in some detail. Others will be mentioned to give some appreciation of the scope.

Forest project. Timber was once one of Tennessee's great resources and Mr. Taylor felt that if a demonstration plot of timber could be scientifically managed, it could serve as an example of what could be done in forestry as a source of community income. There was an 18-acre forest tract owned by a landlord in a distant city that might well serve this purpose. Several conferences were held with interested local people and with state and federal forest service personnel concerning the acquisition and management of the 18-acre tract. With funds provided by a friend, the church acquired the property.

If the forest was to be useful as a demonstration plot, it had to be accessible, which required the building of a road. This was during the period of the Second World War; even if there had been funds to hire road-builders, there was no professional road building labor force available. To overcome this problem, the resourceful Mr. Taylor called a church conference of rural ministers and church leaders. These ministers and lay leaders came to the conference clad in heavy boots and work clothes, equipped with crowbars, a bulldozer and a oneness of purpose—to build a road up the mountain. They did, and the forestry project still protects the area's watershed and furnishes timber which is turned into material for buildings, furniture and wood pulp, bringing in a steady income and standing as a monument to the leadership efforts of these men.

In 1940 the Board of National Missions of the Presbyterian Church in the U.S.A. purchased 1,117 acres of forest land on the Alpine mountain. This purchase was made possible through the cooperative and relentless efforts of several church people, primarily Rev. Bernard M. Taylor, Rev. Charles T. Greenway, Dr. Henry S. Randolph, and generous gifts of Mr. James W. Brown of Cincinnati, Ohio. Leaders in the project were able to secure the interest and assistance of various foresters in the State of Tennessee and of the U. S. Forest Service. Other smaller purchases were made until in 1945 there was a total of 1,600 acres. This woodland was dedicated "The Alpine Forest Reserve" in May, 1941.

The first work in the Alpine Forest began in a small way in 1942. Management was poor until a manager and an assistant were employed in the fall of 1943. In the fall of 1944, the manager left the Alpine Forest project and a full-time forester was not employed until April, 1945, when Mr. J. Edwin Carothers assumed the position. About a year after Mr. Carothers was employed, the project began to make a profit.

The Alpine Forest project was discontinued some five years ago when this woodland was leased to private interests. The woodland continues to bring income to the community from rentals and as a productive outlet for skilled labor. Also, it serves as an example of good woodland management to landowners in the area. This educational feature has contributed materially to people in the area who manage woodland.

Other Projects. During the transition period, other small industries were started under the auspices of the Rural Life Center at Alpine with the prayer that they would become community crafts with a minimum of the evils of factory life, and a maximum of economic benefit. Some additional projects that were started are:

Demonstration Farm. At these farms, which were under trained management, good examples of what could be done to build up farms and to produce more commodities for home use and for the market were in evidence. At the completion of the demonstration period, about 1952, the farms were sold to the hired operators.

Recreational Program. This program was designed to meet the recreational and social needs of young and old. It maintained a gym and sponsored activities including singing, games, pie suppers, musicals with local talent, basketball, etc.

Weaving. This program was started to bring more income into the community. In spite of the limited market, some women in the community made good wages from this small industry. After a temporary lapse of interest in weaving because of better wages available in Detroit and other areas, the weaving program began enjoying a comeback in 1957.

Furniture Shop. This program was started to train returning veterans from the war and grew into a self-sustaining enterprise.

Planing Mill. This program was started to process timber from the forest, making it available as a finished piece for use in the furniture shop.

Pottery. This program was also started to train returning veterans, many of whom later found employment in the occupation in other areas.

In addition to the above type of activities, the Alpine Rural Life Center conducted numerous conferences for the training of Daily Vacation Bible School workers, recreation leaders, ministers and leaders of the Cumberland Mountain Presbytery, Sunday School teachers, and other activities of this nature.

To carry out this work, it was decided that an over-all staff would be necessary. Rev. Bernard M. Taylor was made general director of the staff which usually met every Wednesday night. The over-all staff was to help give guidance and direction to the activities of the above projects in cooperation with persons responsible for the technical direction of the work of each unit. It was decided that the managers of the various projects would work toward making it unnecessary for the Presbyterian Board to continue paying their salaries. The plan was to integrate the crafts with the community as cooperatively-owned community activities and then managers were to be employed by the new owners and operators of their particular projects.

Community-Staff relationships are very important in an enterprise of this kind. The philosophy of the Board of National Missions of the Presbyterian Church, U.S.A., is expressed in the following quotation: "An important prerequisite to happy church and center and community relationships is this: The community must have some voice in the selection and maintenance in the field of special workers. The happy solution of this very particular problem of administration requires a balance at the point where no one who violates the sensibilities of the people shall be appointed to serve there, while at the same time, a good man with new and perhaps surprising ideas is kept free from expulsion by reactionary minorities long enough to prove his worth and win acceptance. In the case of Alpine, the Board's policy had been to give the local Presbyterian Church the voice for approval of the candidate for the ministry in Christ Church, providing candidates suitable to the Board and letting the church congregation choose from among them the one they prefer. Other workers usually come on a somewhat similar basis—making visits to the field to know and be known—going away again to come to a decision with prayer while the local people have an opportunity to express themselves to the minister and through him to the Board. This is not always necessary, but sometimes is valuable. When it comes to a matter of replacement of workers, the same avenue of communication between community and Board is kept open, in order that, together, wise decisions may be made."

Some of the specific elements in the Church-Centered program at Alpine are the following:

Winning people for Christ, with the goal—all the people.

Helping people to become participants in a full church work.

Enlisting and training a corps of volunteers to carry on the "full church program" in which everybody is encouraged to share.

Evangelizing the Church so that it will be helpful to every person in the parish, of all ages, of every social condition, and of a half-dozen denominational backgrounds.

Living and working with the conviction that the Church is the Body of Christ in the community—a unifying influence causing neighbor to help neighbor to the glory of God. This overcomes denominational rivalry, breaking the tendency to divide up the people among themselves, according to "high Church," "low Church," or other standards.

Evangelizing "secular" life by—

a. Preaching and practicing the sanctity of home, school, and industry.

b. Nursing and praying into existence new industries in the community, and contending successfully against destructive ones.

c. Teaching over and over again the truth that these industries are part of our religion, since they make for a better spiritual life.

d. Winning those people especially who work in the church-sponsored industries to full Christian commitment, including participation in the formal program of the church.

e. Convincing more people that it is important to take an active part in the P.T.A., Community Improvement Association, Alpine Recreation Association, and other "secular" agencies for public welfare.

The Dale Hollow Larger Parish

Organization and Early Activities. Thanksgiving Day, 1944, was spent by the Alpine staff studying both the local program and the larger area of responsibility. The increasing spirit and feeling of Rev. Bernard M. Taylor that only by working together could the churches reach all the people with the help that was needed pervaded the entire staff. Much of the day was spent discussing what cooperative steps might be taken to strengthen the work of the ministry in sections of the area where it was weak, and effectively to bring it into sections where it was non-existent. Discussion and consideration of this problem occupied much of the time of staff members of the Alpine Rural Life Center for the next four months. Also, Dr. Henry Randolph, Secretary of the Department of Town and Country Church, Board of National Missions of the Presbyterian Church, U.S.A., who for a long time had an interest in the broader cooperative Christian movement in the area, now gave active support and leadership to it.

In March, 1945, Dr. Randolph, while in the area, and Miss Alice Maloney, his associate at that time, together with Presbytery and synod ministers, national and local Methodist and Disciples of Christ ministers and church officials met for two days in Alpine for a serious study of a larger cooperative church movement. This meeting, which was well attended, was called by Dr. Randolph, who was a frequent visitor to the community and was liked and respected by the people there. Out of the free and liberal discussion at this meeting grew the concept which flowered into the Dale Hollow Larger Parish and its interdenominational council.

In the beginning, the Dale Hollow Larger Parish involved three major denominations in the area: Disciples of Christ, Methodist, and Presbyterian, U.S.A. Churches, which included 18 churches and preaching points in Overton and Pickett Counties. It covered an area of about 200 square miles and influenced some 4000 people living in all the communities and neighborhoods in the area. It was discussed and decided that the entire area be divided into neighborhoods called parishes. In each parish the denomination to be adhered to was determined by the choice of the church people in that area. This prevented numerous small churches with the resulting duplication of effort, and demonstrated an unusually high order of United Christianity. Each parish is served by a minister of the denomination selected by the congregation in that area.

Major decisions that guided the early cooperative activities of the groups were made by the Larger Parish Council. This council, which met each fifth Sunday afternoon, was composed of the staff members and three representatives from each congregation. The Larger Parish Staff, which was composed of the church ministers and employed persons who served the Larger Parish, made and executed plans for cooperative activities that had the approval of the Council. Also, each year, a planning conference was held which was attended by members of the staff and official representatives of the mission boards of the three cooperating denominations. An enormous amount of discussion, and the give-and-take which is necessary for good democratic decisions, were in evidence at all three meetings. Each person entered into the discussion freely, making his or her contribution without fear of ostracism. It was immediately evident that all persons involved were working unselfishly for the goal of the Larger Parish which is: "Every home a Christian home in a Christian community."

With joint resources from this cooperative religious enterprise, some specialized person was employed to work with local churches on projects they could not accomplish alone. The work of an employed director of Christian education has been outstanding in such activities as vacation church schools, leadership courses, and religious education during the "released-time" periods in schools. Also, health work such as eye testing done in conjunction with the public school program, community improvement work, and recreation and personal counseling has been sponsored by the Larger Parish.

Early in the movement a splendid recreational program was organized and carried on the year-round in the gymnasium located on the old Alpine Institute Campus. Together with the growing Scout movement, the program did much toward providing a solution for juvenile delinquency which often results when young people have no constructive outlet for their energies.

Through meetings, paid workers, Larger Parish publications, and other mass media, an early emphasis was placed on Christian stewardship of time, talents, and possessions. Farmers were encouraged to cooperate with agencies such as the Soil Conservation Service, County Agricultural Agents, and Home Demonstration Agents in the interest of more fertile land and good Christian homes. More and more, good results were attained from this emphasis on Christian stewardship. As an example of the benefits of their cooperation with public agencies, several years ago Mr. Taylor and another Larger Parish minister, because of their familiarity with the area and its needs, helped TVA authorities map a system of electric power lines to extend into the territory. One by one, homes of the hill people have lighted up, and the drudgery of many home and farm chores has been lightened by the use of electricity.

Very significant and outstanding work has been sponsored by the interdenominational parish in the area of health. The county health department, along with a health committee from the Larger Parish, had already begun to combat many of the health problems of the area including pellagra and typhoid. However, general undernourishment was still a problem and tuberculosis flourished. Earlier, a parent-teacher organization had studied the problem of undernourishment, and in an effort to combat it, raised funds for a school lunch program. Two of the parish ministers rounded up volunteer labor and dug a basement lunchroom underneath the school building. Since then, school lunches at low cost have helped the children build resistance to illness.

After intensive study and discussion of the health situation, the interdenominational parish decided to sponsor the Dale Hollow Tuberculosis Center. There was none in the Larger Parish and even the distant sanatoriums were overcrowded. The Center was opened on June 29, 1947, with a registered nurse in charge. This, again, was the result of hard work and interdenominational planning and cooperation. The Center was located in a Presbyterian building that formerly was the girls' dormitory at Alpine Institute. The Methodists paid the nurse, and the Disciples of Christ furnished such equipment as an X-ray machine.

For additional support of the Center, patients paid what they could, which often wasn't very much. The Overton County Court made a monthly contribution. Some people outside the area who knew about the Center contributed to it, and voluntary contributions were made by local people at a real sacrifice.

At the Center the Larger Parish carried on a program of rehabilitation for patients in cooperation with the Tennessee Department of Education, so that upon recovery they again became economically useful citizens.

In addition to the work of the Larger Parish Council and Staff, the work of the Education Committee, Evangelism Committee, Finance Committee, Promotion Committee, Stewardship Committee, Health Committee, and many local people who held no official leadership position, made these and many other early accomplishments possible.

Later Activities of the Larger Parish. The Dale Hollow Larger Parish continues to grow and demonstrate outstanding interdenominational cooperation. The purpose of the Larger Parish remains basically unchanged: to undertake any religious or community work that can be done better cooperatively than by the participating churches individually. This included a ministry to each individual in the community in regard to the social, religious, educational and economic facets of life. Larger Parish work continues to include such projects as vacation church schools, week-day religious education, evangelism, leadership training, youth work, recreation, health programs, Christian cooperatives, and other activities that are agreed upon by the Council.

The organization of the Dale Hollow Larger Parish remains essentially unchanged in basic structure as well as in function. However, some very important and overdue changes in operational procedures were written into the by-laws about 1955. Currently each church chooses three lay leaders who serve on the major project committees. The Cumberland Presbyterian Church, which had become a separate group, joined the parish organization in 1956, making four cooperative denominations. Also, the number of participating churches has increased to 27, and the area covered has increased to 250 square miles within which approximately 7000 people reside. The Larger Parish Council is still the administrative unit which determines policy. It is composed of four voting delegates including the pastor from each cooperating church. One of the delegates must be a young person under 25 years of age. The Council holds regular meetings twice a year. Program operation is under the direction of an Executive Committee which is composed of the Council officers, department chairmen, and department secretaries and advisors. The Council president serves as chairman of the Executive Committee.

Four departments have been organized to help plan and carry out the activities. The departments are: Christian Education, Church Development, Community Development, and World Outreach. Special committees are appointed by the Executive Committee as needed to help plan and direct additional activities. All committees are now chaired and run by lay rather than professional leaders.

An Advisory Council, composed of state and national representatives of the cooperating denominations, local Council delegates, and members of the Executive Committee, meets once a year. This annual meeting is held to evaluate the work of the Larger Parish and to discuss future policies and plans of the Council and departments.

Several changes in leadership personnel have occurred since 1951, but the work goes on effectively, which is in itself evidence of good leadership and self-direction. Also, continuation of some of the earlier projects have been rendered unnecessary due to improved conditions. However, some new projects have been undertaken with the same kind of cooperation, vigor and vision that made the earlier ones successful.

Probably the most noteworthy service to be discontinued is the Dale Hollow Tuberculosis Center. The TB Center was closed in 1955, because the need for the service had diminished due to a decrease in number of cases and the acceptance of local patients in state institutions.

Due to increased industrialization and better farming and forestry brought about largely through the efforts of the Larger Parish, centralized development of crafts which were started by the Alpine Rural Life Center has been discontinued. However, some people still carry on crafts in their homes.

Partly through the efforts of the Larger Parish, a shirt factory at Byrdstown was started in 1956, and a box factory was started that same year at Alpine. A shirt factory was started in Livingston in 1944. The number of employees at this factory increased from around 400 in 1944 to over 1100 in 1956.

The activity of the Dale Hollow Larger Parish is a real life example of what Christian cooperation can do to elevate life in rural areas. Of all the agencies serving to improve the welfare of rural people, probably none are in a better position to provide leadership needed than is the church. The ministers and leaders in Overton and Pickett Counties, Tennessee, found they could do more toward bringing Christianity into all the homes, improving education, and relieving poverty and illness among their people through interdenominational cooperation than they could by working separately. Such activity seems to be the trend in rural areas of this type. With such devoted and unselfish cooperative service, the church can continue to be a leading force in raising the level of living for rural people.

Part II

Analysis of the Rural Church Project in Tennessee

Democratic Principles Used. The first portion of this chapter deals very largely with the accomplishments and activities of an individual church which sponsored programs and projects designed to improve the spiritual, educational, economic, health, and recreational welfare of rural people in the Cumberland Mountains of Tennessee. The latter portion of this chapter deals primarily with accomplishments and activities along the same line, but sponsored by an interdenominational group that found that through cooperation, a larger service can be rendered.

In both situations, use of the principles of democratic leadership are in evidence.

There is a somewhat general knowledge that probably the most needy rural people in America are those living in the Southern Mountain areas. Poverty is widespread, which results in many evils such as poor housing, undernourishment, poor education and ill health. All of these evils existed at Alpine, Tennessee, and in the Larger Parish. The Presbyterian minister, Rev. Bernard M. Taylor, had both a *knowledge* of the situation and a motivation to work with people in an effort to improve their status. When situations arose about which his *knowledge* was limited, he sought the counsel of others who possessed the needed technical *knowledge*. Such was the case when he secured information from state and federal forestry agents concerning the establishment of a demonstration forest.

To provide democratic leadership successfully, *knowledge* must be coupled with a *challenge* to improve a situation. This, Mr. Taylor had. This *challenge* to solve the problem led him to share his knowledge with others who were needed to *participate* at different levels in the solution of the problem. His great spirit and enthusiasm *shared* with others caused more and more people to have *knowledge* of the situation and in turn to become *challenged* to help solve the problem.

Use of the principle of *participation* is more evident during later stages of the organization and operation of the Dale Hollow Larger Parish. The *purpose* of the Larger Parish was discussed thoroughly in at least two meetings. Ministers and other leaders present had the opportunity to *participate* fully in the determination of *purpose* at these meetings where a *group mind* concerning the need for establishing the project was achieved. The record indicates, however, that while *opportunity* for lay participation was open, the reality of it was lacking. In about 1955, there developed a responsible *sharing* of leadership roles by lay persons.

The *process* to be used was understood, and a Council and Staff were decided upon to give continued *direction* to the activities of the project. Through Council and Staff meetings, ministers, church leaders, and employed persons had the continuing opportunity to *participate* fully, helping to determine the *process* and *direction*. Also, through these meetings the contributions of the *group mind* were greater and *integration* of the numerous and varied activities was achieved.

Before organization of the Dale Hollow Larger Parish, the Protestant denominations in the area had the *habit* of ministering to their own denominational needs with a minimum of interdenominational cooperation. In this instance, a new *habit of sharing* and organized cooperation has been substituted for the old. To make this change was a *challenge* to the church leadership. It required *flexibility* in the program of the individual church, and a new type of *training* and *experience* never before witnessed in the area. A high type of *integration* had to be achieved among the churches and *service* rather than selfishness had to be envisioned.

There can be no doubt of the *leadership satisfaction* that came to Mr. Taylor, Dr. Randolph, and the other professional leaders who led and participated in the planning and development of Alpine Community and the Dale Hollow Larger Parish. The pride of accomplishment is evident in their reports and conversations. No greater joy comes to men than the fulfillment of their dreams and plans. Certainly the efforts of these leaders and the resources of the church made a major contribution to relieving the burdens of others and helping to enrich the lives of a low-income people.

While the fruits of leadership may be widespread, *leadership satisfactions* are limited to the persons serving as leaders. From the vantage point of hindsight, it seems clear that in the early years the project did not entirely "belong" to the lay leaders and local people themselves. When in later years, noticeably around 1955, local people became more actively involved in the project, they too experienced considerable *leadership satisfactions*. Previous to that time, the enthusiasm, vision and determination of the professional project leaders had been so great as to carry the local citizens along. However, the local leaders seem not to have really understood or accepted the primary responsibility as their very own. Accordingly, as outside support was withdrawn, one program after another weakened and in some cases ceased to exist.

Today the most significant monument to the Board of National Missions' wisdom and investment is found in the firm and secure foundations of the revitalized churches, which are serving an expanded and vastly improved purpose. Probably because the project leaders understood church and spiritual needs and work best, they dreamed and built most soundly in this field of community need. Although improvements were made to the economic and social life of people in the community, they were not as substantial as were improvements in the church. This was probably due to a poorer understanding of methods and procedures in these areas as is indicated by failure to draw sufficiently upon many of the existing resources for assistance, economic aid and development. Perhaps the most serious deficiency was failure effectively to develop and use local lay leadership and support.

Currently the Alpine community projects are based on a more solid foundation with lay leadership as the pillars of support. Their roots go deep and are nourished from within the community. Two very important lessons have been learned. First, rural church leaders can spark and carry forward a measurably successful program of religious and community improvement. Alpine and the Dale Hollow Larger Parish provide a thrilling example of this. Second, those who are responsible for such plans will do well to consider carefully the methods and procedures used. Improvement is more solid and lasting when it results from the direct efforts of the local lay people themselves. Recognizing this, professional leaders make their greatest contribution by helping local people to help themselves. In this way, they can make the lives of people more comfortable and enjoyable, bringing happiness and contentment to all.

PART **IV**

The Leader, the Community, and the Action

CHAPTER XX

The Leader, the Community, and the Action

What kind of leader are you? What are your goals? What are you trying to do to help others? How would you change your community?

In what kind of rural community do you work? Is it made up of families that have lived there for several generations? Is it economically poor or wealthy? Is it conservative or progressive? Is it able to take action on community problems?

How willing is the community to act? On what kinds of problems will it take action? What items are given first consideration when decisions are made? What leadership roles are encouraged in the community?

The answers that you would give to the above questions about yourself, your community and its action would be extremely varied. The kind of person you are affects the action you will take; the kind of community you live in affects the action you can take. The authors believe that the great variability in leaders and in communities has made a study of principles of leadership and a study of their application more significant than a study of techniques and methods would have been.

It is important at this point in our study of leadership that we re-examine the setting in which leadership occurs. To do this we will not review the previous chapters. Instead we will glance back just enough to gain a perspective. This will enable us to look at our leadership today and help us in forecasting what it should be tomorrow.

A Look Back

This book began with you and those factors which make you the kind of a leader you are. If you are a formally elected or appointed leader you will provide your leadership service in a somewhat different way than you will as a professional leader who is paid to provide leadership. If you make an effort to lead without the formal sanction of a group your leadership efforts may be different from both the professional leader and the formally selected community or group leader. There are times when the kind of leadership provided should be identical regardless of the the label placed on your leadership. This is another way of saying that the setting in which you lead, the problem which is being considered and the kind of action begun help determine what your leadership should be like.

It is for this reason that this book reviewed the setting in which the rural leader works. The variations in communities and among a community's organizations make a difference. If we are working among friends and organizations we can do some things that a professional leader cannot do, but the professional leader can do some things that the "insider" cannot do.

The basic setting with which we were concerned was the free democratic society. It is on this base and against the criteria of democratic procedure and the scientific method that your actions can be judged. We have recognized in principle and example that supporting democratic leadership requires of us the acceptance of sacrifice and responsibility. It does not give us a license for an irresponsible liberty. If the authors had used some other basis for this book the contents of most of it would have been different.

Leadership was examined in relation to your dedications. You were asked to compare those guides to action that you have used before with the principles of democratic action described in Chapter V. The importance of leaders working together was considered carefully as was the nature of controversy in the community.

At this point we began viewing communities in different parts of the United States and Canada and observed the leaders at work. We looked for examples of their successes and of their errors. By finding both we might well have concluded that they are no different than any of the rest of us. We saw some things in the leadership in these communities that we would like to try. We saw some things to avoid and we wondered why some other methods didn't work.

A Look at Today

What leadership are you providing in your community? What decisions should your community make to improve the life of its members? What kind of leader are you today?

This book did not answer these questions for you. They are for you to answer. What priorities for work would you establish in your community? Are the organizations, and the other leadership jobs of which you are a part, really important? Will they count for anything in the lives of people? How much do you have to offer and where are you going to place your effort? For example, are you "run ragged" doing a little bit of everything for everybody? Or are you concentrating your efforts on one or two leadership jobs and doing a great deal for a few people? Are you spreading yourself too thin or wasting time on too few? You need to answer this today even though it is assuring to know that some leaders have accomplished much by "spreading themselves thin" while others have done just as much by concentrating.

Are you more effective when you are accepted as a leader by election or appointment than you are when leading from "behind the scenes"? If you are a professional leader, are you more effective in a formal group atmosphere or can you accomplish more with a small group over a cup of coffee at the corner restaurant? Does your formal status as teacher, county agent, superintendent, minister, or executive secretary present too much of a barrier for you to overcome? Are you so informal that you can't take formal leadership action when it is necessary? These are the questions for you to answer today.

A LOOK AHEAD

Since the ability to look ahead is an important characteristic of most leaders, it is appropriate to view briefly the changes that are taking place in rural life. From these changes the implications for leaders, communities, and types of action can be predicted. A final observation can then be made of the use of principles of democratic leadership in this new and changing setting.

Changes in Rural Society. In centuries past, it was normal for change in the nature of society to occur so slowly that persons of any given generation were frequently unable to observe it. This has not been true of the past several decades, and with the speed with which science and society are now changing it may never be true again. We are both fortunate and unfortunate to be living during this period of rapid change. We are fortunate in that we can observe the change first hand and plan to do what is necessary to adjust to it. We are unfortunate in that the adjustments needed to a fast-changing society can be so numerous and complex that leaders will face more crises than under old conditions of slow change. Whatever the advantages or disadvantages of our rapidly-changing times might be, we have them and the problems that arise are ours to solve.

The decline in the farm population in a 20-year period, from over one-fifth of the nation's population to about one-eighth, calls for major adjustments. During this period the relationship between the size of the rural farm population and rural nonfarm population has changed, with rural nonfarm population increasing and farm population declining. All predictions as to the next two decades call for a continuation of the downward trend in the number of farm people.

A higher and higher proportion of people in the United States are living beyond age 70. Projected trends for the next two decades indicate a continued rise in the median age of our population, and a still more rapid increase in the proportion of our adult population in the 50-year-and-over age group. Whereas in 1938, 30 percent of the adult population was in the 50-and-over age group, in 1960, 36 percent were in this group; and it is predicted that by 1970 this age group will comprise 40 percent of the adult population. The rural village has always had a higher proportion of retired people in its population and is likely to continue having this characteristic.

The expanding contribution of science during the past decade leads one to predict that the trend toward greater scientific development will continue with greater and faster change needed by society to keep up. The conquest of the atom, the beginning conquest of space, and the biological scientist getting closer to the production of living cells, tell us how far we've come in a recent short time.

The agricultural scientist has made more changes in agriculture since 1930 than were made since man took up the hoe. This includes our new crop varieties, the hybrids—from corn to chickens, artificial breeding programs, new knowledge of soil and fertilizer compositions, concentrated milk, and tranquilizers to keep frustrated animals happy and producing. We don't know where it will stop—but we do know it is on the way.

Perhaps more significant than any of the preceding changes

are to the rural leader is the increase in the level of formal education. This is both in fact and in expectation. The level of education achieved by rural persons has risen sharply since 1930. Where graduation from the eighth grade was the anticipated termination point of a farm child's education, it has risen to the point where high school graduation is expected. Even more recently we note many rural communities where 40, 50, and even 60 per cent of the high school graduates enroll in college. The prediction for the future is that one-half or more of all rural youngsters will begin college. This change in the level of formal education reached by people living in rural communities will make a difference to the rural leader.

One could continue to list hundreds of other changes that are taking place. Surely there are many others that will make a difference. Only one additional area of change will be identified. This is the change in communication and transportation in rural society and between rural and urban society. We may go back to town roads and telephones as the first major changes in rural communications. This influence did make a difference and did change rural life. More recently the expanding network of all-weather highways has contracted the "time-distance" between farm and city; the radio and more recently television have brought urban culture into the rural living room. The influence of easy communication has opened the door to knowledge, to new questions, and to change for rural people.

IMPLICATION OF THESE CHANGES

The present rural leaders will soon cease to be leaders if they fail to recognize the direction of community adjustment brought about by the changes taking place. These changes will cause problems in rural organizations, in rural schools, in rural churches, and in the relationships between rural and urban people. Leaders or potential leaders will recognize these problems and take the lead in bringing them to solution; adjustments are going to need to be made and there will be some folks who won't understand this. Some people will balk at the change going on around them. They will not believe that it is progress and will wish to go back to "the good old days." They may even attempt to provide leadership for others so they can lead them backward too. Just yesterday an elderly lady commented among a group of adults discussing space travel that she was doing what she could to stop such talk because we shouldn't be concerned with things outside of this earth. All we'll do, she said, is to create new problems and we have too many old ones we haven't settled yet.

The urge to explore unknown frontiers and the urge to change seem to be prime characteristics of man and society. If this is true, then leaders will always be needed to help man and society make the necessary adjustments.

If we refer to Figure 1 on page 12 we will recall how scientific and social changes lead us from a period of balance to one of ferment. It may be that as the speed of change increases, the periods of balance will become shorter and shorter. Thus with the rapid changes of the past two decades a community that attempts to stay in its old balance too long may be faced with more drastic crises than one where leaders are working for a continuing series of smaller adjustments for the community. Today community balance cannot be maintained by remaining static. Balance has become a factor associated with the speed with which a community is able to adjust to the changes of the total society.

The kinds of action toward which leadership effort should be directed will depend more than ever upon the kinds of changes taking place and the present status of your community in relation to these changes. There are changes necessary in both curriculum and administrative organization of the schools as a result of change in society. There are changes in the make-up of the rural church, the program of the farm organization, and the participation of youngsters in 4-H Club work brought about by such things as the increased level of formal education and the declining farm population. Changes in transportation and communication will make their influence felt on these programs too.

Action to be taken by a rural community because of these changes is not a series of isolated actions specific to each specific change. On the contrary, if there ever was a need for wise leadership it is in leadership which can pull together and integrate the effects of a large number of changes and to help the rural citizens to see the entire picture as well as the isolated part.

Solving community problems may often involve looking at the problems on a regional basis rather than restricting your view only to your own community. This is more difficult, but it is one of the outcomes of the progress we observe around us.

We noted in Chapter XIII how leaders in Beckley, West Virginia recognized their problem as involving a region, not Beckley alone. We noted also the success to Beckley which could not have occurred had its leaders looked only to the Beckley community. Leaders in schools, 4-H Clubs, farm organizations, community clubs, and churches need to look beyond their "own community nose" to solve many of today's problems.

PRINCIPLES TO FOLLOW

We have assumed throughout that as leaders you have a strong dedication to a free democratic society. For so long as we remain a free and democratic society, the principles of leadership described in this book will continue to be useful.

You will be able to use the principle of *knowledge* whether you are dealing with an automobile parking problem or a new village landing platform for helicopters.

The principle of the *group mind* was useful to leaders Charlie Remsberg and Maurice Ahalt as they worked with their Middletown 4-H Club during the 1950's. It will be useful to hundreds of other Charlies and Maurices in 1975 even if the meeting places, projects, ages of club members, and their activities have changed.

The principle of *challenge* was useful to Mrs. Carter and Mrs. Oakley in the Alpha Homemakers' Club. Though the challenge may be different in the future, its usefulness to generate and motivate action will be just as important in this club if it is active 50 years from now.

The *sharing* of the responsibilities for community improvement in Carthage, Arkansas, demonstrated the use of a principle which may become more rather than less important as our society becomes more complex. The singleness of *purpose* developed by J. T. Haynes and Lee Jackson in Central Community would have been an important principle to follow whether it was this critical water shortage or had been some other community with a flood problem.

In Cox's Chapel the use of the principle of the *group mind* to stimulate new ideas brought national recognition to its door. In X County, Missouri, little progress was shown until leaders took the responsibility of *directing* certain actions the groups were ready to take. The success of rural church cooperation depended upon the *integration* of ideas that began in an exploration of the problem and led to its ultimate solution.

The use of the principles of democratic leadership has been demonstrated in the examples in this book. These principles can be demonstrated in your organization and in your community. They are not something which work only once and then cease to work. They can be the guide-lines to our action in spite of changes in our total society, in our communities, or in individuals.

The general usefulness of the principles of leadership leads to the conclusion that they would be just as useful to leaders in cities as they are to leaders in rural communities. Should you have been told this sooner?

POSTLUDE

Christopher Columbus discovered America by accident. He was looking for a new route to the East Indies. He sought an easier access to the Orient, fabulously rich for that time. Instead he bumped into North America. Here he found land, forests, and minerals, but none of the spices or jewels that he coveted for his Queen.

Recently I returned to America from a mission to the part of Asia that Columbus wanted to reach. As the engines of our Strato-Cruiser droned on and on across the Pacific they propelled stimulating thought. Why is the area that Columbus tried to locate nearly 500 years ago much the same today as then? Why has there been so little change or progress? Why do teeming millions still go to bed there each night hungry and miserable even now as in the time of Marco Polo? In contrast, the comparative wealth and luxury of today's generation of North Americans seems fabulous indeed. What happened, on the continent that Columbus discovered, which failed to happen where he wanted to go?

I looked backward past the whirling propellers to the footsteps of Thomas Paine, George Washington and Thomas Jefferson. We remember them best for their courageous stand about liberty and freedom. And that was important. But was there something else?

Beginning with the time when Jefferson invented the moldboard plow and Washington bade his countrymen pay heed to their husbandry, a progressive agrarian leadership has emerged. Attention to scientific discovery and the development of enlightened educational leadership have been tenets of our national policy. What are the results?

Within the last century the relative position of farming in the total economy of the United States has exactly reversed. One hundred years ago 87 per cent of all Americans were engaged in producing food and fiber for themselves and the other

13 per cent. Today less than 13 per cent of our population is needed for agricultural production. It is notable, however, that 40 per cent of our total labor force is needed to produce, distribute, process and sell the nation's food, fiber and tobacco. Those released from food production are making industrial or manufactured products like automobiles, washing machines and clothes or they are engaged in providing us with professional, educational or other services. Altogether this trend toward diversification has brought us the highest level of living enjoyed by the people of any major nation.

The development and use of leadership in research, science, education and technology account for much of this progress. Results of that leadership were everywhere about us as we soared in over Golden Gate Bridge. People in America have no greater intelligence or capacities than people in the other cultures I had just left across the wide Pacific. Nor do the mountains, valleys and plains of North America contain riches and resources unknown in those lands of ageless civilization. What manner of miracle can account for the development of this oasis we call America in the few short generations since Columbus made his mistake and planted the first seed of our destiny?

About 100 years ago one great leader used his power and influence to insure universal leadership opportunity through higher education. When Abraham Lincoln signed the Land-Grant College Act in 1862 he declared that this measure would bring the advantages of college training to the sons and daughters of farmers and mechanics. And it would develop leaders for the advancement of those two great vocations. How prophetically he spoke!

Later came extension of the research and educational services of the 70 public-supported colleges under this system. They have paved the way for an era of scientific discovery and educational achievement unparalleled in the world.

Today the United States comprises about six per cent of the world's land area and seven per cent of the world's population. With these resources we are able to enjoy:

    74 per cent of the world's autos
    52 per cent of the world's trucks
    60 per cent of the world's insurance policies
    54 per cent of the world's telephones

47 per cent of the world's radios
80 per cent of the world's TV sets
46 per cent of the world's electric power out-
    put
52 per cent of the world's steel output
32 per cent of the world's improved highways
29 per cent of the world's railroad mileage
92 per cent of the world's modern bathtubs

The people of the United States own almost 50 per cent of the world's wealth. One American in four is attending school. Our agricultural production is increasing at the rate of two per cent per year. We have achieved a 50 per cent increase in total annual agricultural output in the last 25 years. This greater output has been achieved with less manpower. By 1957, the average farm worker produced enough food, fiber and tobacco for himself and 19 others. Farm output per man-hour has tripled since 1910 and has increased 95 per cent since 1940. This increase has been achieved with little or no added land, but largely through improved technology, management and the use of labor-saving machinery.

In short, American farmers are making use of science and are cooperating with other segments of our economy to increase their own efficiency and our over-all level of living. As we move forward further into the second half of the twentieth century one major problem or challenge of rural leadership has been won. The problem of producing abundantly and efficiently has been solved. Further progress still lies ahead and the means for achieving it are available. The leadership exists, or at least the resources for developing adequate technical leaders exists, in our State Agricultural Colleges and in our Federal-State Experiment Stations. Our rapidly expanding population seems to be assured of having adequate food and fiber for the needs of a predicted 220 million people by 1975.

However, even as the problem of production is conquered, other concerns arise. These challenge, with even greater persistency and complexity, the stature of our rural leadership. Agricultural producers are economically distressed. In the face of magnificent individual achievements of highly efficient production they cannot keep ahead of rising costs. In essence the problems of individual families in a pioneer society have now given way to more complex problems which plague agriculture as an industry.

As an example, let's consider briefly the economic problem of surpluses and inadequate prices for agricultural products. The illusive truth is that the law of supply and demand plays queer tricks on American farmers. A summation of the best short-run solutions to the economic problems of individual farmers does not add up to the best advantage of all farmers. The efficient production which helps several million individual farm families to get the highest possible return from a given market in a given year frequently causes a depressive effect on prices at the market itself. A peculiar feature of the farm market, with its relatively inflexible demand, is that it yields a higher gross return to farm producers when that market is not saturated by excessive offerings. A short crop brings a higher total return to the industry than a full or large crop. In the short run, there is a conflict between the best solution for each individual and the best solution for all producers.

To further illustrate this dichotomy, it is generally recognized that a normal or small U. S. production of Irish potatoes in a given year may return a high gross income to all potato producers as an industry. A large crop results in glutted markets, depressed prices and a greatly decreased gross return to all farmers. Yet the individual farmer in either of these two market situations will be in a better position if he has pushed his production to the point where he gets the greatest and most efficient output from his own land, equipment, labor, fertilizer, etc.

Is it any wonder, then, that the present farm problem is not an easy one to solve? On the one hand if all potato producers grew fewer potatoes they would get more return at less cost. But every individual, seeing that prospect, is tempted to increase his own output in order to get an individual advantage. In such a situation there seems to be no easy choice, no best answer for everyone. One road of individual sacrifice hopefully leads toward group welfare. The other road of group freedom may lead to individual ruin. What a dichotomy!

Another new and explosive development is the rapid increase of vertical integration or contract farming. What has already happened to canning crops and broilers seems destined now to spread into many or all phases of agricultural production. More and more of the control of production, processing, financing and marketing of commodities will pass into the hands of fewer and fewer entrepreneurs or "risktakers." Will these risktakers be farm families, farmer-controlled cooperatives, or big corporations? The answer will certainly make a big difference in the nature of farming and the agricultural industry for decades.

In this atmosphere of challenge for the future of rural America, leadership will be given its greatest trial of all time. All our best dedications, principles and skills will be needed for the tasks ahead. Togetherness will be even more important than it was in pioneer days. An understanding of the inter-relatedness of all segments of our society will be imperative, in looking for solutions to rural problems of the next decade. Because no one farmer controls enough elements of the market to insure success, he must cooperate and share with others or perish. Will the required leadership emerge and be recognized at local and national levels?

We have used here only one example, that relating to farm production, prices and income. But it illustrates the need for effective leadership for rural communities in future decades. There will be many problems, not just one—so many that we cannot anticipate them all. Developing adequate leadership to help people solve these problems has been the objective of this book.

As we take inventory for the years ahead let's count our resources and our blessings. What things can we rely on? Where can we place our trust?

First, we can count on man's inquisitive mind. When problems or needs face us we can be certain that men will search to the edges of the unknown for facts and new discoveries. We will seek out better ways of doing things. We will mobilize and combine all knowledge, skills and attitudes to the best of our capacities in order to unlock the door to progress. The trend which was started 5,000 or more years ago probably will be accelerated greatly in our times. In this regard the able leader will find that the Socratic method of raising questions and thus piquing curiosity is one of the oldest and best educational procedures known to man.

Second, we can be confident that 160 years of freedom and democracy has equipped our people with the basic experience and attitudes needed for continuous growth and development. Democracy is not a fair-weather, short-lived institution of pre- scribed and limited destiny. Unlike a crop of annual weeds or a quick summer shower, leaders developed from the sweat and toil of a working democracy have roots that go deep and nourish well. As with the mighty oak, shared democracy is made of sterner, harder stuff. It wells up out of the population. It extends its trunk straight up for divine guidance and sends its branches far out into nourishing sunlight, eventually over- shadowing the weeds that come and go underneath.

Third, although democracy and self-determination may be slow in some of its initial process stages the ultimate objective is accomplished faster than by any other known system. Govern- ment of the people, for the people, and by the people is by no means perfect, but it is so far ahead of the next best system that there is little need to fear for its survival. This applies to the day- by-day conduct of groups and organizations as well as to gov- ernment. Taking care to let people talk out their objectives and talk themselves into participation requires more time in the beginning but less in the end.

Fourth, the Golden Rule is the yardstick and the motivation for good human relations. Know the people you serve. Share their hopes, their experiences and their problems. Start to walk with them where they are. Shine the lamp of knowledge but a few steps ahead at a time. Hesitate while the heavy-laden catch up. Give generous praise for each success. Be willing to share the pleasurable accomplishment of others' goals as the reward for your work. Have faith in yourself, in others, in your job and in the future. These are indispensable working tools for carving out a success.

Fifth, a good leader is one who helps people employ the time-honored scientific method as a blueprint for progress. Together you clarify and define the problems and the needs. You decide on goals and objectives. You work out some alternative ideas or procedures. Next you try them out, evaluate the results and re-try again. You help resolve differences in objectives and goals by thorough discussion and careful communication at each stage.

Sixth, in the leader's personal dedications and motivations there is no room for negatives like hate or waste. The only enemies a good leader should recognize are such things as ignorance, poverty, disease or intolerance. Productivity and more things for everybody derive from positive values like love, cooperation and mutual assistance. The good leader acts as a magnet, generating confidence and togetherness among the persons in his orbit of influence. He counteracts the centrifuge of an explosive environment with qualities of empathy, love and supportiveness toward people—everywhere.

The burden of responsibility and obligation which this view places on your shoulders as a leader is tremendous. We realize that perhaps no human being can attain the ultimate in democratic leadership ability, skills and attitudes. But your load will be lighter and your road will be brighter if you try. You will have many discouragements. We hope that you enjoy many satisfactions, too.

The greatest of these satisfactions may come to you at an unexpected moment—a time of deepest need. As a leader, you may think you are alone—perhaps you are discouraged or dejected. You may be driving home from a meeting—wondering if your efforts were effective or worth while. Suddenly, reassuringly, you realize that you are not alone. The comforting hand of another is holding your hand. A quiet, confident voice of destiny whispers the priceless lesson of time in your ear—

> *"Well done, thou good and faithful servant. For as ye have ministered unto the least of these, oh my brethren, so have ye ministered unto me also."*

When this revealing moment arrives you are no longer troubled. You no longer have doubts. You feel that leadership and service are their own reward. You no longer seek acclaim for your efforts. You find your greatest joys in sharing the progress of others. And in so doing the best in all the world comes back to you across the waters.

INDEX

341